Do You Know This Woman?

It is Friday night and Marcia is feeling blue. She takes a walk and sees couples walking together, holding hands, and it accentuates her loneliness. Finally, Marcia decides she wants to go out for dinner, so she drags herself to a hamburger place around the corner from where she lives, then goes off to see a movie by herself.

Marcia feels blue every Friday night and Saturday night, and all day Sunday as well. But Monday, her world comes alive again.

By now you've probably guessed it. Marcia's boy friend is a married man. And Marcia is a *Married Man Magnet*.

Other Bantam books by Carol Botwin
Ask your bookseller for the books you have missed

THE LOVE CRISIS with Jerome Fine, Ph.D.

LOVE LIVES

*Why Women Behave
the Way They Do
In Relationships*

CAROL BOTWIN

BANTAM BOOKS
TORONTO · NEW YORK · LONDON · SYDNEY

LOVE LIVES: WHY WOMEN BEHAVE THE WAY THEY DO IN RELATIONSHIPS

A Bantam Book / March 1983

ISBN 0-553-22529-4

Published simultaneously in the United States and Canada

PRINTED IN THE UNITED STATES OF AMERICA

O   0 9 8 7 6 5 4 3 2 1

To the memory of Charles Eisner,
and his gift for making others laugh.

I am very grateful to the following psychiatrists and psychologists who graciously supplied me with the information upon which this book is based:

Berta Anagnoste, M.D. The many hours she devoted to this project made this book possible.
Alma Bond, Ph.D.
Carol Galligan, Ph.D.
Wayne Myers, M.D.
Mary Newman, Ph.D.
Michael Rabkin, M.D.
Marcia Rosenberg, M.D.
Robert Sayer, M.D.
Ann Ruth Turkel, M.D.

I am grateful, also, to the many women and men I interviewed who must remain nameless but who contributed parts of their lives to this book.

CONTENTS

CHAPTER 1

INTRODUCTION: WOMEN TODAY

To talk about women today is to talk about many groups. There are modern women—those increasing numbers who seek careers and a place in what used to be called a man's world. Many of these women think of themselves as "liberated" in their attitudes toward themselves and in relation to the world or at least much more liberated than their mothers were.

Then there are the traditional women who still think largely as their mothers did. They believe that being a housewife and mother is the best of all possible worlds. They like being protected. They leave careers to their men.

Finally there are the in-betweens—the large number of women who work for the money because it is needed, but who put family and domestic matters above a job. I heard one such woman, a fiftyish hostess in a restaurant, explaining to her boss that she would have to take a few days off to prepare meals for a religious holiday that was coming up. "It's my duty," she explained, while he kept telling her he couldn't keep her on the job if she was going to take days off to cook.

Another in-between type is the woman who vacillates between her need for independence and her innate desire for dependence on a man, and in the end, is so confused she doesn't know what she wants. One day she yearns to stay home, the next to become a smashing success. Then there's the well-to-do woman who plays at her job or simply plays by different rules from co-workers because of her position in life.

One social worker, a Bostonian married to a very wealthy man, hasn't bothered to collect her pay check in six months. She is saying, in effect, to those around her, "I don't have to work. My husband can support me"—a very traditional female point of view. Nevertheless, this woman is a very good and conscientious worker.

Two other women, both married to movie moguls, recently started a business with a third woman, a divorcée who has to work to support herself. She comes in every day and works around the clock, while the moguls' wives frequently take days off, exasperating her by giving as typical excuses, "I had to go to the hairdresser," or, "I wanted to spend a couple of extra days at our beach house."

There are many women these days who identify themselves as modern career women and, indeed, try to live up to that image, but they continue to think and act exactly as they did when they were housewives.

The rich ladies who play at jobs as Marie Antoinette played with her golden milk pails may not be experiencing much psychological discomfort. As long as they can maintain the illusion that they have careers, they feel in sync with the times. But for the majority of women, whether traditional or liberated, there is a great deal of stress in the current female world.

Traditional Housewives

The traditional housewife today is often a mass of hidden angers and fears. She feels the world has pulled the rug out from under her. Ever since she was a little girl, she was told that fulfillment meant becoming a wife and a mother. Once she attained that status, she was proud of herself and her role, a position that society backed up. She was applauded for being a housewife. But then the mood of the country shifted as the number of working wives increased to over fifty percent. The traditional housewife who felt secure and complacent as a member of the majority now finds herself uneasy and defensive as one of the minority. To those who ask what she does, she mumbles apologetically, "Oh, I'm just a wife and mother." She used to feel superior to mothers who worked. Now she is being made to feel inferior, she thinks.

She is, also, all too aware of the current divorce rate. The fact that one out of two or three marriages ends in divorce, depending on where you live, terrifies her. She is afraid she may become one of those pathetic displaced homemakers she reads about—women like herself, trained only to be someone's wife or mother, who have suddenly been cast out into the world where they have to make a living for themselves and often for their kids as well. She finds herself fearful that among all those working women her husband now comes in contact with, he may find one he likes better than her. The traditional housewife feels increasingly vulnerable and threatened. As a result, she is often defensive and angry, subliminally. She may unleash her anger at the turn of events that now question her version of the feminine role by voting against the ERA Amendment, by attacking feminists for being unfeminine, castrating and the cause of all the messes in the world. Or, in her frightened desire to hold onto her role and the man who makes it possible, she may become the extreme opposite of the liberated women she deplores. She becomes more subservient to her man. She turns herself into a man's slave according to the prescriptions of Marabel Morgan in *The Total Woman*. She may giggle as she does it, or she may feel like a fool, but she knows where her security lies. She bravely puts on a short, baby doll nightgown, pours a martini for her husband, lifts it in one hand, puts a smile on her face and thus greets her husband when he returns from work.

Even if they don't accept Marabel Morgan's advice as to how to hold onto a man, housewives are often uncomfortable and frightened today about their futures.

The Working Wife

The Working Wife suffers from other strains. She earns a salary and therefore may be less financially dependent on her husband than the stay-at-home housewife, but she may remain, nevertheless, just as emotionally dependent. She may change in the wink of an eye from competent brief case

carrier to helpless little woman the minute she enters the
portals of her own home. The changeover is generally an
unconscious process. In a domestic setting she just automatically becomes the woman she was brought up to be. Often
enough, these days, working wives whose husbands are threatened by their new roles purposely act more incompetent than
they feel in order to maintain peace and keep their marriages
intact.

Some wives struggle with the issue of divided labor. A
woman may ask her husband to help out more in the home,
but finds active or passive resistance. He may agree, for
example, to take on certain chores, but forgets to do them or
does them so badly that it comes across as a clear message of
revolt. Some husbands try valiantly to share household duties,
but find themselves inwardly resentful which inevitably they
communicate to their wives.

Other wives try to do everything themselves. They are all
things to everyone—worker, housewife, mother. Eventually
many feel overburdened. Women who take on too much often
do so because of severe conflicts between their roles as career
women and what they feel from their upbringing is the feminine role. These women feel guilty about everything—about
leaving children in the care of others, about not being good
enough wives, about not being good enough career women.

The lack of help is often a woman's own choosing. She
refuses to hire a full-time maid or babysitter. She refuses to
ask her husband to do very much. In this way she can hold
onto her view of herself as "feminine" while she is working.
For other women it is purely a matter of money. Statistics
show that most women work because of economic necessity.
They can't afford more help.

Whatever the reason, the overburdened wife is a familiar
figure in today's world. Burnout is the cause of many cases
of depression, either mild or severe. It also may make a
woman leave the workplace, sometimes in anger and bitterness. She worked hard. She expected more from her career
and from herself as a "new" woman. She did not think that
being wife, mother, and career woman all at once would be
so hard to manage.

Other modern career women carry on with all of their

roles, but because of conflicts and guilt, find themselves unable to take joy in any of their roles. Some mothers are plagued by fantasies of the child coming to harm while with a babysitter. It's a way of punishing themselves for leaving their children. Still others unconsciously fail at their jobs or don't achieve as much as they should because of guilt.

Many women caught in the emotional tug-of-war between career and domestic duties, old roles and new ones, end up feeling personally deficient. A truly modern woman, they feel, should be able to handle all of it without ambivalence or stress.

Although few women today escape conflicts altogether, some are able to manage their multiple roles reasonably well. They get as much help as they can from husband or outsiders, they learn to establish priorities which can shift according to where the need is greatest at the moment, and they become efficient workers as well as good wives and mothers.

The task of trying to work out the sharing of tasks in dual career families is an ongoing problem in today's world. There are no role models or rules to act as guidelines. Women find themselves pioneers in unmapped territory.

Work

Work itself has been romanticized by modern women. Men always knew that the basic purpose of a career was to earn a living. They were aware that there might be grubby, unsatisfying things they would have to do along the way. Women, on the other hand, have developed a romantic, unrealistic view of work. In our times it has become the panacea for all of a woman's ills. A career is not only for making money, it is the thing that will bring a woman self-fulfillment and happiness. When women discover what men have always known, that work can be less than ideal, that there is vicious competition, that there are boring and unpleasant aspects to their jobs, it often comes as a rude shock. They also underrate the wearing toll that prejudice against women can extract.

Although some women are held back by prejudice, there are also those women who stand in their own way. They are afraid to ask for more money or power on a job. Women have not been taught to go aggressively after what they want in the world. Or, afraid to risk true success, some women unconsciously sabotage themselves. A secretary at a large public relations firm was recently offered a job as an account executive. She quit at that moment. Soon, she was looking for a job as a secretary elsewhere.

Another woman already in a middle-management job in a large corporation, when asked to prepare a report that would bring her to the attention of the company president, kept finding one excuse after another why she couldn't prepare the report in the prescribed time.

Some women climbing the ladder of success find they work harder and harder for meager returns. Tired out, they leave the working world in a state of disenchantment. Others become disillusioned about other women. The sisterhood support they had counted on simply wasn't there. They may have discovered that many successful women are as sexist as any man in terms of lending a helping hand to women.

Women who want to start careers in mid-life are sometimes unrealistic about their goals. They want executive jobs right away and are unwilling to take smaller ones and work their way up. "At my age how can anyone expect to be a trainee?" snorted one 47-year-old woman. Some of these women keep looking for acceptable jobs and not finding them. For them, job hunting becomes a career in itself.

It is interesting that while men talk about work-related matters among themselves, women, even when they have significant careers, sometimes don't inquire about each other's work, and don't volunteer reports from their work world. If work does get discussed, the subject is closed quickly in favor of talk about relationships. With their husbands, though, it is often the reverse. Many wives want to talk about their new careers all the time, either out of excitement or because they want ongoing reassurance and advice from a husband who may begin to resent the same topic awaiting him night after night when he comes home from his own trials and tribulations at work.

When a job turns out to be disappointing or difficult, for a single or divorced woman, or even when she is simply having a "bad" day, it is common for her to revert to old habits. She may fantasize about a man rescuing her from all of this.

The Single Woman

The population of single women is larger than ever before in history. There are currently about forty million single, divorced, separated and widowed women in the United States. According to the 1980 census, women are marrying at later ages. More women are never marrying at all. A large number of women find themselves divorced and alone once more. There is a new and significant population of middle-aged or older divorcées. Women continue to outlive men, so widows are abundantly represented in the female singles population. For many of these women, the single state is less than satisfactory. In our society females were never reared to live alone. When they find themselves without a man, many women feel lost, lonely, perhaps a little bewildered by their fate, and sometimes bitter.

Many single women who work to support themselves don't attach real importance to their jobs and fail to provide for their own futures because they feel that working is a temporary state. They are ladies-in-waiting. They feel, often unrealistically, that somewhere, sometime, a man will take care of them. It is not uncommon for these women to feel victimized and outraged by the fact that they have to work.

As they get older, if a man has not appeared, they often begin to panic. What will become of me, they wonder, as they toss and turn in countless sleepless nights. Fear is a common part of many single women's lives. They are afraid of being alone forever, they are afraid of being destitute, they are afraid to walk the streets after dark by themselves, they are afraid to go into restaurants alone, they are afraid to go to the movies or to the theater by themselves.

Many single women suffer from identity confusion. They are not sure who they really are. They hinge their identity on that man in the future, and they feel their problems can be solved only by attaching themselves to a man. If they don't have a permanent relationship with a man, many women feel as if something is wrong with them.

Some single women stay single by choice. They feel they want to remain unattached until their careers and identities are firmly established. These women, to their surprise, often find themselves panicking as well. They may be good at taking care of themselves, at investing, saving for their own futures, but they forgot about the passage of time in terms of the functions of their bodies. They often wake up with a start in their mid-thirties. They realize they want children and that time is running out. As nature's clock runs down and the forties loom, they feel more and more desperate. Some of them at this point start looking for a husband—a father for their children—rather frantically.

A few brave ones decide to have the child they want without marrying. Single mothers are no different from other mothers in that they often approach motherhood quite unrealistically. There is a tendency to think of babies as cute little things to play with. Many women don't take into account the sleepless nights, the constant calls on one's attention and time that are part of life with infants and young children. Unprepared for the hardships that await them, single mothers sometimes find themselves under greater stress than they counted on. It comes more from within than from society. They hadn't realized when they made their brave decision and picked out the man to sire their child how much it would take out of them. It is not easy to supply all the love and attention of two parents, as well as all the money needed to support a child.

Divorced mothers who have to support their children and assume all responsibility for their day-to-day care, are also under great stress today. Many find there is never enough time or money. "Who is going to take care of me?" wailed a divorced mother of three young children. "I take care of them, but, damn it, I need someone to take care of me, too!"

Middle-aged divorcées and widows face their own problems. They find themselves unexpectedly lost and vulnerable without a man. A divorced woman, newly sprung from a bad marriage, may at first look forward to meeting and sleeping with new men. It looks like fun. But she soon tires of the game and yearns for a steady relationship again.

Middle-aged divorcées and widows soon discover the problem that all single women have to face—the man shortage. In every age group above the twenties, single women outnumber single men. There are seven million more single women than single men in this country. The male gay population cuts further into the number of men available to women.

Statistically men become even scarcer the older a woman is. The shortage of men in older age groups is exacerbated by the fact that men of a suitable age often go out with and marry younger women. A man like Cary Grant, in his seventies, can marry a woman in her early thirties. The reverse is rarely true for older women. They don't and can't marry young men.

Women, even liberated ones, even those with good jobs and salaries, continue to feel inferior and incomplete without a man. Women of all ages who cannot find satisfactory, committed relationships often feel cheated by life. And they find it hard to create a life of their own apart from men. Even if they do, it seems second best to many. "I take classes, I go to the theater and the movies and to dinner with girl friends. I travel. It's okay," said one forty-year-old computer operator. "But I still feel something is missing—and that's a man. It isn't the same without one." Her sentiment is echoed by many single women today who feel disappointed in a world that hasn't turned out as they expected.

Nevertheless, adjustments in life among women are diverse and there are a growing number who are beginning to enjoy their friendships with other women as much as their relationships with men, or at least much more than their mothers or grandmothers did. They exchange confidences they often wouldn't dare reveal to a man. They draw emotional support from one another. They laugh about their lives, even their disappointments about men and love. "You know," said one of these women, "I'm disappointed sometimes when a friend brings a man along. It means there are so many things we can't talk about."

Growing up Female

How we grow up female in our culture influences the way we feel and think of ourselves in terms of our relationships, our self-images, our attitudes towards work and being single and on our own. As women we receive messages from society and are shaped by certain forces that are hard to escape.

Various studies of infants and very young children reveal that girls tend to be somewhat less active physically and to display greater verbal and perceptual skills than boys. Boys are more prone to act out aggression and are more impulsive physically. On top of what appears to some scientific observers to be natural tendencies, the way boys and girls are socialized, the way they are trained to fit their roles in society, magnifies and distorts whatever differences naturally exist between the sexes.

The factor that is most important as far as women and their future fate is concerned is the way mothers prepare sons for independence and autonomy and daughters for passivity and dependency. Both sexes start out dependent on mother, but after the age of two, a boy is encouraged by his mother to stray from her side and explore the rest of the world. Boys are discouraged from clinging. The opposite is true for girls. Dependent behavior is not only permitted, it is even encouraged. At the same time that a boy is pushed to separate from his mother, the little girl is encouraged to remain tied to her mother and not risk independent activities. Girls are expected to be their mother's companion, to help with her tasks, in general, to be compliant, cooperative, passive, dependable and dependent. Girls learn what sociologist Jessie Bernard has called the Love-Duty Ethos, that to be loved and approved of, a female must serve others.

When boys venture out, they learn different ways of coping in the world besides trying to please important people like mother. Girls never give up their earliest way of coping. They keep on trying to please others, and they persist in basing their sense of self-esteem not on doing productive things, but on the way others react to them. Throughout the rest of a female's life this will be true.

In school, girls are briefly allowed to achieve good grades and derive self-esteem from that, but this stops abruptly at adolescence. The girl now becomes interested in boys, and she is warned that to be too competitive or to appear too smart might endanger her relationship with the opposite sex. Her own parents often discourage academic achievement as the girl reaches her teens. A girl's attention now shifts from schoolwork to winning approval from the new important people in her life—boys. She concentrates on her looks and popularity.

Throughout a girl's growing-up period, what is reinforced is not her value as an individual but her skills in interpersonal relationships. From trying to please her parents and teachers, she goes on to try to please men. In this way women learn to become overly dependent on attachments. They frequently don't know who they are as individuals apart from their relationships. This is a fact that must be recognized as working concurrently with personal psychodynamics in individual women's actions and interactions. Women act in a society which requires certain kinds of behavior from them.

In addition, girls have to cope with other factors in their homes that will influence their future relationships. Many women in this country are the daughters of overinvolved mothers and absentee fathers—a combination of parents that social scientists have pointed out is very common in the United States.

In one sense, the overinvolved mother is created by the absentee father—the husband who works long hours, travels a great deal, or is emotionally aloof and withdrawn when he is home. The average father spends 12½ minutes a day with his child, according to one study. The absentee father throws all responsibility for the children on his wife's shoulders. This often makes her anxious, which in turn makes her worry and hover over her children.

Overinvolved, anxious mothers are also created by male experts, generations of whom have told mothers to ignore their maternal instincts and listen to what the experts had to tell them about the right way to raise children. As a result, mothers in this country are often afraid they may harm their children, and they spend too much time and attention trying to do the right things.

Overinvolved mothers have also been created by technology. Before the turn of the century, women had a productive role. Father and mother and children all worked together to support the family and keep it going. With the industrial revolution men left the home for jobs in the outside world, and women's roles became less productive. A woman's world began to center on purely domestic matters. She became solely a mother and wife. Hours that used to be spent in attending to domestic chores gradually lessened as machines came in to take over tasks formerly done by hand. Women now had washing and drying machines, vacuum cleaners, dishwashers. Food did not have to be prepared for storage when supermarkets supplied frozen, canned, and other kinds of food. The contemporary housewife simply has more hours to fuss over her children than her grandmother or great-grandmother did.

Overinvolved mothers are also created by the narrow female role in our society. When a woman's identity is based only on her role as wife and mother, raising good, successful children becomes very important. When mothers have the major responsibility for children, there will always be anxiety over how well one is doing as a mother and overidentification with her children.

The overinvolved mother with an absentee husband frequently resents her husband's lack of involvement. She may take her resentment out on her children. She becomes overcontrolling, binding children to her by submission.

A girl who is raised by an overinvolved mother is frequently ambivalent about her mother. She may interpret overinvolvement as distrust. She thinks her mother has no faith in her abilities to operate as a separate person. A girl begins to distrust her own competence. She finds herself bound by ties that she struggles with, but cannot break. She ends up both needing and loving her mother, but also resenting and hating her.

Many women in this country have double-edged relationships with their mothers. They dislike their mother or are frequently angry with her, but they keep on returning to her nevertheless.

Such daughters may also incorporate their mother's version of love as their own. They think of love as overwhelming or as a fusion with another rather than as loving coexistence of two individuals.

Even if a girl did not have an overcontrolling mother but simply an absentee father, the ties to her mother may be hard to break unless the mother encouraged her daughter's independence. A more active father acts as a buffer between daughter and mother, helping the girl create her own separate identity.

An absentee father, because he was inaccessible to his daughter, may also create in her a vision of men as elusive or unobtainable. Many women in our culture are really searching in their love relationships for the father they never had. Many women also go through life feeling defective, because they were never able to capture their father's attention or love.

As women grow up, they learn also that the world which started out as most valued, the female world, the world of the mother, is not the most highly regarded in the larger universe. They find out that men, the doers, are thought of more highly than women, the pleasers. When they accept and adhere to their female role, women create a bind for themselves, because they are also accepting an inferior position in life.

Because men have more power and status, a fact that becomes abundantly clear early in life, women in our society either consciously or unconsciously learn to envy men. They feel that men have what women don't have. It is this envy that causes many women to seek alliances with powerful men, harboring the illusion that in their relationships with men they will find power and status to make up for what they lack within themselves. Envy of men also keeps a woman from valuing herself or other women too highly. Some psychiatrists call this penis envy, but penis envy is more a metaphor for a woman's desire to have man's position in our society, than a desire to actually have the male sexual organ, as Freud saw it.

Dissatisfaction with Appearances

Most women in our culture have a hang-up about some part of their body or face, if not about their total looks.

Wanda secretly hates her breasts. She thinks they are too small. Each time she slept with a man before her marriage, it was worrisome. She was convinced that she would be spurned because of her breasts. This never happened, but her anxiety never abated. She is now married to a man who tells her her breasts are beautiful. She is glad he thinks so, but one part of her really doesn't believe he is telling the truth.

Cecile, on the other hand, dislikes her big breasts. She thinks they droop too much. She hates having to take off her bra when she gets undressed.

Danielle always worries about her thighs. She thinks they are too fat. For Mandy, it's her legs; her ankles are too thick. Jennifer thinks her nose is too big. Carla hates her hair which hangs limp no matter what she does with it.

Why do so many women dislike their looks and their bodies? Why do women want to be bigger, taller, shorter, thinner, more buxom, less buxom?

First of all, women value looks because women know that men do. Beauty of face and form is an important attraction for men. Many men, of course, can go beyond a woman's appearance and like her for what she is as a person. Nevertheless, it is true that in male society at large, the possession of a beautiful woman automatically confers status on a man and makes him the envy of other men.

There is a basis in reality for the importance that women attach to beauty. As sociologist Jessie Bernard points out in her book *The Female World,* "It is certainly true that beauty in women became supremely important when there was little place for a woman outside her home, and few opportunities for economic survival, much less comfort unless provided by a husband. . . . until recently a woman could do better for herself by way of marriage than through her own efforts. Beauty matters."

Because of this, many mothers are always trying to improve the way their daughters look, thereby transmitting a sense of dissatisfaction which their daughters internalize. According to a passage in Nancy Friday's book *My Mother, My Self*, "Almost from birth we see mothers conveying to their daughters that they aren't good enough as is. Mom doesn't fuss much with her son, but she is constantly adjusting, fixing, trying to perfect this little female picture of herself in the same way she fiddles with her never-perfect appearance."

The influence of the cosmetic and advertising industries on women's dissatisfaction with their appearances has been enormous. Women grow up being bombarded with messages about various creams, cosmetics, shampoos, deodorants, lotions, polishes, conditioners—an ever increasing array of products for women, designed to make them into more desirable creatures. The subliminal message behind most ads is that the woman seeing it is defective. She can and should improve herself. It's a message that women take to heart.

The cosmetics industry is a multimillion dollar business. Diet books regularly become best sellers. The offices of plastic surgeons are so crowded these days with women who want to look younger or better with more beautiful noses, different chins, larger breasts, or fewer wrinkles that in New York City there is a six-month wait for a mere consultation with some of the better known surgeons.

Few women in our culture remain entirely unaffected by the sense of imperfection that the advertising industry fosters in women. The media in what it presents to women as the female role, helps contribute to the dependency, helplessness and dissatisfaction with their appearance that most women feel to some degree.

Media Images of Women

As a girl grows up, she is subject not only to the influence of her parents and teachers, to the message of ads, but also to the feminine images coming at her from the media. A group called Women on Words and Images studied the representation of women used in school textbooks and found that the majority of the stories in them centered around males. Male biographies outnumbered female ones. Even in fantasies, male heroes far exceeded those with leading female characters.

In children's textbooks, males are portrayed as doers who figure things out on their own and make money; females are shown as fearful and incompetent, relying on others to solve problems for them.

From an early age on, the picture girls receive about being female is that women are helpless and dependent on others, and they see also that women even accept derision from males.

Derision is the female's lot if one judges by popular humor. One survey revealed that anti-female jokes outnumbered anti-male jokes by six to one in our culture. Women pictured in jokes are talkative and silly, dumb, sex objects, anxious to trap men into marriage, dominating or exploiting men for money, unable to handle money, and nags.

Television is the most powerful communication medium in contemporary culture. By the time the average American child reaches adolescence, he or she has spent more time in front of the tv set than at school. And what is the message that girls and women receive about themselves? Women on Words and Images found that three-fourths of all the leading characters on tv are male. The male heroes are generally involved in action dramas. They are brave and clever and are doing a job. The women in these same shows are pictured as largely interested in romance, families or helping their bosses out. Most women on tv do not have jobs and careers. Recently Mary Tyler Moore and shows like *Wonder Woman, Policewoman,* and *The Bionic Woman* have shown women as doers instead of dependents or manipulators, but as Carole Tavris and Carole Offir point out in their book *The Longest War,* ". . . it is interesting that Wonder Woman when she isn't saving the world works as a secretary, and the Bionic Woman teaches elementary school. Heroines such as Charlie's Angels usually take their orders from an authoritarian man instead of figuring out whodunit. Even Angie Dickenson's competent Policewoman is often bailed out of jail by her male partner. Heroines typically unmask the villain by accident or luck. When women succeed, these programs seem to be saying, it is not by virtue of their own talents."

If one turns to tv situation comedies, one sees women pictured largely as manipulative. Women get what they want by deceiving their husbands or by other indirect methods that often make their men seem like little boys or fools.

In addition, if one looks at the women who are heroines on tv shows, they always turn out to be slim and beautiful. One study revealed that eighty-five percent of the women on television are under the age of forty.

Television commercials also present to girls and women a distorted, hard-to-match or poor image of themselves. A large number of commercials show women in kitchens polishing floors, doing laundry, baking cakes with maniac devotion. Only recently have tv commercials begun presenting women as career women, but when a career woman is shown it is often in a trivialized or sexual context. For example, one recent commercial showed a man waking up in a rumpled double bed. The phone had rung. The person calling was obviously the woman who had shared his bed the night before. She was already off traveling for her job.

Other commercials show that women who are admired or loved are always perfect beauties often with long hair blowing in the wind—an image most women can't measure up to.

The Mental Health of Married Women vs. Single Women

For all of the single woman's feelings of unhappiness because she isn't married, for all of her exaggerated feelings of loneliness, for all of her fears about the future or even about sleeping alone in her apartment at night, for all of what she perceives as her disadvantage in life because she doesn't have a man of her own—it turns out when you look at various studies comparing the mental health of single women with married women that single women are in better emotional shape. (Single women are also in better shape than single men.)

Why is this so?

The single woman's mental health is superior to that of the married woman because she has a job and is out in the world among people, and she is taking care of herself, doing things.

At the same time that the single woman may bemoan her autonomous state, she is actually benefiting from it.

New brides may feel happier than they have ever been, but their sense of well-being is short-lived. In terms of various symptoms used by psychologists to indicate distress—things like nervousness, inertia, nightmares, headaches, palpitations, feelings of impending breakdowns—wives have more symptoms of distress than single women. Many social scientists have concluded there is something about marriage that is unhealthy for women.

This does not mean that all wives are unhappy. Contented, thriving wives do exist. But who are the ones who suffer in marriage, who account for the statistics? Various studies have shown that wives who work, even in low prestige jobs like waitress or supermarket clerk, are happier than those who derive their sole identity from being wives and mothers. One survey done by *Psychology Today* magazine in 1976 showed that housewives were more anxious and worried than wives who worked. Housewives also felt more lonely and more worthless. The *Psychology Today* magazine study sampled relatively well-educated and affluent women, but other surveys of less educated and less affluent women also showed similar results.

The tangible reward of paychecks for work done and some sense of accomplishment in doing even low status, relatively undemanding work creates a greater sense of well-being than doing housework. Housework, sociologists have pointed out, has no clearly defined criteria to judge oneself by, and there is no visible reward comparable to a paycheck for the stay-at-home wife. Adding to the housewives' mental health problems is the social isolation and the lessening of a sense of autonomy that often takes place the longer a woman is married and taken care of by her husband. "Women who are quite able to take care of themselves before marriage may become helpless after fifteen or twenty years of marriage," points out sociologist Jessie Bernard.

Housewives also become very dependent on their husband's continuing love and often fret about losing it. A variety of studies have shown that wives, more often than husbands, say that they feel unloved and unvalued, which can certainly lead to depression.

The unhappy housewife is so common in our society that medical doctors, psychiatrists, and social scientists have a term to describe it—"the housewife syndrome." The housewife syndrome is characterized by feelings of depression and incompetence, and is often accompanied by a variety of psychosomatic ailments.

Although wives seem to suffer in marriage, husbands thrive. Statistics show that husbands are in better mental and physical health than either single men or their own wives. Theorists maintain that this is because a man does not derive his identity solely from his marriage. He knows who he is by his job. Men also do not suffer from the social isolation of many wives, since men go out into the world every day.

Going back to work appears to be a solution to the poor mental health problem of wives—and in one way it is. It does improve a woman's emotional state. But, as pointed out in other portions of this book, work creates its own conflicts for women, particularly the more ambitious women with demanding jobs. Women get caught between their duties to their careers, their duties to themselves as women, and their duties to their husbands and children. It's a conflict a man does not face since his identity as a man was never traditionally associated with his domestic functions.

Husbands who work have wives. Wives who work don't have wives. Even today, most wives still do the lion's share of the housework, leaving a husband to pursue his career unencumbered by peripheral matters and able to rest up on weekends—the time when most working wives get around to taking care of their homes.

Perhaps this lopsided arrangement will change sometime in the near future. A recent poll done by the General Mills Corporation showed that both men and women are starting to believe that decisions about housework and family activities should be shared.

But we aren't there yet. In the same poll working wives reflected their ambivalence about full-time careers and the pressure they feel juggling household duties and careers, by reporting that if they could, they would prefer working part-time rather than full-time.

Women and Sex

Although there is much more casual sexual activity among women than in the past, casual sex turns out not to be terribly satisfying for most. The majority of women find they do not enjoy one night stands, brief affairs, quick sex. They don't like sleeping with two or three men at the same time while they try to find one man to settle down with.

It may be biological or it may be our social conditioning, but for women, sex is still linked to emotions. Sex becomes an unsatisfactory experience when it is not. The act of sex itself can make a woman emotionally attached to a man. How to have an active sex life and remain true to their values is a problem that many single, divorced and widowed women have to grapple with today. Most women feel entitled to a good sex life yet they don't know how to achieve it without an ongoing relationship. Many women vacillate. They go through periods of sleeping with men casually for sex, then withdrawing and refusing sex for another period of time because they find it humiliating or unfulfilling.

Although many women find sex unsatisfactory without a partner to whom they are emotionally attached, recent surveys show that there is a great increase in the number of wives who are having extramarital affairs. Some women, once they have emotional lifelines and the security of a man in a steady, committed relationship, then find they can play more casually with sex. More often wives look to sex as an antidote for a faltering marriage or an ailing ego. Most women, however, even in extramarital affairs often find themselves more involved emotionally than they intended. Wives tend to get more attached to their lovers than do husbands who play around. Wives also often feel more guilty about their affairs than husbands do.

No matter how much they try to act differently, sex for most women remains an act of the mind as well as of the body.

Women, Men, and Love

Whether a woman is traditional or modern, with or without a career, in or out of marriage, love still remains a paramount issue. An increasing number of women, particularly younger ones, now place as much emphasis on careers as on relationships, but traditionally women have spent their whole lives rehearsing for love, yearning for love, endlessly pondering over the quality of love, needing reassurances of love, mourning for lost love. The famous psychiatrist Karen Horney has written extensively about what she calls the overevaluation of love among women in contemporary society.

When a woman is in love, it often infects every other area of her life. Unless she is one of the new determined career women, at work she daydreams and waits anxiously for him to call. Reports may be neglected, memos may not get written, research may remain undone, schoolwork may suffer when a female is involved with a man.

At home the woman waits for a man's appearance or at least to hear from him. She may be afraid to leave the house in case he calls. If he doesn't call when she expected or hoped he would, she becomes distraught or worried. A woman interested in a man may plan her wardrobe with an eye to whether he will find her appealing in a certain dress, blouse, pair of pants. She wants to look good for him and suddenly none of her clothes seems right, or she thinks her hair needs to be fixed up. She concentrates on what she thinks are her defects and prays he won't notice or care, but fears otherwise.

A woman in a new relationship will frequently invite the man to dinner and then spend hours planning and cooking an elaborate meal. The hidden, often unconscious goal is to impress him so much that he will fall in love or love her all the more. It's also to show him how accomplished she is and what lovely meals could be in his future. She may buy pretty sheets she can't afford for them to sleep on together. Unless, of course, she is very liberated—but how many women are?

When she's with friends, a woman is liable to talk about her current romance endlessly, going over every detail of the relationship, analyzing conversations, trying to figure out what her man's actions or words may mean in terms of what he feels or doesn't feel about her.

Women don't know how to compartmentalize love the way men do. When a man is involved with a woman, he generally works as well as ever. He doesn't spend time daydreaming about her when he should be helping clients, working on briefs, making sales. He knows that love is one part of his life and work is another. He doesn't let one area of his life slide over the psychological barriers to another, as a woman frequently does.

Women also tend to obsess about relationships in a way that men do not. Rare is the man who thinks about a woman as continuously as a woman thinks of a man.

Even when they have good jobs, women are often unhappy, even frantic between relationships. They may man hunt in all of their spare time, bemoan their fate to friends, ask for introductions. Making a new connection becomes their prime business in life. Even when everything else may be going along fine, if a woman is without a man for any length of time, she feels there is something definitely wrong with the quality of her life. Men are able to take more enjoyment out of their work, and most don't feel that their whole world has fallen apart if there isn't a woman around—even if they intensely wish for a relationship.

When a new man does come into a woman's life, she may suddenly shed a few pounds. She begins to worry about how she will look naked or in a bathing suit. She may have eaten her way through the anxious period of being without a man, so a diet is in order. Some women do the reverse. They diet madly when they are without a man—sprucing up their appearances to find someone. Only when they have a man will they slowly gain a few extra pounds.

Other little things connected to appearance become more important with a man on the scene. Legs that have gone unshaven, hidden under pants, suddenly are tended to meticulously. Hair that used to go unwashed or unset for days at a time is suddenly shampooed and blown dry every day, or at least every time she expects to see him.

A woman in a new romance suddenly may look better for

no concrete reason. There may be a new sparkle in her eye, a zesty look on her face. Her skin may seem smoother or rosier. People tell her she looks marvelous and want to know what she's been doing to herself.

A woman with a new man is quick to broadcast the news to the world. The telephone is the bearer of good tidings. Women's telephone conversations are generally longer than men's anyway, but when a woman is "involved," conversations become interminable. A woman goes down her list of friends and calls them all to tell them about the new man she's met. She continues to call her friends regularly to give them blow-by-blow descriptions of what's going on, or to enlist their advice.

Men would be shocked at how indiscrete women can be. Women among themselves will often talk quite openly about whether a man is a good or bad lover and back up their assessments with concrete details. A woman is liable to talk about a man's psychological problems, his financial condition, reveal his faults along with his good points. She may even give friends a historical perspective—telling them about old girl friends and ex-wives.

Women are capable of revealing all to their friends about a man. Men still retain a sense of chivalry, even these days, and they reveal very little about the women in their lives.

Many women, once they become involved with a man, tend to lapse into one or a combination of the roles traditionally assigned to women in our society. They may become motherly and nurturing, looking after a man, listening to his woes, doing him small favors. They may become helpless and enlist a man's protection. They may become subservient, putting the man's needs first, perhaps even ignoring their own needs. They may become concerned about their value as decorative or sex objects, becoming overly involved with their appearance, or trying to be sexy or seductive. They may become passive, letting a man do all the work in a relationship, from calling for dates to being active in bed. They may become very emotional or moody.

In marriage, a woman's drive for power may come out within the context of her family interactions, if she has no other outlet for it in the outside world.

The various ways that women interact in their relationships are described on the following pages of this book. When women are neurotic they often act in ways that are exaggerations and distortions of what they perceive their traditional role as women to be—servers, consumers, passive and helpless creatures, nurturers.

Aggression, and the desire for power are not included in what we think of as femininity, and so these drives get played out indirectly and covertly. They are often disguised in more acceptable forms for a woman—service to others, helplessness, an alliance with a powerful man which gives a woman power she wouldn't dare seize herself.

The behavior and motivations within each classification in this book are generalized descriptions of the way many women act. Specific individual women will rarely fit a category totally. Women will find, though, that even if all of the characteristics described don't apply, a good number do, and they will recognize themselves to be Big Mommies, Technicolor Ladies or any of the other kinds of females I write about. Within the categories there are, of course, degrees of behavior. Some women are more Bitchy, more Chameleonlike, more Princesslike than others.

Many women will discover little bits of themselves in many female types or that they are combinations of two or more categories. A woman, for example, may have some Princess in her in terms of what she expects from men in the way of material possessions. She may also be something of a Martyr expecting people to read her mind rather than stating directly what she wants, or she may also be a Chameleon at times, changing her tastes to suit a man's. She could be a combination of Big Mommy and Technicolor Làdy, Bitch and Enslaver or other categories of women found on the following pages.

The purpose of this book is twofold. It is to help women understand why they act the way they do in their relationships with men and to more fully comprehend the behavior of their friends. It is also to help men understand the women they have known, do know, and will know, and as a result understand something of their own reactions to women. If men really want to know, as Freud did, "What do women want?" this book should help give some of the answers.

We are in an age when many women are trying to change their behavior and create more satisfying, self-fulfilling lives for themselves. In order to move ahead with our lives it is not enough to only understand how we have been molded by society's expectations of us as women. We must also understand our own individual pasts, the early family interactions that caused us to like or hate ourselves, to feel that love can be counted on or is always denied, that men are elusive or accessible, that women are friendly or competitive, that caring is dangerous or gratifying, that a relationship is a partnership of two individuals or a melding into one, that being vulnerable is a way of gaining power or a risk of losing it that must be avoided at all costs.

This book means to give women the knowledge of hidden motivations so crucial to the outcome of all relationships.

CHAPTER 2

THE PRINCESS

He met her when he was finishing up his residency at a large hospital in Chicago. It was at a party given by another doctor he knew from medical school. He noticed her right away. She was the best-dressed woman there. Her clothes were casual, understated, but in superb taste. Even from a distance he could see she had a polished glow, a "presence" about her.

He was shy, but he finally managed to force himself across the room. He placed himself in front of her, grinned, and said, "Hi, I'm Arnold." She looked at him tentatively. Her large blue eyes surveyed his tweed suit, his shoes, his watch, his hair. "Dr. Arnold, or Mr. Arnold?" she asked. "It's hard to tell in this crowd."

"Dr. Arnold," he confessed, "but you can call me plain old Arnie."

Her smile broadened. Instantly she became attentive and gracious. Within ten minutes he decided that she was as charming as she was good-looking and toward midnight he offered to take her home. The next day he called her at the public relations firm where she worked as an assistant to an account executive. He insisted they have dinner that night. Arnie had a wonderful time. He found her bright, lively, intelligent, attractive. What more could a man want? Arnie started to see her regularly, and the more he was with her, the more convinced he became that this woman was someone very special.

She took him to marvelous little restaurants with terrific food. Her taste in everything was perfect. Her judgments about people seemed so wise. He had a hard time getting her into bed, but that was all right. He had to agree with her when, in answer to his pleading, she said, "Arnie, you wouldn't like it if I were the kind of woman who fell into bed with just anybody. Sex is something precious to me. It has to be with the right man." She looked at him meaningfully.

Finally he was able to convince her that he was "serious" about their relationship, and they did have sex. But by that time he was already in a daze, and the sex merely sealed the spell she had cast over him. He asked her to be his wife.

He wanted to get married right away, but she resisted. She told him she always had dreamed of a big wedding with all of her friends and relatives present. Such affairs took time to arrange, she explained. They would have to wait at least three months.

She had a hard time choosing the place where the wedding would be held. She changed her mind three times. She had an even harder time choosing her wedding gown. It seemed to Arnie that she and her mother went to every expensive store in Chicago, but still she couldn't decide. "Don't you want me to look perfect?" she argued when he suggested she settle on any one of several dresses. She obviously looked good in all of them with her tall, slim figure. "Even if you don't care, I want to look perfect for you. I want you to be proud of me," she said, placing her hand on his. He was touched. When she finally did decide on a dress, then she had a crisis at every fitting. Something always was not quite the way she wanted it. She would call Arnie with her complaints about the dress, the dressmaker, the veil, the shoes, the floral arrangements.

One day after trooping from store to store together in search of suitable bridesmaids' gifts, Arnie left her still undecided. He flung himself across his bed exhausted, and began to think. A sense of uneasiness that had been growing since the wedding preparations began, came to the surface. Arnie envisioned his future life—endless nit-picking and infinite attention to small details presided over by his wife. He had to ask himself if this was what he wanted out of marriage. To his horror he found himself saying, "No, no, no, this is not what I want." The next day in the kindest and gentlest way possible he told her that the wedding was off. She, of course, never forgave him, but Arnie figured that her undying hatred was a fair price to pay for avoiding a lifetime of misery.

Arnie was lucky to have spotted a Princess, one of a royal breed of women, in the nick of time. A Princess is the kind of woman who runs her life according to the principle of entitlement. A Princess feels herself to be superior and therefore entitled, just by virture of being who she is, to whatever she wants. The best of everything is none too good for the Princess.

Princesses are almost invariably attractive, if not by virtue of what nature gave them, then because they have polished up, worked on, fixed via dieting, cosmetics, plastic surgery, and hairdye, what they have.

A Princess's appearance is quite identifiable. She is always dressed immaculately and stylishly. She looks totally put together even if you catch her picking up her kids at school or dashing down to the supermarket. A Princess may be in jeans but the jeans will fit perfectly, be well pressed, and generally sport a designer's label.

No matter what color a Princess's eyes, they are always a combination of radar and microscope. They monitor the field in front of them picking out the significant detail, the telltale sign, the fatal flaw. Nothing is ever accepted at face value by a Princess. She is a regal judge of everything. What are her standards? Herself. Things have to be the way she thinks they should be or they are no good.

When you meet a Princess for the first time, you may not realize it, but the radar and microscope are being turned on you. Your clothing, your manners, your escort are being scanned and rated. If you are a man and are wearing a double knit leisure suit or are hiding white socks beneath the trousers of your business suit, the Princess will mentally record these strikes against you in the calculator always clicking away in her attractive head.

If you are a woman, don't think you can get away with last year's dress at a party. The Princess will recognize it as such instantly.

She will also note the right things and give you gold stars if she finds them—an Yves St Laurent suit, for example, a

Halston dress, a Missoni sweater, Perreti jewelry. A Princess can spot the difference on sight between a silk blouse and one made of synthetic. She can guess at the labels sewn into your clothes.

Based on how you look and your standing in the world, the Princess will decide whether or not to bother with you, whether you will add luster or tarnish to her carefully tended image.

The Princess is eternally concerned about how she and others look to the rest of the world. If she feels you will be a valuable acquisition, she will turn on what can be great charm. If, however, she figures you have nothing much to offer her, she is liable to be rude, turning away abruptly. For example, if Arnie had answered at the party, "I'm Mr. Arnie. I own the cleaning store down the block," his Princess would have reacted as if he had bleeding sores and fled. Unless, of course, she felt the cleaning store was but one of a national chain that Arnie owned.

What a Princess Wants in a Man

First of all, a Princess wants a man to be presentable. She needs an escort who will look good on her arm. After establishing that he is the right height and that his looks are acceptable she will quickly try to find out what a man does and how much he earns. What the man represents in terms of status and her material needs is much more important to the Princess than what kind of a human being he is.

If you could peek into a Princess's fantasies from an early age, you would see no torrid, X-rated drama—just a serene picture of a beautiful suburban home with manicured lawns and elegant furnishings. Princesses dream about their home more than their man. Prince Charming is simply the one who will give it to them.

Rarely is sex allowed to get in the way of a Princess's goals. Sex may be something the Princess enjoys. She may even be good at it—after all, it is one of the weapons in her husband-hunting arsenal. But sex is essentially a means to an end rather than an overwhelming need or interest. A Princess would trade orgasms with a dashing ne'er-do-well any day, for a man who is an ox in bed but who considers her to be a goddess and is willing and able to place suitable offerings at her well-shod feet.

It is the rare Princess who allows herself to be an easy lay, even in this sexually liberated age. She may not wait for marriage as Princesses of yore did, but she is reluctant to give herself sexually to a man until she is certain that she is involved in a relationship with a future.

A Princess's consort or candidates for that position are never aware that beneath the gracious, polished exterior they find so attractive lies the steely heart of a scheming, determined woman. Since the prime ambition of her life from childhood on has been to marry the right man, she has cultivated the skills of courtship and they provide excellent camouflage for her true nature. She looks good on any occasion, is a lively companion, converses well, drawing upon a smattering of knowledge about many things. She may even have a wicked sense of humor. She seems interested in a man's affairs. All of this is surface adornment and hides the fact that in reality she is critical, demanding and totally self-absorbed.

So dazzling are the Princesses' attributes to the men they capture, however, that they often remain ignorant of her true character even after many years. Husbands remain continually in awe of how smoothly their households are run, how stylish their furniture is, what a good hostess the wife is, how neat and well-mannered their children are, and how good-looking at any age their Princess is compared to other women. The Princess's conviction that she is special rubs off on her man, who eventually shares her sincerity on this score. One consort summed it up for many when he said recently, "I not only love my wife, I'm enthralled by her."

Since Princesses do most things with style, they are often gourmet cooks—when they decide to cook, that is. One Princess makes it into the kitchen only twice a week, but she invests those occasions with such importance that her husband for fear of offending her with too small an appetite won't let a crumb pass his lips beyond ten o'clock of the morning that his wife prepares dinner. Fear of his wife's disapproval or displeasure is common among husbands of Princesses.

Although her husband may remain for the most part adoring, this does not mean that Princess's marriage is without stresses and strains. To the contrary, it is often full of fights caused by the fact that there is never an end to what the Princess wants and she is so critical. Although arguments are commonplace, they rarely end in disillusion. The Princess is clever enough not only to get her own way, but also to make her husband believe that even if he gave in, it was in his best interest to do so. For example, if she wants a new fur coat, it is because a business competitor's wife just got one and he wouldn't want her to look shabby by comparison, would he?

One Princess didn't want her husband to hire a man he was seriously considering because she didn't approve of his manners. She managed to put the whammy on him by telling her husband that the prospective employee would be a threat to her husband in business.

But as shrewd as Princesses are, even they occasionally make mistakes—sometimes fatal ones. There are two times in the life of a Princess when this is most likely to occur. The first time is before marriage, soon after the engagement has been announced. During courtship she has either consciously or unconsciously been smart enough to keep a rein on her critical, demanding, self-centered nature, but once she feels she has her man, she may relax a bit. One man to his horror discovered what his fiancée was all about during a telephone conversation a short while after the formal announcement of their engagement. While they were chatting, his Princess casually mentioned that she had gone shopping that morning for table linens. He was surprised. He presumed she had been at work. "Did you take the day off?" he inquired. There was a pause at the other end of the wire and then his bride-to-be said matter-of-factly, "Oh, I forgot to tell you. I quit my job two weeks ago."

The fact that not only had the Princess thought it unnecessary to consult him about whether she should leave her job or not, but also that she hadn't even thought it important to tell him when she did, was enough for this man to break his engagement.

From the Princess's point of view there was also shock and surprise. She didn't know what all the fuss was about. After all, Princesses (at least until recently) aren't supposed to work after marriage. He should have known without her having to tell him that she would be leaving her job.

After she is married, a Princess may show her true stripes when demands of one kind or another are placed upon her in hard times.

Not long ago a successful businessman had the veil lifted from his adoring eyes after he suffered a heart attack. While in the hospital, he asked his wife to go to the office to keep an eye on things until he recovered. She was outraged by his suggestion. He was appalled that after a lifetime of catering to her, the one time he asked her to do something for him, she balked. This caused him to spend his remaining time in the hospital reviewing his marriage with new eyes. He suddenly realized how one-sided their relationship had always been. To her dismay, he decided to retire because of the state of his health, sold the business from his hospital bed and asked her for a divorce soon after.

Another example of the undoing of a Princess occurs in the movie *Ordinary People*. The husband of the movie's central female character, Beth, had his eyes opened only after one son died in an accident and another son, out of guilt, tried to commit suicide. On the day of the son's funeral, Beth noticed that her husband was wearing the wrong color shirt and told him to change it—a typical action of a Princess who, no matter what the circumstance, is concerned about outward appearances and what people will think. She also was unable to give any comfort or love to the surviving son, which caused a final rupture in the marriage.

Since *Ordinary People* is about a WASP family it points out the mythology attached to Princesses. They are thought to always be Jewish; in popular culture they are referred to as JAPS, Jewish American Princesses. Princesses can and do belong to any religious or ethnic group. As proof that not all Princesses are JAPS consider the names of these Princesses: Jacqueline Onassis, The Duchess of Windsor, and, in fiction, Scarlett O'Hara.

Princesses are actually very traditional women with very

rigid notions about the roles of men and women. Women
have to be taken care of, men have to take care of them. Even
when a slight infraction of this basic rule occurs, it can
disturb them greatly. One widower courting a widow found
this out during a long automobile drive to a resort. He was a
man of seventy and became tired after a couple of hours
behind the wheel. He asked her to please drive while he took
a short nap. She did as she was asked, but told him after-
ward, "I will never forgive you for that." He decided not to
live out his golden years with such a woman.

The Kind of Men Princesses Attract

What type of man finds a Princess irresistible?

Let's look at Harry. Harry is a man who left school at
fourteen. He had to help support his very poor family. By the
time Harry was twenty he was on his way to becoming a
millionaire. He spent most of his waking hours working and
had little time to educate himself. He rarely read anything
beyond the financial pages of the daily newspaper. Nevertheless, because of his wealth, Harry soon began mixing in
social circles in which cultural matters were important, albeit
in a superficial way. It was a circle, also, in which people
always wore the most fashionable clothing, behaved with
proper manners and lived at good addresses. When Harry
was thirty, he met Valerie, the daughter of a lawyer. Harry
was a tall, well-built, nice-looking man and Valerie seemed
attracted to him instantly. Harry soon found that Valerie
was everything he was not—she could talk about the latest
books and the latest plays, she dressed impeccably, her
manners were beyond reproach. They soon married. Valerie
was a Princess happy to educate Harry about the finer
things in life in exchange for a wonderful lifestyle. Harry
is typical of the husbands of Princesses. Many of them are
successful men, or men with the potential for being very
successful, but no matter how rich or successful they are,
they feel somewhat inferior because of something in their
background. It could be, as in Harry's case, that they
come from very poor families or left school early or their

mothers and fathers were immigrants or their background was
blue collar.

Because they feel deficient socially, Princesses are enormously attractive to them. The Princess is seen as a social
asset. She represents what they feel inwardly they lack—class.

If a man needs pointers in his social life, a Princess is
able to help him polish up his act. She gets him to the right
tailors, she improves his social graces by giving him instruc-
tions in the better way to do things. The Princess can be
counted on to push her man to become more and more
successful, often insisting on maintaining a standard of living
that forces her husband to work harder and harder to maintain
it.

A typical attitude of a Princess was expressed by one
young woman who told her husband she was going to buy a
fur coat. "We can't afford it," he warned her. "Where will I
get the money to pay for it?" he asked. "You'll just have to
find it," she answered and sailed out to buy her coat. Princesses do not have empathy for the struggles of their husbands.

During courtship, the Princess can generally sense very
early on which kind of man will be right for her. The man
who will let her have a lot of say about where they will go
and what they will do stays in the running. The man who
insists too much on having his own way will eventually be
rejected. Either consciously or unconsciously, she sorts out
her suitors pruning them down to those she will be able to
control as a husband.

In marriage a man gets his Princess, but, alas, so do his
friends. The Princess will reevaluate a man's chums once she
has a ring on her finger, knocking out those who don't meet
her standards. If a husband stubbornly insists on continuing to
see those the Princess considers undesirable, she banishes and
isolates them. She will never mix the friends she approves of
with those she considers unfit. They will be seen separately,
entertained less lavishly than is her custom and they will
never make a Saturday night with the Princess. She will see
them on weeknights when everyone has to go home early.

Although husbands of Princesses may consider themselves
to be either happy or unhappy depending on how they read
her demands and criticisms, they remain, through it all,

admirers of her appearance, her taste, and ability to run a household.

What fights there are, are always kept in the strict confines of their private life. To the outside world they appear to be a united and serene couple, an image the Princess is eager to foster. Everything connected to her must appear perfect. In her own mind, the Princess almost always considers herself to be happy and her marriage to be just right. The Princess is a master at the art of denial. If something is wrong, she either denies it, forgets it, or rationalizes it.

Nevertheless, sometimes a Princess finds herself married to the wrong man. It is often because a Princess's demands escalate as the marriage continues, and if a husband cannot meet her new demands, he becomes progressively more inadequate in her eyes.

If divorce occurs, it can cause immense, unforseen problems for the Princess. Even though she may have initiated the action, the Princess may find herself very angry at her ex-husband. Even when he gives her a large settlement, alimony or child support, she feels that her husband is not giving her enough. This is typical of the Princess who always feels under any circumstances that no one ever gives her enough.

In addition to experiencing anger and a sense of deprivation, the Princess may find herself unable either to look for a job, or to keep one.

Generally, a Princess divorces when she is in her forties. Marriage is sacred to her and no matter how dissatisfied she is, she cannot break it up until the children reach a certain age. It is very hard for a Princess in mid-life to start a career and accept a beginner's low status job and salary. She considers this to be a humiliation. So she either finds reasons why she cannot begin a job search, or she finds she cannot hold onto a job. One Princess told her friends she couldn't possibly begin to look for a job until she had finished wall-papering her new apartment, after that it was carpeting, then it was lining her kitchen closet shelves. One excuse followed another and three years later, she still has not started seriously looking for a job.

Another Princess never lasts in a job more than three months. She is always telling her peers and her superiors at work what to do. She considers herself above them all and eventually gets herself fired because of "personality problems".

Another Princess procrastinated a whole year, then finally found a job. She lasted exactly one week. She felt she wasn't being given enough power, and when her boss asked her to water a plant for her, it was more than she could take. She quit.

Princesses Who Never Marry

Some Princesses, to their everlasting dismay, never marry at all. Although they tend to have personality problems at work, just as divorced Princesses do, unmarried Princesses often compensate for their abrasive manner by being very good workers. They may have a reputation in their firms for being hard to get along with, but their eye for detail, their perfectionism and orderliness—all the traits that come with being a Princess—can also make them very competent. However, they scatter the demands they would ordinarily concentrate upon a husband if they were married, instead upon those who work with them. They are full of orders to underlings to shut doors, open windows, stop smoking, bring pencils. They also don't know how to keep a proper hierarchical distance with their superiors and act as if they are on the same level as the chairman of the board, the president of the company and the head of the department.

Throughout the unmarried Princess's working days, she cherishes one ongoing fantasy. She dreams that a suitor will appear who will recognize her marvelous qualities, rescue her from a degrading career, and allow her to assume her natural role—that of housewife.

She shares with the young Princess the dream of a spacious, suburban, elegantly furnished house—her future kingdom.

The Princess Career Woman

Today's Princess approaches work more seriously than her older counterpart. Princesses are always the first to catch onto a new trend, and today they see that having a career is high fashion for women. The new Princess also understands, perhaps with a sigh, that her most cherished role has been downgraded to that of mere "housewife." Therefore to achieve the high status image she covets, the new Princess is apt to become a Princess Career Woman.

Princesses of the past often learned a profession at the behest of their mothers "just in case"—just in case calamity befell them, God Forbid, and their husbands died, or just in case there was—bite your tongue—another depression and their fortune was wiped out. Because Princesses took up their careers with a just-in-case attitude, they didn't take them seriously. Careers were secondary. First, of course, came marriage and family.

Vintage Princesses generally abandoned careers when they snared a husband. Before marrying, they worked at something with a little glamour attached to it, something that would make them an even more desirable catch. They dabbled at being actresses, they worked in the fashion industry or public relations; young Princesses played at being production assistants in television or the movie industry. If a mature Princess wanted to do a little something after her kids grew up, she would generally choose interior decorating, drawing on her natural taste, her eye for detail and her vast experience decorating and redecorating her own home.

Today's Princesses can still be found in the above professions, but they call themselves interior designers rather than decorators. They are no longer content to be production assistants, but want to be producers instead. Contemporary Princesses are entering many of the currently fashionable high status fields for women—law, for example, and medicine.

Having a serious career doesn't change the Princess's basic way of thinking one whit, however. Not only are Princess Career Girls just as demanding of their husbands, they now feel justified in being even more so. The working Princess insists that her husband bring home a big income, no matter how much she earns herself, and he must also take over a large share of the household duties and child care. Although his job may be at least as tough or more time-consuming than hers, it is she who makes the decisions as to what he must or must not do. Mutual decisions? Not for a Princess in any era.

Today's working Princess demands constant sympathy and consideration for her career problems. It doesn't occur to her to return the favor.

The working Princess feels justified in indulging every whim for luxury she may have. If her husband objects, she reminds him that, after all, she is earning an income, too. As a result, husbands of today's working Princesses feel as much financial pressure as those whose Princesses stay at home.

Princesses who don't choose to work are almost always involved in community activities and charity work. The Princess does not do it out of altruism. She does it to enhance her image in the community. She wants public recognition for her efforts in the form of plaques or a high position in volunteer organizations.

The Princess as Mother

Although a Princess would rather perish than admit it, many of them have some doubts about having children. Their hidden fear is that children will make too many demands, ruin their carefully tended figures, get all the attention in the household.

Generally the Princess resolves this initial conflict about motherhood by making the children her property. She sees her children not as separate identities but as extensions of herself. She appears to be a devoted mother, but in reality she uses her children to reflect glory upon herself. She teaches her children to keep their rooms neat, to be clean and well-dressed. They must do well at school and have proper manners at all times.

The Princess has no understanding of what makes her husband tick as a person. She judges him by how well he does as a provider and how well he conducts himself as an escort and host in their home. Similarly, she hasn't the foggiest notion of what her children, at any age, are thinking or feeling. She is not concerned about their emotions. She is concerned only with how well they are performing.

The Princess pushes her daughter to be good-looking, to watch her figure, to wear the clothing that is considered fashionable for her age group as she is growing up. When a Princess's daughter arrives at college, she always brings more clothes in the latest style than her schoolmates. The Princess teaches her daughter to observe others with the same critical eye that she has, and instills a rigid set of "shoulds" in her daughter's psyche that she will never shake until the day she dies.

Sons are pushed in a different way. Whereas daughters are brought up to be consumers, and objects worthy enough to be traded to the right man, a son is trained to be like his father—a workhorse, a man who knows that his sacred duty in life is to provide well for a woman like his mother. A son is always being reminded of the realities of having to make something of himself.

The Princess's message to her daughter is that she simply has to be. As a result, Princesses' daughters become their mothers' carbon copies, their think-alikes and shopping companions. Sons are more likely to recognize their mother for the selfish, manipulating woman she is. After a childhood spent believing what he has been told—that Mother always knows best—a son suddenly may rebel as a late teenager or young adult.

Adolescent rebellion is something the Princess handles not by trying to explore the real reasons for the teenager's actions, but by crossing the whole thing off as being unimportant. If he's mixed up, the problem is his. It is not because of her. She draws solace from the fact that the rest of the world won't judge her badly even if her son is scruffy, hostile and bad-mannered, for she has always been a devoted mother. Everybody knows that teenagers rebel, therefore, it can't be a reflection on her personally.

If a child becomes too rebellious, a problem that even the Princess can no longer ignore, she handles it in her usual way. She makes herself comfortable. She encourages him to stay away from home during vacations, to visit classmates, to take trips, to go to young peoples' resorts, to take a job away from home. In effect, the Princess abandons a child who gives her too hard a time.

Why the Princess Is the Way She Is

At the moment of her birth, the Princess is crowned. Her mother, determined that she shall have the best of everything, proceeds to give it to her. Often the mother is a Princess herself, and she is simply creating another. There are dynasties of Princesses that go back for generations. Sometimes, however, the mother is simply a woman who never had enough of what she dreamed of for herself and so she is determined that her daughter shall have it instead.

In infancy the Princess has to have the best crib, the best toys, the best tricycle. In childhood, she goes to the best schools, the best camps, the best music teacher. As an adolescent, she is taken to the best dermatologist—pimples are not for royal skin. She is allowed, as a teenager, to shop at the best department stores and boutiques. If, heaven forbid, her nose or chin is not the right shape, it's no tragedy. She is taken to the best plastic surgeon to have it fixed. When she arrives at college, she will always have several pieces of gold jewelry to complement her extensive wardrobe. The Princess who has received so much from as far back as she can remember inevitably comes to expect everything as her due.

Along with an unending stream of goodies, the Princess also has been treated to an ongoing chorus of praise. Everything the young Princess does is wonderful. This creates the air of self-confidence typical of Princesses.

However, indiscriminate praise also creates a problem for the Princess. You will never see it on the surface, but eating at her silky insides is the worm of doubt. Even as a child, the Princess senses that she cannot be all that wonderful. She secretly wonders to herself if she really deserves all the praise she is receiving. Inadvertently reinforcing this doubt is her father, off on the sidelines, indulging her but not praising her verbally as her mother is. The young Princess feels that her father, by his silence, is disagreeing with her mother. "See!" she says to herself, "I am not that perfect after all. Or am I?"

Mother's adorations have been for things connected to external appearances, not internal values. The Princess is not praised for being understanding, kind or helpful. No, she is wonderful and her mother's darling because she is pretty, doesn't dirty herself like other children, has a nose that never runs, and has learned to twist her daddy around her already manicured little finger.

She has been taught the screwed up, superficial values, the credo of the Princess: what matters is outward appearance, what counts is getting what you want. External, rather than internal values, the fact that she has been turned into a praise junkie, yet harbors doubts about her worthiness, all cause the Princess to search continually for applause, appreciation, recognition.

As anyone who comes in close contact with a Princess knows, a Princess is also very rigid. Things have to be her way and only her way. Even if she would like to, she finds she cannot bend or change. Her rigidity is a by-product of her close relationship with her mother. Mother was her original source of self-esteem—the one who told her how wonderful she was. She needs her mother to feel okay about herself. Emotionally she has never separated from mother. She runs her life according to what her mother told her was right. To deviate from her mother's standards would constitute a betrayal. She would in effect be abandoning her mother and would risk punishment for it. It is separation anxiety that makes a Princess fear change and cling so rigidly to her own preferences. By remaining faithful to her mother's values, she remains close to her and in her favor. This unconscious clinging to her mother exists whether the mother is alive or dead. Even if the Princess discovers later in life that there are values other than what she was taught which also net praise from people, she finds she is unable to change.

The Princess has very selective hearing. She will hear praise only for the things her mother told her were good; she will not hear praise for things her mother did not value. For example, one very intelligent woman derives little pleasure when praised for her intellectual capabilities. If someone tells her she looks beautiful, however, she glows.

The Princess carries with her a whole set of "shoulds" from her mother. If the Princess finds herself in circumstances which make her run counter to the "shoulds," she often finds herself in trouble. For example, Princesses who end up having to work often have problems. Mother told them they should be housewives, not workers, so they devalue work and act on the job as if they were made for something better than their current tasks.

Mother's admiration is also the source of an underlying rage found in many Princesses. They resent having to rely on attention and admiration from others. They are in a fury because they have to depend on others to make them feel good about themselves. Their anger comes out in ambivalent feelings about loved ones. Princesses love and need their mother, for example, but on an unconscious level they are also furious, because without her attention and applause, they feel helpless. They love and need their husband's salary, but at the same time are aware that they are not capable of earning it themselves, which makes them frustrated. They love their children, but are also angry at them because they take so much energy and keep them a prisoner. A Princess's ambivalence is unconscious but it is a source of typical fantasies. She is plagued by dreams and inexplicable fears that her loved ones will be involved in a car or plane accident or harmed in other ways. It is quite common for a Princess to feel a sudden sense of panic and call her mother to ask, "Mom, are you all right?"

Princesses also turn their anger inward. No one on the outside knows it, but they go through regular periods of feeling incompetent, helpless, distraught. They suffer from subterranean bouts of depression. As these feelings come closer to the surface, they are transformed into a sense of being unrewarded for all of their efforts. This, in turn, allows Princesses to feel justified in getting angry and making more demands on others.

If a Princess is not in a family situation, she will turn her anger, now converted into demands, on others—tradespeople and even their doctors. They may threaten physicians, for example, with suicide if they don't make them better.

In a business office a Princess's underlying anger will come out in impatient, arrogant replies. "Why are you asking me about that report? I did it two days ago!"

The Princess's basic feeling of helplessness is reinforced,

of course, by our society which has taught women to think of themselves as incompetent.

Although the Princess at the most profound level pictures herself as helpless, she is often extremely competent. Princesses are always very thorough at their tasks. They generally are good at what they set out to do, but they never believe it. This accounts for their perfectionism. Orderliness, discipline, organization are ways of counteracting innate helplessness.

Meticulousness can become a compulsion for Princesses. It can reach the point where they resent anyone else messing up their neat universes. One Princess, talking about her college-age kids, admitted recently, "I can't wait until they leave after they have been home on vacation. They always get everything out of order."

The Princess and Other Women

The Princess gets along very well with other women. She generally has many friends, particularly if she can act as a mentor to them. A Princess's following may include younger, admiring women for whom she is a role model or instructor.

If she has a sister, the Princess is often very close to her, transferring to the sister the same sense of oneness that she felt with her mother. One man has had to put up with his sister-in-law's constant presence. For twenty-five years his wife wouldn't make a step without her sister. Wherever he and his wife went, the sister-in-law was invited to come along. Finally the husband bought a home in a faraway resort thinking that at least there he could rid himself of his sister-in-law's constant presence. When his wife invited her sister to buy a condominium in the same resort, he knew he could no longer preserve his marriage.

The Princess's tendency to glue herself to another as she was glued to her mother extends in a different way to her husband. She feels she is part of her husband's competence and success. In other words, if her husband is a judge, so is she. If he's a lawyer, she is one, too. The Germans used to call the wives of doctors Frau Doctor—nothing could be truer than that appellation for the Princess.

What Happens to Princesses

What happens to Princesses? If they are lucky and lead the charmed lives they think they should—and many do—nothing happens to them. They live out their lives with the same adoring husband, surrounding themselves with ostentatious displays of material goods and die happy.

Some Princesses grow a little restless in middle age. They may then have an affair, a very discrete one, in which they will get the admiration that is like a narcotic for them. If a Princess has an affair, she will generally choose a man who will add status to her life or who can help her husband's career. One Princess had a long-term affair with the head of her husband's large company. She knew her husband was kept in a cushy job because of her. He was also sent out of town a lot so that the wife would be freer to see her lover. When her husband died from a heart attack, she remarried a successful lawyer, but continued her old association with her lover whose status position in life she found irresistible.

Other Princesses handle middle age by going back to school. They are generally excellent students and sometimes they go on to prepare themselves for a career in mid-life. If this happens they often develop a sense of competence for the first time in their lives, putting the energy into their new career that they used to put into clothing and material goods. Their households remain meticulous, however, and you can count on it—they are the best-dressed employee wherever they are.

How a Princess Can Help Herself

The Princess is a woman with many strengths. She is often very intelligent, articulate, well read in terms of current books, actively involved in the community and interested in cultural happenings such as art exhibits or the theater. Despite whatever shortcomings she may have in terms of point of view she is also devoted to her children and family life in general.

If you are a woman who recognizes herself as a Princess and you feel you would like to change, here are some tips:

First of all, it is important for you to become aware on a conscious level that what guides you in life is the notion that you are entitled to whatever you want. It's an attitude that gets you material things, but prevents you from getting others—like internal satisfaction. For all you have acquired over the years, do you ever really feel truly satisfied? Be honest.

Your guiding principle of entitlement is not your fault. It's an attitude that was handed to you by your family long before you were old enough to be given a choice of whether you wanted to have to live this way for the rest of your life. If you give up the idea that you are entitled to everything the world has to offer, you are really only giving up an attitude handed down from another generation. Once you give up entitlement, your relations with others will improve. You will stop having to demand things—or expect them too forcefully—from those around you.

Second, if you give up your dependence on externals, you will feel better about yourself. Concentrate on your real strengths—your excellent taste, quick mind, good eye, talent for handling details, active involvement in the outside world. Your feelings of worth will come from these strengths rather than from still more stylish clothing or new furnishings. You won't know what true pride means until you attach it to yourself, rather than to things that look good to the world.

Next, think about those around you. Begin to wonder about the inner life of your children and your husband. What do they think inside themselves? What are they feeling? Pay attention to them instead of yourself. Does your son look unhappy? Ask him why. Try to find out what he is feeling and listen sympathetically when he tells you. Try to imagine what it would be like to be him. The same goes for your husband. If he comes home from work a little crabby try to find out what went wrong to make him feel that way. Or, if he is in a particularly good mood, let him know that you notice it. Your husband may have missed such personal concern from you in the past.

The next time you start to demand something from your husband, ask yourself three questions: (1) Do I really need this? (2) Why do I really need this? (3) Am I asking for this or issuing an ultimatum?

You will find your relationships with your loved ones more satisfying if you start caring about the way they tick, if you communicate with them on a level that grants them respect, if you show you really care.

If you are a Princess, your life is probably pretty good now, but it could be much better. Develop an inner sense of worth so your self-esteem doesn't depend on external trappings, and stop paying attention only to your own wants and start tuning in to the needs and wishes and inner life of those who admire and love you.

CHAPTER 3

THE LITTLE GIRL

Jane is a talented artist. Her paintings have been exhibited in some of the best galleries in the country. She is very competent at what she does, and yet for several months preceding each gallery opening while she is finishing up the paintings to be shown, she becomes helpless and dependent. She phones friends, asking them to come over and view her latest works, seeking reassurance that the paintings are really good. Friend after friend troops into her loft, views the same painting, tells her it's beautiful, but it is never enough to reassure Jane. Her husband holds her hand through the whole process. He soothes her, brings her cookies, cake and other nourishment while she works late into the night.

Jane's sixteen-year-old daughter runs errands during this period and keeps the house neat. She also makes sure her mother gets up early after a late night's work. The household runs around Jane who is always close to tears, afraid that her work isn't good enough, or that she will never finish what she has to do on time. Her phone bills are enormous. She calls everyone she knows from the gallery owner to her father in Seattle.

Jane's behavior before gallery openings is just an exaggerated version of the way she acts all the time. Jane can never seem to get her life together by herself. Her husband is constantly reassuring her about the many things she doubts; her women friends are all surrogate mothers, listening to Jane's problems, offering her advice, meeting her for cozy lunches where they talk mostly about Jane.

Jane's friends generally don't mind because Jane is such a fascinating talker and she makes them feel—well, needed and loved. Jane enthralls them with stories from her past, tales in which she often appears as a waif adrift in a world that was always ready to take advantage of her, a world that was and is too much for her to cope with.

Jane is a Little Girl. Little Girls are extremely dependent women who refuse to grow up. They use a helpless, I-can't-do-anything stance to get others to take responsibility for them and to obtain the nurturance, attention and reassurance that is as necessary to them as water is to a plant.

Some Little Girls, like Jane, seek the caretaking they need from everyone, man or woman. Others, a more common breed, look for it only from men. They are reasonably competent when around female friends and even brag about accomplishments, but the minute a man comes into view, they become incompetent before your eyes. The Little Girl dissolves into a mass of scattered pieces, and she can only be put together again by this wonderful man who has just appeared. The man does not have to be anyone special in her life, any man will do. And when her special effects light goes on, she becomes coy, naive, seductive, flattering, pouty, smiling. She gazes at this man with wonderment in her eyes.

The women who reserve their babyish, help-me act for men make one exception to this rule. They also become a piece of mush looking for behavioral directions from a female authority figure, such as a woman boss.

Typically, Little Girls have a wide-eyed look and a high-pitched childish voice. Some of them look younger than their years and dress accordingly in a rather girlish manner. They wear an air of vulnerability and helplessness the way another woman might wear a designer dress. Many men find the Little Girl to be an altogether adorable and irresistible package. Other men, however, run like hell.

A journalist in his thirties got into an elevator with a woman he had just met. She looked at him with her big green eyes and asked him to push the button, please, adding, "I just get so confused by things like that." He knew it was all over between them at that point. Men like this journalist who find the Little Girl has all the charm of a rattlesnake, don't want a lifetime dependent who will lean on them for everything. They want a more independent woman and the Little Girl in no way fits that bill. Other men run because they sense the insincerity of the Little Girl's manner. Little Girls are really not helpless or incompetent. They just pretend to be in order to control people and manipulate them into giving them what they need and want.

The kind of man who can't resist the Little Girl is a man with a rescue fantasy. He will take Orphan Annie out of the orphanage. He also needs her dependence on him which makes him feel important to offset hidden doubts about himself.

The Little Girl is always ready to adore. When she looks at a man, her eyes see an image that is totally flattering. She sees him as big, powerful, completely competent, a take-charge person who knows everything. It's a picture that is understandably hard for a man to resist.

Most often Little Girls attract successful men. Very occasionally, though, a Little Girl will hook up by accident with a Little Boy and then they become two orphans clinging together in life's storm. They get into so much trouble and have such a tough time dealing with life that one of them sooner or later has to become competent.

The Little Girl has a lifetime fantasy of the perfect man that precedes the entrance of any specific man in her life. When a candidate arrives on the scene, she simply makes him fit the preexisting picture and endows him with the qualities she is seeking. Specific requirements vary from one Little Girl to another. Some Little Girls want an authoritarian man who will order them around. Others just want a sweet man who will reassure them. There is one quality, however, that all Little Girls insist upon. A man must provide the Little Girl with the feeling that she is being looked after and cared about.

Little Girls are very good at quickly sorting out the men who can give them the kind of attention, guidance and reassurance they need from those who can't or won't. After three or four dates, they generally will eliminate the ones who don't fit their agenda, dismissing them with a vague statement, such as, "Oh, he's not right for me." Little Girls, in spite of their scatter-brained appearance, are cognizant of their own needs and at bottom very practical about obtaining them.

In relationships with men, Little Girls are very demanding. They need a stream of assurances, insisting on support for the least little thing they attempt, wanting a myriad of things done for them. Their demands and complaints are clothed in pitiful little whines or hidden behind tears, but are delivered in such a sweet way, accompanied by such respect and worship, that they win rather than alienate. Little Girls are never branded demanding bitches.

Little Girls often play out their great dependency needs with chronic psychosomatic illnesses such as backaches and headaches, and can demand as much from their doctors as they demand from their lovers or husbands.

One doctor who has been treating a Little Girl for many years described her effect upon him. "She called me the other night at 11 PM to complain about pain. I had been on call for a straight twenty-four hours and had just fallen asleep. I was about to get angry with her when suddenly her little face came into my mind. It was so adorable and she is so helpless and needs me so much, I just couldn't shout at her. Instead, I told her what to do."

Little Girls don't need much to satisfy their demands and complaints. A little reassurance calms them down. A compliment or a gift goes a long way. They are grateful creatures and a man sensitive enough to know what makes them tick finds a Little Girl relatively easy to deal with.

Men involved with Little Girls give a great deal, but they also reap their own rewards. A Little Girl supports her husband or boy friend, too, by handing him an image of himself as Mr. Wonderful. As one man explained, "She makes me feel like the most important person in the world." If a man marries a Little Girl when he is quite young, she may be very instrumental in making him into a successful person because he tries so hard to live up to her image of him.

The Little Girl is not a materialistic person per se. She doesn't demand great wealth or success from a man as long as he can assume the caretaker role and be loving, supportive and understanding. Nevertheless, Little Girls often end up quite well off simply because they appeal to obsessive-compulsives many of whom are successful, career-oriented men.

Obsessive-compulsives are often highly organized, driven men, with little spontaneity and imagination, who can't show or even locate their emotions. To them the Little Girl is a delightful contrast. She gives color to their drab, gray world. As opposed to an obsessive-compulsive's emotional control, she spills emotion all over the place. She doesn't have a logical thought in her head. She is vivacious and fun, and she provides him with what he lacks in himself.

As wives and girl friends, Little Girls are affectionate, kind, sweet, and loving. They find it easy, generally, to attract men and get married. Whether they stay married is another question. Some husbands get tired of having to play daddy all the time. They start to want a more equal relationship and may begin an extramarital affair with a more mature kind of woman. It is common in these circumstances for the husband to leave his Little Girl for the other woman. Little Girls tend to blame the whole thing on the other woman, refusing to see their own role in the marital drama. The dumped Little Girl can be heard complaining about that horrible, aggressive, organized other woman. What can her ex-husband possibly see in her?

Sometimes the Little Girl drives a man to leave her in another way. If, for example, she starts to live with a man and the fantasy in her head doesn't match what he is like in reality, she may do things that force him to change. After living with her boy friend for a year, one Little Girl decided that she wanted him to be more authoritarian. She tried to provoke him by telling him she was going to go out with other men. The man she chose for her first fling worked in the same office with her boy friend so he couldn't help but know. Finally the boy friend was so challenged and irritated by her provocative affair that he became, indeed, more force-ful. He told her he wasn't going to put up with her behavior any more. The Little Girl immediately stopped seeing the other man, but by then it was too late. Her boy friend left.

A Little Girl is capable of leaving a relationship herself if something suddenly makes it clear that she has endowed her man in her fantasy of him with qualities that were never there in reality. It happened when one Little Girl became ill and had to be hospitalized. Her man only came to see her sporadically and never brought her anything more than a magazine, making her realize he was a lot less caring than she assumed.

When a Little Girl leaves a man she often does it in such an ambivalent way that he is left with the impression that the relationship might be resumed at some future time. Instead of saying, "Get out of my life," "I can't stand you," "I don't love you anymore," or "You are a rat," she will say something like, "I don't want to see you anymore. It hurts too much to see you." This means, of course, that the man still plays a role in her affections.

Little Girls will stay in contact with men they aren't particularly interested in. They see them a few times, telephone, and withdraw, then keep repeating this pattern. They give men just enough attention to create false hope.

When Little Girls get dumped, they don't fall apart as one might expect. After only a brief period of despondency, they are able to pick themselves up and start searching for a new man. Most of them are successful in finding one fairly soon. It is rare for a Little Girl to be without a man for long. For one thing, they demand less of men than many other women do. Success is often not too important to Little Girls. They are able to see qualities in a man that other women don't necessarily value as much, qualities such as the sweetness and patience to deal with Little Girls, the ability to soothe Little Girls in moments of disorganization or panic.

Why the Little Girl Is the Way She Is

The root of the Little Girl's attitude lies in her early relationship with her father. Most Little Girls were very close to their fathers. Daddy treated the Little Girl as something special. He was full of little attentions; he beamed with approval. Other Little Girls had a father who was aloof and whom they were always chasing after. But the actual character of the father is less important than the Little Girl's view of him as the most important person in her life and the fact that she could never separate from him emotionally. Because she remains fixated on father, she never grows up. The Little Girl in young, middle or old age is still Daddy's Little Girl. It is no accident that many Little Girls wind up married to older men.

The Little Girl first learned to play the game of helplessness with her father. Through a pose of incompetence, she found she could get her father to do things for her and pay attention to her. When the Little Girl couldn't tie her shoes, for example, she discovered that Daddy would do it for her. If she or her mother was sick, she noticed that Daddy would become more attentive. If Daddy was careful with money, she overspent and couldn't stay within her allowance which caused father to worry about her and try to teach her how to handle money better. Being a helpless Little Girl proved so gratifying that even as an adult, she remains a child with men.

The Little Girl tries to make every man fit her father's shoes and gives him whatever characteristics she associated with her father. Many of her relationships fail because the men can't live up to her expectations. She wants men to be eternally giving.

A Little Girl's relationship to her father is very important to her as long as he lives and he never loses his glamor in her eyes. It is to him, not her mother that she goes for help when she is in trouble.

Although the Little Girl strongly desires relationships with men, she is also afraid of them. They might interfere with her daddy's interest and affection.

Sometimes a Little Girl lives out this central drama with her father by finding someone who is a duplicate of him—a much older, married man. In one case, a Little Girl found a man who was exactly her father's age and as powerful and well-known as her father. The affair went on for many years and with her lover, she felt like the second woman rather than the first in a man's life, just as she had felt when her mother came first with her father. It was only after many years of therapy that this woman had the courage to break off the affair and take up with a man of her own age for the first time in her life.

The Little Girl has not forgiven her father for choosing her mother over herself. There is a residue of anger at him that spills over in her relationships with other men. It comes out in the way a Little Girl swiftly rejects men whom she feels won't give her what she wants or who want to treat her as an equal rather than a special little girl. It also comes out in the ambivalent way she ends romances, leaving men with false hopes.

The Little Girl's relationship to her mother is distorted by her adoration and longing for her father. She has never forgiven her mother for winning her father's affections and throughout the Little Girl's life she remains ambivalent about and competitive with her mother.

"My mother's a basket case," said one Little Girl with derision. "She can never go anywhere out of the house without my father."

Little Girls' Relationships With Other Women

The Little Girl's feelings about her mother are reflected in her relationship with other women. Some Little Girls are unable to have close relationships with women. Others can have tight friendships but they use their women friends as additional support systems, parental figures to whom they turn often for reassurance, soothing words, and advice to get them out of their confusion and turmoil.

A Little Girl's friend remembers a phone call. "I'm lost here at the airport," the Little Girl began without saying hello.

"What do you mean, you're lost?" asked the friend.

"It's so big and confusing here, I can't find my way out," the Little Girl said, close to tears.

Her friend snapped to attention. "Go outside, get in a cab, and tell the driver to bring you here."

The Little Girl did as she was told and had no further trouble. Little Girls only need directions from someone else to be able to function quite adequately.

Although the Little Girl's friendships with women appear to be close, they are always secondary, inconsequential, when compared to her friendships with men. Women don't make a lasting impression and they leave few traces in a Little Girl's life. She is quite capable of using a woman friend for awhile as a source to turn to for support and encouragement, but will drop her abruptly when her usefulness is over or she finds a serviceable male ear.

Little Girls also have problems with men who outlive their usefulness. With men who aren't as supportive as they once were, there is disillusionment and anger. A Little Girl always idealizes a man initially, investing him with all of her daddy's qualities which have become more wonderful with time. If the man doesn't come through as a perfect daddy figure, then this man who only a short while ago was so fantastic is converted into a monster. Little Girls are unable to assess their relationships realistically, because they tend to regard people on an all or nothing basis.

Little Girls as Mothers

The Little Girl can be a reasonably good mother because she is loving, and she gives her children attention and kindness. Often, however, the Little Girl may force her children, particularly an oldest daughter, into a parental role. Mommy is such a scatterbrain that the daughter becomes the organized one who looks after her. Because Little Girls tend to suffer from chronic psychosomatic ailments, children often have to help out or take over because their mother is out of commission with a headache or she can't lift things because of her bad back.

Sometimes a Little Girl's relationship with her daughter can be an instrument for insight and change. If, for example, the Little Girl's daughter refuses to take on the responsibility her mother wants her to have, then they both end up as competing Little Girls, vying for the husband's attention. At that point the Little Girl may become dimly aware that something has to give. It is then that some Little Girls decide to take courses, or start to think more seriously about a career. They begin to grow up a bit themselves, leaving their daughters to be the primary children in the family. The original

Little Girl, though, is left with a residue of anger toward her daughter whom she feels encroached upon her rightful territory.

Little Girls' sons are often filled with guilt about themselves. A Little Girl looks upon her son, as she does on all men, as a replacement for her father. She loves him in a very special way because of this, but she also expects a great deal from him. She makes him feel guilty, because he could never be as perfect as she expects him to be.

Little Girls as Workers

The Little Girl who is a helpless creature at home may be quite competent in the office. Most Little Girls choose jobs in which others make the major decisions and they simply follow orders. There are lots of Little Girls among secretaries, for example, and they are good at what they do.

If life circumstances dictate that the Little Girl become self-supporting, however, she is generally able to shape up and do what is required. Little Girls are neither stupid nor incapable, although they often act that way.

Little Girls' meetings with men, however, even in a professional atmosphere, are charged with eroticism and office romances are common.

Sometimes a Little Girl will be interested in her career while she is single and feels she must earn a living for herself, but when a man comes onto the scene, her career suddenly becomes much less important to her. Soon after she marries, if she is financially able to, she generally will quit her job.

If the married Little Girl maintains a job, she may operate with two distinct sets of behavior. In the office Little Girl does her job in a very capable manner. The minute she returns home, however, she dissolves into the helpless Little Girl again. The same woman who can run computers from nine to five can't change a light bulb in her apartment. Even husbands are aware of the split in behavior. A husband can respect his wife's competence at work but still treat her as a child at home because he accepts her total vulnerability there.

The Unmarried Little Girl

If a Little Girl doesn't marry, she finds other ways to remain a Little Girl. She transforms her boss into a father figure or, even more commonly, she turns to chronic illness to provide her with a whole set of doctors whom she uses as daddies. Little Girls are notorious in the medical profession for shopping around for doctors and changing them frequently. They look to the medical profession for the perfect man to be dependent upon.

Little Girls have symptoms that are stronger than their illness warrants and they resist all attempts to help them recover permanently.

When a doctor is not available, it is a trauma for the Little Girl because she feels her father is deserting her. She becomes angry and resentful that her doctor had to take a vacation or tend to business elsewhere.

The Little Girl and Society

Little Girls are quite common. Our society has fostered the role they play in women. The Little Girl stance is an exaggeration of the old-fashioned feminine role. Men thought of women as frail, incompetent creatures in need of help and protection and women thought of themselves in that way, too.

It is a deeply ingrained attitude attested to these days by the fact that so many women can have successful careers but fall apart and become Little Girls in their social life with men.

As long as men find naiveté, helplessness, coyness and general childishness attractive, some women will continue to behave as Little Girls because they feel it is to their advantage. The only hope for Little Girls to grow up and vanish as a species is for new models of femininity to replace the old ones. Little Girls would gradually disappear if more men found competence as sexy as helplessness.

How a Little Girl Can Help Herself

Little Girls are women with many positive features. They can be affectionate, sweet, loving, charming and can make a certain kind of man feel like a king. The problem is while the Little Girl is being taken care of and has someone to lean on, she remains fearful and uncomfortable about herself and life.

If you are a Little Girl, you are stronger than you think, stronger than you let the world know. Review your own life for proof. How are you when you're alone? You manage to eat, sleep, shop, maintain a home, travel around by car or public transportation. If you work or have worked, you manage to hold down a job and earn a salary. If you were totally incompetent, you would have been fired. You have survived all these years—even the years when there was no man to look after you all the time. You are competent. All you have to do is learn to believe it.

It will help you to realize that your behavior as a Little Girl was learned way back before you can remember. Early in your life, you discovered you could get what you wanted by acting helpless—notice the word *acting*. Helplessness is a device, not a reality for you. But, between childhood and adulthood you began to believe your own act. Now is the time to start touching base with your own reality again.

Pay attention to your actions around men. You can catch yourself, if you are very alert, in the process of going into your act. Observe yourself changing your manner, your voice, your attitudes simply because a man—or your man—came into the room.

Start tuning in to what you want from men. Think first about what you have always felt you wanted from your father. Now think about the significant men in your adult life. Do you notice a similarity between what you expected or wanted from your father and what you expect and want from men in your adult relationships? Do you often begin your relationships with fantasies that are hard for a man to fulfill? These fantasies can create destructive behavior on your part in relationships.

If you have a husband or boy friend in your life now, start to think of him apart from his role as the strong man on whom you lean. What are his needs? If he didn't keep reassuring and coddling you, would you still like him as a person? If he fell ill and you had to take care of him for a long time, would you be able to help him?

Your task is to separate the men in your adult life from your original childhood love, your father. Then you will be able to establish a mature relationship and begin to feel like an adult. Inevitably this will make you feel much better about yourself, and life in general will become less fearful. Your health will improve too, when you start thinking of yourself as a competent, independent adult rather than someone who cannot survive alone.

CHAPTER 4

THE BED HOPPER

When Ben met Chloris at a party, he had just separated from his wife. Chloris was almost twenty years younger, a very attractive woman with a seductive manner. Ben went for her in a big way and the attraction seemed to be mutual. They danced together for a good part of the evening. They talked, then parted to socialize with others. At one point in the evening Ben went in search of Chloris and found her in the kitchen with another man who was coming on strongly to her. She seemed pleased to see him.

At the end of the evening when Chloris was at the door saying good night to her host, Ben managed to be there, too. "May I drive you home?" Chloris asked. Ben accepted. Once in the car Ben felt overwhelmed by the sexuality she had exuded all night. He pulled her toward him and kissed her. No one could have been more surprised or delighted than Ben when her fingers began fiddling with the zipper on his pants. He considered himself a lucky man to have elicited such a response from this attractive woman.

"Let me take you home," he murmured, and soon they were speeding toward her apartment. She took him by the hand and led him through her darkened living room. Her roommate was asleep. Silently, she pulled him into her bedroom where she undressed instantly. Ben noticed that it seemed like the most natural act in the world to her.

He saw her again two nights later. She didn't have an orgasm either night, but she was a sexy woman and Ben was sure that with time and practice that would come, too. By his third date Ben felt a terrific relationship was beginning. On their fourth date Chloris told him that she had a sporadic, long-term relationship with a married man. Ben continued to see her.

By the end of a month Ben knew more about Chloris's sex life than he wanted to. He realized the quick consummation of sex which he felt was something special was commonplace to Chloris. Gradually, he realized that there were always a series of men in Chloris's life—shadowy creatures who came and went. It seemed to Ben that sex was Chloris's whole life.

But Ben found himself fascinated by Chloris and her wild ways. He had never known anyone like her. Chloris continued to tell him about her sexual escapades. He found out that Chloris had not only an active sex life but she also fantasized about sex constantly. She tried to act out some of her fantasies with Ben. She enjoyed outrageous or daring scenes. One Sunday she met Ben at his office where he was working on a rush project. Chloris insisted that they have sex right then in his office, even though they could hear the sounds of other men working down the hall. Once when he visited her at a resort where she was renting a house, she met him at the train station, naked except for a bathrobe. She took him to visit her hometown in New England and seduced him on the lawn of the minister's house.

Throughout their entire affair, Chloris was totally unreliable. She would disappear to spend time with her married lover; she broke dates at the last moment. Ben realized it was because she had become involved in yet another of her impetuous affairs.

By now, Ben also knew that she had occasional affairs with women as well as men and that she enjoyed group sex. There was nothing Chloris wouldn't do.

Ben, at his wife's pleadings, finally went back to her. He broke up with Chloris but continued to think about her. He was very turned on by her, although at times, he was disgusted by her behavior as well. Finally, he called Chloris and saw her once in a while. He was only able to break off the affair altogether when he left his wife again for the final time. After his divorce he saw Chloris once but he realized that he wanted a woman with whom he could have a serious relationship. He knew that this was just not possible with a woman as promiscuous as Chloris.

Chloris is one of several types of Bed Hoppers. Bed Hoppers are women who compulsively run from man to man, from one sexual liaison to another. Wherever Bed Hoppers find themselves, they will find men also. If they arrange to meet a man at a museum, for example, they will have a flirtation going by the time he arrives. If they go into a store they may not emerge with what they wanted to buy, but they will with a man.

Bed Hoppers are constantly on the prowl. Men are attracted to them because they exude sexuality. Some Bed Hoppers blatantly advertise; they dress in tight clothing with plunging necklines. They go without bras. Others don't have to rely on provocative dress. Sex is implied by the way they walk, the way they look at a man, the way they interact with him. They are experts at the art of seduction, and they do it unconsciously and automatically. The age and appearance of a man makes little difference. It can sometimes be ludicrous but you see Bed Hoppers acting seductively with very young boys, very old men, and any age in between.

One Bed Hopper who frequents nudist colonies explains her indiscriminate eye. "I like every man there. It doesn't make any difference if he is tall, short, skinny or fat—I like them all."

Another Bed Hopper unconsciously plays her game of seduction with the nine-year-olds she teaches in an elementary school. She succeeded in overwhelming one by whirling in a flared skirt so that the full length of her legs and part of her underwear were exposed. He was so overcome by the experience that he exclaimed, "Oh, Miss Coleman," and rushed out of the room. Miss Coleman wasn't ashamed. On the contrary, she bragged about the incident to one of her current sex partners.

Not only do Bed Hoppers send their message of sexual availability to males of all ages, they commonly get involved with inappropriate sexual partners—rough men, men from lower social classes, men of different races. This is not accidental. Bed Hoppers are women with a very poor opinion of themselves. They feel undesirable as human beings and as women in particular.

One reason they have to keep snaring men is to prove they can. As one Bed Hopper put it, "I just have to see if I can pick up a man. I feel I have to try." This woman spent her teenage years feeling ugly because of a bad case of acne and hirsutism. The acne is cured, the excessive hair removed by electrolysis. She is now an attractive woman but the feeling of undesirability lingers on. Because Bed Hoppers feel so vile, they set out to prove they are by taking up with men they unconsciously look down upon.

Sometimes Bed Hoppers get into trouble with men like this. They catch venereal diseases, they get beaten up, or in the case of the heroine of *Looking for Mr. Goodbar,* they get murdered if they have the bad luck to pick up a violent man.

These rough men and men from different races or classes are the very ones they choose to flaunt in front of their families. One young woman spent a vacation in Europe hanging out at the enlisted men's club on the army base where her brother was stationed. Her family was an aristocratic one from the deep South, prejudiced against blacks. The only men she chose to be with were blacks, to the embarrassment and fury of her brother.

There is self-destruction and a search for humiliation in much of what the Bed Hopper does. Her search for sexual partners is to prove she is attractive which she really never believes, and she is also always trying to validate her intrinsic low self-esteem. Because the promiscuity of Bed Hoppers is quite open, both men and women often look down on them for it, even in this sexually liberated age.

One man tells a story which illustrates how people talk about Bed Hoppers. A woman he met while writing speeches for the head of an advertising agency had been put in charge of editing his speeches. When he called to say the first speech was ready, she suggested she pick it up at his apartment. "It wasn't more than half an hour after she arrived that we were in bed together," he remembers. "I thought she was kind of nice and I wanted to see her again. I told this to a friend of mine who worked for the agency. He answered, 'You like her? Then for Christmas buy her a gallon drum of vaginal jelly. She's screwed every man in the agency. If you're thinking of falling in love with her, forget it.' I never called her again after that. She called me a while later to find out what had gone wrong. 'Was I too easy?' she wanted to know.''

Bed Hoppers alienate their roommates. Roommates don't like strings of men parading in and out of the apartment.

One Bed Hopper, a professor, has been openly seductive with students, with fellow teachers. She is known to be sleeping with the head of her department. Without being entirely aware of it, she has even come on to members of the janitorial staff. She can't understand why the school custodians treat her like a tramp and make offensive remarks to her. Men often treat Bed Hoppers as objects of derision; a Bed Hopper is not a woman they take seriously.

Bed Hoppers come in several different varieties. Although their behavior is the same—they all sleep with an unending stream of men—they can be distinguished by what makes them act the way they do.

The Mother-Love Lover

Chloris, in the opening story of this chapter, is a prime example of a Mother-Love Lover. Like Chloris, Mother-Love Lovers are often polymorphous perverse, a term psychiatrists use to describe the undifferentiated sexuality of a baby. Mother-Love Lovers have sexual liaisons with women as well as men and would just as soon tumble into bed with two men or a man and another woman as with a man alone. They can and do participate in orgies if the occasion presents itself.

Despite the quantity and diversity of their sexual experiences, they rarely have orgasms. ''After awhile, I just didn't seem to have much feeling left,'' sighed one Bed Hopper.

In truth, the Mother-Love Lover is not in pursuit of sex at all. What she is unconsciously after is the kind of love she had from her mother. Mother-Love Lovers had overinvolved Moms who refused to let their daughters separate from them and establish identities of their own. They were discouraged from asserting independence at about the age of two when children normally start to separate from their mother. As a result, they are stuck in an infantile state with the emotional needs of a baby. They want what an infant perceives as life itself, an endless stream of motherly love and devotion.

Grown up physically but not emotionally, Mother-Love Lovers still want what their mothers gave them, only now they want it from men. For these women, sex is not an end in itself, although they often protest that sex alone is what they are after. In fact, sex is a tool to trade for what they interpret as nurturance.

Mother-Love Lovers respond to the beginnings of their liaisons with pleasure. They dote on the things men do when they are in the process of seducing a woman. They like the kisses, the holding of hands, the touching, the flattering attention. Their baby nature makes them love to be fed. It is not only going to restaurants that appeals to the Mother-Love Lover, it is the actual intake of food. They are reminded how good it felt to be fed by mother.

When a man stops seducing, gets what he wants—sex—and doesn't kiss her, hold her, compliment her or hover over her as much, and maybe starts to want to go right to bed, she finds herself feeling disappointed and disenchanted. Unconsciously, the Mother-Love Lover equates the lessening of preliminary physical stroking with rejection by the man. "He's just like the rest of them," she says with bitterness. "He only wants sex. He's not really interested in me."

She suddenly notices faults she hasn't seen before. He wears socks with holes in them. His stomach protrudes a little. Hair grows in his ears.

The process from a man's initial interest, when Mother-Love Lovers feel they are getting the intimate attentions they want, to the end of the affair, when unreasonably these women feel rejected, which makes them want to move on to another man—gets quicker and quicker over the years. Eventually the Mother-Love Lover goes from the pleasure of seduction to disillusion after consummation in a matter of hours or even minutes. They go through men so quickly they can find themselves hopping from bed to bed in the course of a day.

Of course, Mother-Love Lovers have all kinds of rationales

for such speedy bed hopping. One woman said, "I need three men to make one whole man. I need one to laugh with, another to talk to, another to get my juices flowing for the next one, and so on."

Unfortunately, Mother-Love Lovers set themselves up for the feelings of rejection that repeatedly and inevitably occur. They ask for the impossible from men. Their need for displays of caring are insatiable. They must have a concentrated stream of physical affection before, during, and after sex. Their sense of repeatedly being rejected when they don't get it, whether imagined or not, contributes to the depression which is always a pattern of their personalities.

Their life runs in a circle. They get depressed when they don't get what they want from men, then they run after men still more because catching a man's interest gives them a lift. But it always ends in more disappointment and more depression, which makes them continue to chase men.

The Mother-Love Lover's close tie to her mother continues into adult life, but it is fraught with ambivalence. She is full of hostility toward the mother who made her into an eternal dependent. She bristles with resentment, but she always goes back to her mother.

The great rage toward their mothers that Mother-Love Lovers harbor was shown by two of them in typical ways for Bed Hoppers—through sex. One, while traveling with her mother, picked up two men at the hotel bar after her mother had gone to sleep early, brought them back to her room, and with her mother next door, had sex with both of them. Another woman played with a man's genitals underwater in a pool while her mother sat beside the pool unaware of the sex games. A third woman took her current lover—a female—to the theater with her mother to see a play about lesbians. While her mother watched the stage, the Mother-Love Lover put her hand on her lover's thigh and stroked her sensually. This same woman was mixed up with a married man and didn't want her mother to know. When her mother dropped by unexpectedly, as she sometimes did, she would make the married man hide in the bedroom.

Often, the men who hang around for any length of time with Bed Hoppers are married men or men who are equally promiscuous. Some analysts theorize that the man who has latent homosexual tendencies is attracted to a Bed Hopper because of her repeated experiences with other men in which he vicariously takes part.

Mother-Love Lovers are basically insecure, lonely women walking around with a great deal of repressed rage that spills over in all directions. They lie, cheat, and act outrageously with men. One woman shows her anger and contempt for the men she sleeps with by lying inert and unresponsive while they make love to her. Another gets pleasure from sleeping with one man, then getting him out of her apartment just before she expects another man. She feels she is putting something over on both men. The relationship with their mother interferes with their ability to have orgasms, as well. Mother is in the bedroom with these women, as she is everywhere else.

The anger Mother-Love Lovers feel toward their mother is transferred unconsciously to other females and they find it impossible to have women friends. "I wish I could," explained one, "but I react to women as competitors." The truth is that with their infantile needs, Mother-Love Lovers are unable to have mature relationships with anyone.

The relationships of Mother-Love Lovers with other women can be catty and competitive. They try the patience of their family and become sources of worry and shame to them. They are often deliberately provocative with those near and dear. One woman's mother always tells her that she dresses in too sexy a manner and that she should at least wear a bra. She always makes sure when she goes to see her mother that she is wearing her most revealing clothing without a bra.

These women generally end up all alone, living unhappy, empty lives. Although they start out believing they will get married, at some point in their chaotic lives marriage may begin to seem like a foreign territory. "I wonder what it would be like if we could marry," said one young woman to her lover, and then quickly followed this statement with, "I can't ever imagine myself married."

Occasionally, however, life circumstances make Mother-Love Lovers look at their lives in a new light and settle down. One woman who had been subsidized financially by her father, suddenly found herself cut off when his business went bankrupt and he could no longer send her money. At this point she realized she had to do something about her life which had largely been spent careening around with men, with little attention paid to her work. She found a man forty years older than she was. Because of the great age gap, she felt she had the upper hand in the relationship, and it gave her enough of a sense of security to marry him.

Occasionally the Mother-Love Lover is able to find a man who can give her enough of the motherly nurturance she craves and she marries him. If she does, she may run into another kind of trouble. She will generally want to have the tightly bonded, symbiotic relationship she had with her mother. One such Mother-Love Lover is devastated every time her husband wants to go anywhere or do anything without her. She sulks each time he leaves the house to play tennis. She is even sad when he leaves the house in the morning to go to work. She finds she cannot tolerate having sex with her husband, for he has become a mother-figure to her.

If the Mother-Love Lover has children, she may do the opposite of what was done to her by her mother. Instead of being overinvolved, she becomes a remote mother who keeps out of her children's lives as much as possible. She promotes a strong relationship between the children and their father. Said one, "Well, I'm not a great mother. I find I just can't get close to my daughter. I hope I'm doing her a service. Maybe she'll be better off than I am."

Many Mother-Love Lovers choose not to become parents at all. Said one, "I still need my own mother. How can I possibly become a mother myself?"

The Attention Seeker

A second kind of Bed Hopper, one of the most common, is the Attention Seeker. Attention Seekers share certain characteristics with Mother-Love Lovers. Both are self-centered, both are unable to perceive another's needs. Both doubt their desirability and worth. Both compulsively seduce men and use sex to validate their acceptability. But, beyond that, there are some important differences.

The Mother-Love Lover looks for private shows of tenderness from the men she encounters, but the Attention Seeker looks for public displays. Both get what they want only at the beginning of their affairs. The Attention Seeker loves the feeling of having the spotlight on her, of being the most important woman in a man's life during courtship and seduction. She adores flirting, likes to be hugged and kissed publicly. She dotes on external signs, such as flowers and gifts, to prove that she is his number one lady.

She loves to go to restaurants. But, while the Mother-Love Lover likes eating because of its nurturing connotations, for the Attention Seeker, it's the act of being taken out that gives pleasure. What the Attention Seeker wants from a man is to be center stage with him forever.

In contrast to the Mother-Love Lover whose problems originated with her mother, the Attention Seeker's trouble is with her father. He never gave her enough of what she needed. Her aloof, rejecting, rotten father gave all his attention to his wife and not to his adoring daughter. Or he was distant from everyone, or he was away from home a lot.

Attention Seekers learn quite early in life that sex can be used to be noticed. A relationship with an Attention Seeker can last from one night to a couple of months. Rarely can the Attention Seeker hang onto a man for more than six months.

During the time they are involved, they appear to be monogamous. But there are always the shadowy figures of other men in the background, for Attention Seekers are constantly attracting other men to have them around as backups. The Attention Seeker may not be sleeping with any of her backups, but if she is, she does not consider it very important. She is as casual about sex as she is about going to the supermarket. Her emotional attention remains focused on the primary man, not on all those others.

If an Attention Seeker does tell a man about her exploits with other men, you can be sure she is doing it for a purpose. It is either as a show of independence (''See, I can do very well without you.'') or it can be an attempt to nail a man down. Attention Seekers are always after marriage. If a man is really interested in her and doesn't like her sleeping around, then he should do something about it, like marry her. If he doesn't get angry at her, and she still isn't ready to give up on him, then she decides it is another one of his wonderful qualities—he is so understanding. If, however, she feels she is never going to get what she wants from him, then he's a bastard. "What does he expect? He never tells me when he's going to call. Does he think I'm going to sit around waiting for him?" She may continue the relationship but she wants to punish him.

Attention Seekers generally have an easy time attracting men. They tend to have attractive personalities. They can be funny and charming. They express themselves in colorful, dramatic ways. Their minds jump from thought to thought. Their attention span is short, but this can give them a whimsical, amusing quality. They are emotional creatures—they laugh and cry easily.

Like the Mother-Love Lover, the Attention Seeker is rarely orgasmic, in spite of her busy sex life. She never fakes orgasms as some women do. Basically, the Attention Seeker's approach to men is honest. She doesn't want to fool them. She just wants their undivided love. Even though the Attention Seeker rarely has orgasms, she needs frequent sex as proof of her desirability which she basically doubts and as proof that the man still cares.

When the Attention Seeker finds herself without any man in her life, she reacts in the same way that the Mother-Love Lover does—she becomes frantic. Anxiety and depression overtake her. One Attention Seeker in such a state went out in search of a cure. She walked into a neighborhood book store and picked up the man who worked behind the counter. They made a date to go to a party he knew about that evening. At the party he started to talk to friends, while she could only think about having sex. She knew it would make her feel better. She grew impatient and angry with her escort, who was unaware of what was happening. Finally, she picked up another man at the party, and they started to leave together. The first man saw what was happening and a fight broke out, but she left with the second man anyway.

With all of her men, the Attention Seeker goes through a

series of transitory infatuations. Initially, when she meets a man, she idealizes him. But her continued adoration rests directly on his ability to deliver a constant display of affection. If he fails, in her eyes, in this sacred duty, she suddenly starts to find fault with him. His attention may not have flagged at all. He may simply be taking her more for granted, but she perceives this as a dereliction. She becomes furious. He has failed her. Yet another man has not kept the spotlight shining on her. She changes quite suddenly from being warm and charming to mean and hostile. The man finds himself under attack. There is always a knife hidden away in the psyche of the Attention Seeker, who has a basic hostility to men. Once her displeasure is invoked, she uses it to castrate the man. She may belittle him, make fun of him, attack him in whatever way suits her. She is out for blood. Her underlying anger at her father is unleashed on the man who in her eyes has repeated his sins. Her hostility to men is also why she doesn't have orgasms. Unresponsiveness is another way to castrate.

An affair with an Attention Seeker may end, also, because she expects a decision to be made much too fast. She demands quick gratification. She gets disgusted and angry if a man won't commit himself completely and irrevocably in a very short time. One Bed Hopper explained her attitude by saying, "I don't have much time to waste. I waited four months with this one guy. I wanted to marry him. He couldn't make up his mind. Well, if he can't make up his mind in four months, then he'll never be able to. I'm not going to hang around forever." Since there is always another male in the background, she did a typical thing. She switched to another guy.

Even if she doesn't become disillusioned, her man generally does. He begins to realize that for all her charm, the Attention Seeker is not really interested in him or his needs. She will talk about his job, for instance, only to keep his interest focused on her, not because she cares about his problems at work.

The Attention Seeker at Work

Attention Seekers can run into trouble if they take the wrong kind of job. They cannot pay attention to details, so a job that requires precision of any kind will turn out to be disastrous for them. They can't sit still for very long, so they do poorly in any kind of structured work that necessitates staying behind a desk or in one place. Attention Seekers do better in jobs that deal with the public, since they have pleasant personalities, but even then they have problems. Behind the counter, for example, they are always creating inappropriate dramatic scenes. As secretaries, they can drive their bosses crazy with melodrama that alternates with moodiness. They are apt to complain, "This terrible report! You mean you really want me to type this awful thing?" Then they resign themselves with a sigh, and say, "Oh, all right, I'll do it."

Many Attention Seekers are found among actresses and they can do well on stage or screen where their natural flair for the dramatic helps rather than hinders; they get the attention they crave from public recognition and applause.

Attention Seekers' Relationships With Other Women

Relationships with other women are better for the Attention Seeker than for the Mother-Love Lover.

The Attention Seeker goes through a period in her early years when she cannot tolerate other women because she sees them as rivals who may swipe her latest man. Eventually she gets over this, because she has a basic trust of women that she doesn't of men. Mommy could be counted on. Daddy couldn't. The Attention Seeker makes women friends who give her support and to whom she can tell her troubles. She may pick older maternal figures to confide in because they pose less of a threat, but she may also make friends in her own age group. You can bet that a good part of her conversation with her female friends will be complaints about the latest rat in her life who let her down.

Beginnings and Endings

The sex life of the Attention Seeker generally starts early. Rarely is the motivation lust. Sex serves a dual purpose for the teenaged Attention Seeker. Sex gives her the attention and acceptance from boys that she didn't get from her father. She also feels that by engaging in sex, she will be accepted by her peers who are doing the same thing.

A good example of this is Joan, who grew up in a home with an alcoholic mother. At a very early age Joan started to take care of her brothers and sisters because her mother was unable to. Her father relied on Joan to keep the house running in his absence. During this period, Joan received all the attention she needed from her father. He hurried home after work and Joan knew she could call him during the day if she needed to. Joan's mother eventually joined Alcoholics Anonymous and stopped drinking. She resumed taking care of the children and running the house, and Joan now felt out in the cold as far as her father was concerned. He no longer had to rely on her and he paid less attention to her now.

Joan had lacked friends because of her responsibilities at home, but now she tried to become like the other kids. She found it difficult though, because she couldn't be as carefree as her peers. Her experiences had given her a sober outlook. In adolescence the girls she wanted as friends started to sleep with boys. Soon Joan was sleeping with boys, too—anyone and everyone. It wasn't until Joan entered therapy as a young woman that she understood the reasons for her promiscuity.

Very rarely is the first affair for either an Attention Seeker, or for a Mother-Love Lover based on sincere affection. Typically, Bed Hoppers are afraid of losing a man. They are haunted by a fear of abandonment and so when a man pressures them, they give in, rather than risk losing him. The pace of their sex life picks up as the years go on, and by the time the first flush of youth is past, they've led frantic existences.

While Attention Seekers were young, there was minimal discretion in their sleeping around. The Attention Seeker feels she is looking for a suitable husband. Early in her life, she may discount two out of ten men as unsuitable prospects, then sleep with the other eight. By middle age, even this small amount of selectivity largely disappears.

Bed Hoppers of all kinds age badly. They feel they need their youthful good looks in order to attract men. When wrinkles or sagging start to appear, there is much anxiety and they tend to sleep with any man who comes along. They have needed verification of their desirability all along, but when their beauty begins to fade, it assumes the proportions of a life-and-death matter.

An Attention Seeker stands a better chance of marrying and finding marital happiness than a Mother-Love Lover. If a decent man comes into an Attention Seeker's life, a man who is authoritarian enough to control her behavior, who is able to give her a sufficient amount of consistent attention, and who is completely reliable, she may become a devoted wife and excellent mother.

Their husbands tend to be serious men with regular habits who are devoted to their careers. Their reliability and regularity make the Attention Seeker feel secure.

These men, generally logical, orderly, methodical types are attracted to the Attention Seeker precisely because she is opposite to them. She brings color and emotion into their lives. They enjoy her vitality, easily expressed emotions and affection.

As a mother, the Attention Seeker can be wonderful. Her home may not be neat, but she takes pride in it. Her children's meals may not be on time and she may let them go to sleep any old time but her children will get lots of what the Attention Seeker feels she missed—love. If she can't help with homework because she can't concentrate, she's still great with hugs and kisses. Somehow, in her emotionally messy way, the Attention Seeker manages to create well-behaved children. She values their good behavior as a favorable reflection on herself.

The Sex Addict

A third group of Bed Hoppers have an obsession about sex itself. Unlike the Mother-Love Lover and the Attention Seeker, the Sex Addict is able to have orgasms regularly. Sex is not only pleasurable and gratifying, it becomes the whole world to her—it's something she must have.

Some Sex Addicts have a much stronger sex drive than ordinary women. Their pursuit of sex appears to be a biological necessity. One woman claims that if she is without a man, she takes care of her demanding sex drive by dreaming of a sexual liaison and having an orgasm in her sleep. Such supersexed women with uncontrollable drives are extremely rare. The average Sex Addict has a psychological motive behind her sexuality—the search for power.

Some Sex Addicts are housewives; others are women with careers. Unfortunately they don't find their jobs satisfying. They feel they could do better but are unable to put their energies into making a greater success for themselves. Sex Addicts view women as powerless and themselves as belonging to a powerless class. Whom do they see as possessing power? Men, of course. Sex Addicts envy men and their promiscuity is a way of identifying with them. By aggressively seeking sex, they believe they are acting like men and deriving the same benefits as men do from sexual activities. Their unconscious rationale goes like this: If a man is considered a superior male when he has a strong sex drive and many sex partners, then I will be considered superior if I have a strong sex drive and sleep with as many men as possible. Sex Addicts are macho females. During the sex act the Addict feels she is incorporating or taking away a man's power.

The Attention Seeker and the Mother-Love Lover feel victimized by men. They set it up so they are. By contrast, the Sex Addict feels as if she is in charge. Sex gives her a sense of control over the ruling class—men.

The Mother-Love Lover and the Attention Seeker find that sex brings them little joy. They are stuck with no orgasms, continual disappointments, no sense of fulfillment. But the

Sex Addict derives pleasure and a sense of accomplishment from the whole bed-hopping process. You hear it in the Sex Addict's description of her exploits. "I just met a terrific lover! We stayed home for three days and never left the bed the whole time! It was fantastic!"

Sex Addicts judge a man not by what he can offer them as human beings, but by how many times he made love to them in one session and how many orgasms they achieved. Tenderness? Attention? The hell with that! What is his body like? Does he want to make love all the time?

Occasionally, Sex Addicts are scorekeepers, women who keep track of how many men they have slept with, how many times they made love, how many orgasms they had. For some the bookkeeping involves how many important men they are able to inveigle into their bed.

The daughter of a famous theatrical producer languished for his attention during her childhood because he was always traveling, always working in other parts of the country. Today she keeps a list of her conquests—famous authors, well-known politicians, publicized tycoons. Another woman keeps an on-going diary of her sexual exploits with well-known men, and she brags about the number of Pulitzer prize winners who have shared her bed. The mechanism of Sex Addicts is quite clear with these women. If they sleep with powerful men, they feel more powerful themselves.

Sex Addicts often marry and more than once. They have extramarital affairs and their marriages break up. Sex Addicts are able to maintain a relationship only as long as the initial phase of strong desire is there. While they are enjoying frequent sex with their partners, all is well. However, if sex slows down and their mate wants sex only five times a week instead of seven, for example, they feel gypped. They find other men to fill in the gap. Sex Addicts very often have a husband and several lovers besides. Men are sex objects, not human beings to them.

Generally, Sex Addicts do not become mothers. They realize that children would interfere too much with their sexual activities.

There is another kind of Sex Addict who doesn't have sex with a variety of men, but instead demands that her husband make love to her at least once a night if not more. For these women, sex is a reassurance that they are loved. Without sexual reassurance, they feel rejected, unhappy, insecure. These wives can be a terrible strain on their husbands. Sex becomes a duty, a command, rather than a natural expression of caring and desire.

Occasionally, a woman uses sex to emasculate and belittle her husband. No matter how much sex they have, it is never enough.

The On-the-Side Bed Hopper

Betty has been married for seven years. She has never had an orgasm in that time. On a business trip last fall, she became friendly with a salesman from a rival firm and to her surprise ended up going to bed with him. She experienced her first orgasm with this man. Since then Betty has been making excuses to her husband about working late and has been picking up men in bars regularly. She obtains the sexual satisfaction with these strangers that is missing from her marriage.

On-The-Side Bed Hoppers like Betty suffer from what one psychiatrist dubbed the saint-or-sinner syndrome. They have steady relationships or are married to men whom they value. These men become "saints," good men like their fathers. Fulfilling sex is impossible with good men. They respond to sex only with sinners, the casual pickups whom they have no feelings for.

Other Bed Hoppers

Some women sleep with every man they go out with because they feel this is the way to act in our society. They assume that's what everybody else is doing and so it is expected of them. Some women do it out of acquiescence. They have never learned how to say no to a man. Women who acquiesce have little sense of their own identity. They have been praised for having pretty faces, for being good and obedient girls. Their approach to men is to do what they ask.

If a man wants to sleep with them, they do it automatically. They fall into relationships, they don't choose them. Because they are unable to shape their lives with personal goals, they can't make relationships into anything more than transient, empty encounters.

Other women bed hop because they feel they are particularly unattractive or because they are overweight or suffer from a disfigurement or physical handicap. Because they feel they can't attract men or compete with other women in the usual ways, they try to compensate by offering themselves sexually.

Some women from especially strict religious backgrounds rebel against their upbringing by choosing the most forbidden sin—promiscuous, extramarital sex.

Situational Bed Hoppers

Finally, there are women who bed hop only at certain times, and not as a way of life.

Sometimes a woman will be promiscuous when she is very young. As she matures, discovering that it is not a satisfying or fulfilling way of life, she becomes more selective and gives up her promiscuity.

Other women first become promiscuous in middle age, often at the onset of menopause. Afraid they are losing their attractiveness, they set out to prove that they still are desirable to as many men as possible.

Many women bed hop right after they are divorced. They do it to test out the new sexual climate, to see if they have been missing any fun. But mostly they bed hop to verify their desirability, particularly if they have been rejected in the marriage. Most divorced women, after an initial period of frantic sexual activity, give it up. They grow tired of empty relationships. They want to settle down into something more steady and with more meaning. They start looking for a mate rather than a variety of sex partners.

Wives who feel abused or rejected or those who discover that their husband has been having affairs may bed hop to give themselves reassurance that they are needed, wanted and admired.

Bed Hoppers and Society

Bed Hoppers have always been around but they certainly seem to have increased in today's world. For one thing, Bed Hoppers are simply more visible. Women used to hide their sexual activities in the past. Today's Bed Hopper can be quite open about what she is doing.

Since our society has made sex into a panacea, a cure for anything that ails you, the general atmosphere today encourages women to act out through sex whatever problems they have.

The sexually promiscuous woman also is able to rationalize her behavior by drawing on women's liberation themes. Today, a liberated woman actively seeks sexual pleasure. The promiscuous woman thinks that is what she is doing. With no insight into the psychological motivations that are driving her, she often considers herself to be simply more liberated than other women. Bed Hoppers sometimes also feel they are liberated simply because they are doing what men have always done.

Bed Hoppers, for all of their rationalizations, are really less liberated than other women. They are in the thrall of a compulsion that makes them slaves to sex rather than mistresses of their own bodies.

How a Bed Hopper Can Help Herself

If you recognize yourself among the Bed Hoppers and you would like to change your life-style, you should fix the answers to the following questions firmly in your mind: What am I getting from all of my sexual activity?, Am I getting orgasms?, Am I getting love?, Am I getting long-lasting admiration?, Am I getting a man I can count on in life?, Do I feel satisfied instead of continually restless?

Chances are you will have answered no to all the questions. Knowing that you are not getting lasting good feelings from your adventures with men, you can begin to modify what you are doing.

It's important to start to believe that you are an attractive, desirable woman. You have tested it out enough by now. You know you have a track record of being able to attract men, so stop proving it over and over again.

Believe what your experiences have shown; believe that you are attractive and desirable. Pin a note in a prominent place that says, "Believe it!" You'll know what it means every time you pass it.

The next time you begin to feel restless when you meet a man, when you feel that undefined urge to get him into bed quickly, try to first consciously identify the feeling that is propelling you. Then attempt to resist it. It may not work the first few times, but if you continue to ask yourself, "What am I really going to get out of this?" each time you get that old urge, it may make you pause and eventually will help you change your mind.

You may feel dimly that this brief encounter could lead to something more than sex, but you have enough proof from the past that it won't. Bear this fact in mind when you are ready to hop into bed with the next stranger.

If you give into your urges, try to examine what you are feeling throughout your entire experience with the man in question. Pay attention to your emotions. Do you start out with a sense of excitement and hope? Does the excitement disappear soon after the sexual part of the relationship begins? Do you always seem to want more from the man than he delivers in the way of attention, love, touching, caring, commitment? By keeping your attention focused on your thoughts and emotions with a man, you will learn more about why you are bed hopping. You should recognize that you are searching for something that sex alone will not deliver.

You may find it hard to be more patient, to let a relationship develop before engaging in sex. You may miss that instant body contact which momentarily seems to soothe you.

If, despite your best efforts, you find you are not changing, get additional help in the form of therapy. Therapy will help you find a way to live and love that will bring you more happiness and satisfaction than you now have.

CHAPTER 5

THE CHAMELEON

Dan first met Sandy when they were both seniors at the same college. At that time it was common knowledge that she was having an affair with one of her professors. He was a leading radical in the middle of the upheaval and politics that dominated campuses in the late sixties. Sandy, along with him, would take part in demonstrations. At his behest, she would circulate petitions for signatures. They would smoke marijuana together. She wore crazy costumes. Her hair was frizzed around her pretty face.

Several years later, after graduating from law school, Dan started to work for a very prestigious, very conservative law firm. He was surprised to find Sandy working there as one of the paralegal aides. She looked altogether different. Her clothing was tasteful and subdued. Her hair was pulled back into a neat bun. He soon discovered that Sandy was having an affair with an older, married man who was a senior partner in the firm. Occasionally Dan would have lunch with Sandy. Her opinions had changed as much as her appearance. Her radical ideas had disappeared. She now espoused arch conservative views. She ranted against the people on welfare. She voted for Republican party candidates.

After a couple of years Dan got another job and left the firm. He lost track of Sandy again until he bumped into her one day on the street. They had a drink together and he discovered that her married boy friend had had a heart attack and the affair was over. He filled her in on his life. He had become a leading figure in liberal politics and was planning to run for office in the fall. Sandy looked at him with new respect and interest. She listened to him, enthralled. She told him how exciting it all sounded. She looked especially pretty that day and Dan remembered what a very sweet person she was. He asked her out for the following night. Soon Dan was having an affair with Sandy. As their relationship progressed, Dan realized that Sandy had a whole new set of beliefs and opinions—his. His own words were coming back to him out of her mouth. Suddenly it became clear to him that her abrupt switch from radical to conservative politics was not because of a change of heart on Sandy's part, but rather because there was a change of man. Sandy seemed to borrow her attitudes and convictions from whomever she was currently attached to. Dan got bored with Sandy very quickly. He didn't want a parrot. He wanted a woman with a character of her own.

Sandy is a Chameleon, a type of woman some men think are made in heaven and others feel are for the birds. In the animal world, chameleons are lizards whose skins change color according to their surroundings. Chameleons in the female world change their entire set of values and interests according to the man they are interested in.

One Chameleon, frightened of small planes, nevertheless enthusiastically took up flying with her current boy friend, an amateur pilot. On a recent trip when their cabin filled with black smoke, she fainted. Fortunately the trouble was minor, but she was soon up in the air again, smiling and raving about the wonders of flying.

Another Chameleon was raised as a Jew. She married a Catholic and became an enthusiastic convert. She divorced him and remarried a man very interested in Eastern religions. Now she is an expert in Yoga, meditation and Buddism.

Basically, Chameleons have no sense of themselves as people. They don't know who they are or what they are interested in. It is only when a man enters their life that they are sure of what they are supposed to say, think, and do because they echo him.

Chameleons are totally submissive to men. They anticipate a man's needs, never ask anything for themselves, let the man make all the decisions. Although they are totally passive with men, Chameleons don't allow themselves to be chosen by just anyone. They actively seek out powerful men with status and financial security, two things the Chameleon needs. Only strong, powerful men can turn them on. Men whom they see as weak and ordinary either bore them, or worse— they find themselves repulsed. One Chameleon described a man she knew, "I don't know why I don't like him. He's nice, he's sweet, but he's kind of . . . well, I guess the word is soft." Her mouth screwed up in distaste.

The reason strength is so crucial to Chameleons is because they feel so weak and helpless themselves. A weak man mirrors their own insecurities which they are loathe to face up to.

Chameleons tend to get involved with their immediate bosses or other executives in their offices, successful businessmen, heads of companies, the rich and/or famous. Their ability to attract such men is helped by the fact that many Chameleons are very attractive women. They know how to guard their assets. They take good care of their skin, watch their diets, keep their hair well-groomed. They tend to look younger than their years and often have a rather childish, waiflike appearance, a look which has enormous appeal to certain kinds of men. They dress conservatively. Flash, in any sense is not their style. Very often the men they attach themselves to are considerably older than they are.

Chameleons generally had powerful fathers who captured their daughter's total attention within the family at an early age. All the adoring young Chameleon wanted was love and attention from her fascinating father. All she got, unfortunately, was neglect or rejection, but she kept chasing after her father, vainly hoping to win his affection. When Chameleons seek out powerful men who will love them, and whom they can serve dutifully, they are really trying to make up for their past wounds. They are getting admiration and affection from a father figure that they should have gotten from Daddy himself.

The Chameleon's mother was much less interesting to her as a child. Weak, dependent, and passive, her mother always seemed at the mercy of her father. One way the child tried to differentiate herself from her pathetic mother was to turn her full interest upon father and interject his strong presence as a wedge between mother and herself. Otherwise, since she was so much like her mother, she wouldn't know where her mother ended and she began.

Nevertheless, in spite of all her efforts, the Chameleon ended up just like her mother. She attends to men's needs with the same devotion her mother lavished on her father. She thinks of her mother, herself, all women as weak. In her mind, power resides only in men. Therefore, to achieve power as woman, and to feel complete as a person, she must ally herself with a powerful man. She will be safe with such a man, no longer helpless and oppressed by the frightening task of life. One Chameleon described her fantasies as episode after episode of being rescued from disasters like fires, earthquakes, and burglars by the strong arms of a man.

The only way Chameleons know how to relate to men is by becoming a slave. They totally sublimate their own wishes and desires. Whatever the man wants them to do is acceptable, even if it goes against their natural inclinations. One woman, for example, learned to cook fiery Mexican food for her boy friend even though, until she met him, she had liked only bland foods, hating anything heavily spiced. Now she raves over hot chili that secretly makes her wince, and attacks piquant enchiladas with the same enthusiasm as her boy friend. If the future brings her a man with an ulcer, she will start to love soft, bland foods again.

Not only are Chameleons capable of acquiring brand new tastes, they are also able to give up things they truly like for the sake of a man. One heavy drinker met a man with a strict moral view of the world that lumped drinking among the mortal sins. It was a terrible deprivation for her but she forced herself to give up the martinis, wine, and beer that had been an important part of her life for eighteen years.

The desire of Chameleons to please has a dark underside the man never sees. Inwardly, they are constantly worried about whether they are succeeding. They monitor, they search for clues. How is their beloved reacting? Any hint of displeasure is enough to send them into depths of despair. They experience it as a personal rebuff. Wounds from their father's rejection in the past are reopened. Frantically, they set about trying to please their man with renewed energy. Chameleons are constantly improving on their own performances as dutiful slaves.

Although marriage is the ultimate goal for some Chameleons, it isn't that important for others. What matters is the attachment to a man with power and the feeling that he is not going to leave them. Marriage may be better, but they will settle for less without much protest in certain circumstances. Many a Chameleon becomes the long-term mistress of a married boss, allowing him to take advantage of her docility. He knows he can see her only when he wants to and she will accept it. The association with power that he brings to her is enough to keep her in line. He can count on her being discrete. Chameleons may get talked about in such situations, but they never open their own mouths about liaisons. Their aim at all times is not to cause trouble for their man.

Unfortunately, the Chameleon who has been a mistress for many years frequently finds herself dumped when she gets older. The boss takes up with a younger employee. Getting tossed aside after twenty years would depress most women, but for the Chameleon, it is disaster. Without a man the old feeling of helplessness and incompleteness returns and overwhelms her. The Chameleon feels fearful, frantic. She doesn't know who she is anymore. She worries until she can find another man to make her feel okay again.

The only time a Chameleon will leave a relationship with a powerful man is if he loses his power either by getting fired, through severe financial losses or from illness. The Chameleon who has until that moment worshipped him—treating him like the grandest man in the world—suddenly changes her mind. She has made a mistake. He's a "nothing" after all.

She who was his total slave yesterday, suddenly feels she cannot stay with him another minute. A Chameleon can only be counted on to remain loyal if she is getting what she wants. She sticks like glue during good times and is gone in a flash in hard times. She may be sympathetic and reassuring to the man in trouble, but while she is sweet-talking him, she will be looking around for a replacement. When she finds another man with power, she will pack up and leave.

Chameleons are basically monogamous. They generally

only enter affairs as transition measures—when they are preparing to leave a man who already has lost luster in their eyes.

One woman was happily married to an important government official until it was discovered that he had taken a bribe. A true Chameleon, she had been completely faithful to him while all was going well. After his disgrace, she started an affair with a business tycoon for whom she soon left her husband. She was equally loyal and faithful to the tycoon until his business ran into trouble and he was on the verge of bankruptcy. By this time she had met the president of a university and left the tycoon for him.

Occasionally a Chameleon will remain married to a man she no longer idolizes, but only if she can replace from another source the sense of power her husband once gave her. A woman married to a well-known politician in Europe came with her husband to this country. Once here he decided not to look for a job, but to write a book instead. At that point the romance was over. To her, he no longer had status. She began working, met the married head of her company, and started an affair with him. They traveled together for months on end on business. She was thus still plugged into power, but able to tolerate staying with the husband who no longer commanded her respect.

When disenchantment comes, a Chameleon will rarely tell a man directly how she feels. She simply goes about the business of self-preservation by finding a new man.

In direct contrast to her disenchantment in times of trouble, the Chameleon will put up with all kinds of abuse from a husband as long as he remains in a powerful position and she feels financially secure. It is not uncommon for Chameleons to marry tyrants, but they are able to accept a certain amount of abuse and remain submissive because they feel they are getting what they want out of the deal.

In the right circumstances, Chameleons have even been known to put up with perversions. One Chameleon's husband was caught molesting a child while he was on a business trip. She stuck by him, even when he lost his job, because he came from a wealthy family and they were able to live in comfort until he found his next job.

The following story may sound incredible, but it's true. A Chameleon came home unexpectedly one day and found her husband wearing her makeup and one of her dresses. She handled the situation by simply leaving the room. He washed off the makeup and put his own clothing back on. Neither one of them mentioned the incident, but she accommodated to his needs by buying him makeup of his own so he wouldn't use hers. She left the makeup in an obvious place where he was sure to find it. She also put a selection of clothing she no longer wanted in a bag and left it in a place where he couldn't fail to find it.

Chameleons have an amazing knack for excusing behavior that might drive other wives crazy. They simply write off tyranny, oddities, peccadilloes, even perversions by saying "Well, he may have problems, but I will never find a more wonderful man."

• They can endure almost anything except stinginess. A stingy man is seen as withholding what she must have—his power. Assuming a man is reasonably generous, however, Chameleons feel quite happy and good about themselves and life. It is only when they are stripped of money and power through some failure of their husband's, or through their husband's death, that the Chameleon's innate sense of worthlessness and incompleteness comes to the fore and depression overtakes them.

The Kinds of Men Chameleons Attract

Chameleons often attract men who have a great deal of underlying rage toward women. These men may give lip service to wanting independent women, but what they really need is someone to dominate. On an unconscious level, this is the way they think. "I want a blob who is going to do exactly what I want and who will always be available and malleable and never question or cross me because if she does I'm going to beat her up because I hate her so much underneath." Because the Chameleon is so compliant, she doesn't invoke the rage against women this kind of man harbors. Because she does exactly what he says and never makes him angry, he is able to fool both of them into believing he's a normal man who likes women.

Many men who are attracted to Chameleons have rescue fantasies. They feel powerful when they can care for and protect a helpless waif who adores them.

Chameleons often marry men whose real partners are their work. Dedicated to their careers, motivated toward success, they can be unscrupulous. Husbands of Chameleons can find it difficult to establish relationships. They have little capacity for closeness and intimacy. When they talk with a woman they talk at her, not to her. The Chameleon is a perfect listener. She admires whatever he tells her.

These men are able to pursue their careers with full dedication because their Chameleon tends to their needs, making no demands for time, or attention. Because these men are very busy, the Chameleon is again made to order. They can call at the last minute or whenever they want, and she will always be available without complaint. The Chameleon is the kind of woman who is afraid to make plans of her own. She hangs by the telephone, for she wants to be ready when and if her man calls. She will always break a date with a woman for one with a man.

She may need periodic reassurances from her man that he loves her, but if he gives these to her, she will accept his lack of time, his ineptitude for intimacy, even his paucity of physical affection graciously. She is able to take care of herself in other ways without putting demands on a man. If she wants some affection, she has pets; if she needs companionship, she has friends; if she is intelligent—and Chameleons can be—she will find intellectual stimulation in other pursuits. All of her other activities will take second place, of course, to her man. She can be very competent in running a house, dealing with neighbors and storekeepers. She runs a smooth ship for her man.

Her husband's basic rage toward all women may come out indirectly. It is not uncommon for a Chameleon's husband to leave proof of an affair where his wife will stumble upon it. But he will rarely leave the clue until the affair is finished.

One Chameleon's husband left a packet of love letters in a

drawer his wife used periodically. Although she was upset by her discovery, he soothed her by saying it was all over and the other woman never meant anything to him anyway. Because she wanted to continue her comfortable life-style she forgave him.

What drives a Chameleon's husband to an affair is the fact that his passive, compliant wife does not excite him physically as much as a more aggressive woman. The husband may give in to his yen for her opposite personality, but he will always return to his adoring Chameleon. In the end, the Chameleon is less threatening to him than these other women for they have expectations of their own and make demands.

Although Chameleons marry men whom they perceive as powerful, often these men suffer from a poor sense of self-esteem. The Chameleon makes them feel good about themselves because they see the aggrandized image that shines in her eyes.

Sometimes Chameleons pick men who, although they are very successful, are not very attractive physically. What matters to the Chameleon is not a man's appearance but his standing in the world. If a Chameleon describes a new boy friend to a female confidante, she will give a Dun and Bradstreet report rather than describe what he looks like.

Because they may be fat or short, with bad skin, bad manners, or have other features they are ashamed of, these men find the Chameleon pleasing—she adores them despite their shortcomings. They are afraid no other woman will find them as appealing as she does.

Chameleons' mates are generally proud of their attractive, well-mannered wives. They like to show her off as the prize package they have captured.

The Chameleon and Sex

The Chameleon is not interested in sex per se. The right "chemistry" doesn't matter. So what if a man doesn't excite her physically? All he has to do is take care of her. Many Chameleons are not orgasmic. One reason they have trouble reaching climaxes is the unconscious fear that they are taking something from a man—his power as symbolized by his penis. If that happens, he would no longer be able to give them what they need. By not having orgasms, they leave their man intact as well as their future with him.

In addition, Chameleons are so intent on pleasing a man that they often disregard their own pleasure. And since they find it difficult to be assertive with a man, they are unable to tell or show what pleases them sexually.

The Chameleon as Mother

Chameleons are relatively good mothers. They try to limit the number of children they have to one or two. Since they tend to devote themselves to their children, they realize they can spread themselves too thin with too many.

Chameleons often get involved in their children's interests. One mother whose son was very talented musically took piano lessons herself in order to better understand his interest. There is a tendency among Chameleons to idealize their sons just as they do their husbands. In the Chameleon's eyes, a son can do no wrong.

Chameleons like their daughters and are good to them, but they don't treat them with the same sense of importance that they attach to males, young or old. As mothers, they often turn out to be poor models for daughters. They emphasize submissiveness as part of the feminine role, and tend to create other Chameleons.

The Chameleon's relationship with her own mother continues into adulthood. Together they seem like helpless, hapless sisters, rather than mother and daughter. Neither is aggressive or successful in her own right. They operate together on a level of mutual dependency. They share each other's difficulties, particularly if one or both of them is without a man. Chameleons often lose their husbands early in life because they marry much older men or they dump them because of some loss of power on the man's part.

The Chameleon's Relationships with Other Women

The Chameleon's relationships with other women are cordial and superficial. Chameleons are thoughtful, always aware of social niceties. They never forget birthdays or other occasions.

Any friendship with a woman is secondary to what a Chameleon has going with a man. She sees her female friends only when her man is busy or out of town. If a woman friend is good-looking, you can be sure that the Chameleon will never let her man set eyes on her. She will meet the friend for lunch or dinner when her man is otherwise occupied, but she will never invite her home or on a double date.

To the outside world, Chameleons appear agreeable, pliable, and sometimes a little boring. One of the reasons the Chameleon bores some people is that she keeps her mouth shut more than other women. She doesn't talk in deference to a man. Her silence also covers the fact that she is quite immature in her attitudes and opinions. If she doesn't talk, no one ever finds out. With outsiders, Chameleons are guarded, which makes them uninteresting to be with.

The Chameleon sometimes improves as she gets older. She may gain insight into her own need for power, security, and status. She can sometimes talk wittily on the subject to close friends. If the Chameleon does have wit, however, she will never reveal it to her man. She feels he may be threatened by her humor.

The Chameleon and Aging

The Chameleon exhibits a strong interest in boys very early in life. As a teenager she will often develop crushes on leaders and older figures. She may spend her time trailing after a teacher, for example, or daydreaming about a priest. These men, of course, are father figures.

The Chameleon ages well, but not without stress. She will never allow herself to get fat. Chameleons hang onto the illusion of youth longer than many other women. A Chameleon is conscious of her looks as an asset to be traded for power and security, so she worries a lot about wrinkles.

As she advances in age, the Chameleon may become practical and settle for a man she might not have while she was younger. For example, instead of a man with a high status profession, she may settle for someone who is merely rich. One woman after being widowed by the head of a company, then a department chief at a major hospital, married the third time an automobile dealer who was undistinguished but very well off.

Another Chameleon allowed a younger man to move into her large house with her. He didn't have a distinguished job, but since she was close to sixty, she contented herself with the fact that he brought home a decent salary and was very handy, so her house was maintained in splendid condition.

As long as they are attached to a man who can give them some measure of security, Chameleons will survive better than if they had to face old age alone.

The Chameleon at Work

Chameleons are not career women. Women's liberation has barely touched them. A career success requires a certain amount of aggressiveness and the ability to tolerate competition, neither of which is part of the Chameleon's character. They may have to work but work remains unimportant in their value system unless, of course, work and love are intertwined. This is often the case when Chameleons are involved with a boss. Some Chameleons come with a job. One boss/lover may leave, but they immediately get involved with his replacement.

Chameleons leave their jobs as soon as they marry. However, in their dedication to their husband, they may learn all about his business and become informal experts in his field. They do this to be good helpmates, not to shine in their own right.

The Indiscriminate Pleaser

Another version of the Chameleon is the Indiscriminate Pleaser. Indiscriminate Pleasers, like Chameleons, are women who change interests and tastes, who do whatever it takes to please a man. But for Indiscriminate Pleasers, this will happen with any man. Chameleons please only powerful men. The Indiscriminate Pleaser will change her character for a starving artist, a high school teacher, a salesman. One Indiscriminate Pleaser took up photography while she was dating an impoverished photographer. She became good enough to have some of her pictures shown at a museum, but she abandoned photography to study the recorder when she exchanged the photographer for a music teacher.

Another Indiscriminate Pleaser's wardrobe changes with each man in her life. She wore slightly eccentric clothing with an advertising copywriter; she wore tailored suits and conservative dresses with a management consultant. For a novelist, she switched to blue jeans and plain shirts. For her current beau who loves long walks in the country, she wears corduroy pants and sturdy hiking boots.

The Indiscriminate Pleaser watches Lawrence Welk on television if that's what her boy friend likes, or she watches no tv at all, if he thinks all television is trash.

Although Indiscriminate Pleasers act similarly to Chameleons, the origin of their problem is different. They feel themselves to be personalities without boundaries, undefined. They don't know where they start and where they end. Often this began with domineering and strong parents who gave them too many orders while they were young.

Sometimes their homes were run according to strict rules based on a religion that spelled out what you could or could not do. While in their own homes, Indiscriminate Pleasers knew who they were. They defined themselves by the rules that bound them. Once outside their original home, however, Indiscriminate Pleasers find themselves in trouble. The old rules don't apply anymore. Lost, the Indiscriminate Pleaser either adopts any man's viewpoint in all respects, or in other cases, the Indiscriminate Pleaser joins a cult, therefore finding a new set of rules to follow.

In addition to giving too many orders, the Indiscriminate Pleaser's parents were sometimes irrational about what they expected from their child. Without considering whether or not she had any musical talent, for example, they may have wanted her to become a pianist. The Indiscriminate Pleaser studied and practiced because she wanted to be a good kid, not because she enjoyed the piano. If directed into too many activities foreign to her nature, the Indiscriminate Pleaser becomes permanently confused about where she belongs naturally and who she really is.

Overdirected children never develop their own tastes or discover interests on their own. Therefore, they spend their lives looking for others to tell them what to do. The orders must come, however, from men or from a higher power like a guru or a cult leader. Indiscriminate Pleasers don't accept women as authority figures.

Chameleons and Society

Until recently, it was considered natural for a woman to subordinate her own personality to a man's. It was part of our female role. Most women, at one time or another, have tried to please men at the expense of their own feelings and tastes. The Chameleon and the Indiscriminate Pleaser simply turn this into a full-time profession. Chameleons and Indiscriminate Pleasers are two more examples of the female role as defined by society, carried to an extreme, and turned into a caricature of itself.

How a Chameleon Can Help Herself

Chameleons may live in the shadow of their men but there are positive things about these women. They are generally pleasant women, and they can be loyal and devoted wives as well as concerned, caring mothers. Marriages of Chameleons and powerful men can be very successful. However, if you are a Chameleon and you realize that you may be cheating yourself by living through someone else rather than for yourself and if you would like to alter your life-style, you can become a more exciting, self-confident woman.

The first thing you must do is pay attention to your self-image. You think you are a weak and helpless person. It's time you start reassessing yourself to see the strengths and independent qualities you already have, but have overlooked.

Chameleons are known for running their households very smoothly. That fact already makes you a more competent person than many other women who live in constant chaos and disorder. You are also able to accomplish things when you put your mind to it. For example, to please your husband, you may have picked up a lot of expertise in his business. Put the same determination that you use to please your husband into learning and doing things for yourself.

It is a good idea for you to take courses to give yourself an independent activity and to learn something that has nothing to do with the man in your life. Any knowledge that you gain independently will enhance you as a person.

You must learn to speak up and ask for some things for yourself in your relationship. Start out by asking for two things a week just to get the hang of it. You'll find you won't lose your husband if you do. Make sure you don't worry about whether or not your request will please your husband. In the beginning, ask for inconsequential things so you will be sure to succeed.

Your task is to establish yourself as a person in your own right. Start expressing opinions that are your own and not borrowed from someone else. Start slowly. Express one opinion a day for three weeks, then increase it to twice a day until you feel more comfortable saying what's on your mind. Opinions can be positive or negative just as long as they are yours and not your husband's. Begin by expressing yourself about minor things.

You must eventually learn to say "No" to your husband occasionally. It does not have to be done in a nasty way. Just a quiet no will do; it doesn't have to be about anything very important until you feel comfortable doing it. For example, if your husband asks you to get the briefcase he left in the hallway, you might reply, "No, I can't get it now. I'm busy in the kitchen."

Thinking for yourself, doing things for yourself, and having opinions of your own will make you like and respect yourself more as an individual apart from your man, and people will end up responding to you with more enthusiasm rather than as that nice bland, Mrs. X down the block.

CHAPTER 6

THE EXPLOITER

The best place to observe Cynthia if you want to understand her is at a party. As you watch her move from person to person, you will eventually be able to pick out all the people in the room with power—those whom Cynthia feels can help her in her budding career as a film director. She turns a full smile, presents a respectful manner, is all charm to the producers, the influential screenwriters, the prominent actors and actresses. Occasionally, she finds a few words for other people she knows, but her conversation is perfunctory. Her true attention is riveted on those she feels can be of use to her, and her eyes dart around the room seeking them out.

In her private life, Cynthia has a history of quick, intense friendships with women that either peter out or end in angry breakups because Cynthia is continually putting demands on her friends. She becomes angry and vengeful when they don't do what she wants.

Cynthia is an expert at alienating people. An acquaintance remembers the one and only car trip they took together. Cynthia sat in the back seat issuing a series of orders: "Open the window, please. Turn on the radio. Can you turn down the radio? It's too loud. It's getting cold. Would you shut the window? Would you mind not smoking?"

Cynthia's relationships with men are marked by her desperate need to have a man in her life and her knack for driving men away. She is always hammering at her boy friends with a series of demands. She wants too much from them whether it is time, attention, or sex. In one case,

Cynthia insisted that the man treat his young son more firmly. Cynthia has a hidden motive in all of her relationships. She wants to control, to take things from others without having to give much in return.

Cynthia would dispute the last statement. She feels she tries to be generous and helpful to her friends. But everything she does has a price. Cynthia feels her friends are obligated to her. She calls in the debt when it suits her, and she is furious when friends don't come through as she expects. For example, when Cynthia is ill she becomes angry and resentful if her friends don't drop everything and come to see her. She is irritated, angry, and disappointed when a girl friend starts a new relationship with a man and doesn't have as much time to spend with Cynthia as before.

Cynthia desperately wants power. She wants to be at the top of her profession, and she is constantly working to get what she wants. It creates a lot of strain for her. She is tense at parties and other social occasions when she is working on contacts for either immediate favors or possible future use. On the surface, she seems to generate a lot of charm. She works hard at trying to impress the right people. But astute observers who have observed Cynthia recognize a quality of phoniness about her. Cynthia is an Exploiter. Exploiters come in two basic forms—Power Exploiters and Mercenary Exploiters.

The Power Exploiter

Power Exploiters are people who see themselves as weak, helpless, insignificant, inferior. Their behavior is an attempt to guard against these feelings and to compensate for them. They also want to avoid feeling humiliated or abused by others—something they fear.

Power exploiters try to dominate and control people. They use others to reach positions of status or wealth which they fantasize will automatically give them the power and grandeur they lack.

There was always something in the Power Exploiter's early background that made her feel deprived. Sometimes it was lack of love.

One Power Exploiter felt abandoned at a young age by her mother who was institutionalized. She felt rejected by her father who, after he remarried, paid more attention to his new wife and stepchildren than to her. She never felt she counted in her family and vowed never to feel that insignificant again. This was converted into her overriding ambition to be a "somebody."

Some Power Exploiters grew up in Spartan homes. Their parents felt that children shouldn't be spoiled and so, out of principle rather than poverty, they were deprived of everything except what was needed to survive. Still other Power Exploiters were poor kids who lived in rich neighborhoods, or were the poor relatives in rich families. Feeling worthless and deprived, Power Exploiters think they have to force people to give them things.

The Power Exploiter is quite different from other career-oriented women who try to advance through their own efforts. A normally ambitious woman may sometimes use networks and contacts to go after what she wants, but her use of others is moderate and her actions don't have the desperation and anger of the Power Exploiters. The Power Exploiter will trample on any bodies in her path, if necessary.

Her hidden motto is, "I'll show the world," and she goes about her business with hostility and combativeness. She feels life is a constant battle. She has to break down barriers to get where she's going. Her determination is not healthy ambition. It is neurotic, conflict-ridden and vengeful.

A Power Exploiter generally divides her love life in half. There are the men she sleeps with for contacts and favors, or because they represent status. They can be catered to, slept with, and forgotten the next day. Then there are men who fulfill her emotional requirements. The Power Exploiter is a very needy woman emotionally. She wants an endless amount of admiration, encouragement, love and for these needs, she may turn to an altogether different kind of man with whom she expects to develop a more long-term, possessive relationship.

There is a self-inflicted, continuing sense of deprivation in the Power Exploiter's relationships with men. She becomes angry or upset if a man goes out of town, doesn't telephone, is occasionally late. She feels, on the surface, that he doesn't love her, but what really angers her underneath is the fact that he isn't complying with her wishes for him to be with her, to call regularly, to be anxious to get there on time.

Her relationships with men rarely work out in the long run, because she operates in her relationships the way she does elsewhere. She tries to force what she wants from a man. She is a continual, unending stream of demands which eventually drive men away.

Some men leave a Power Exploiter when they finally wake up to how she operates in career matters. They get turned off by the fact that she is always trying to use others.

In marriage, the Power Exploiter is quite capable of being an unfaithful wife. If it is advantageous for her to sleep with someone while she is away at a convention, for example, she will, without a twinge of guilt or regret.

On the other hand, there is her opposite number, the Power Exploiter with an ongoing sexual relationship with one or more powerful men in her company who sleeps with casual pickups when she isn't with the power brokers.

Unless they marry very passive men with consuming interests that allow them to ignore what their wives are doing, marriages of Power Exploiters generally end in divorce. These women become spiteful toward their husbands. If for some reason, a husband isn't giving them what they think they need or want, they may begin to flaunt their affairs with other men.

It is rare that Power Exploiters understand what their own role was in the demise of their relationships. They generally end up feeling abused, and they paint others as villains.

Power Exploiters have female friends, but there is little continuity in their relationships with women. They rarely keep the same women as friends over the years because of the demands they put on them, or because they feel that they aren't getting enough from them.

Power Exploiters are always weighing their relationships like pharmacists weigh ingredients in a prescription. They measure what each person can give them, and so their friendships shift according to need. They are friendly with those who can offer what they need at a certain time. If someone has entrée to people a Power Exploiter wants to know, the Power Exploiter will be warm and attentive until her goal is accomplished. If she needs someone to bitch or brag to she will pursue friendship with the person who can be an ear and an audience.

All her relationships are one-sided and all are poisoned by the forcing, demanding quality that emanates from her. One Power Exploiter has lost innumerable friends after sharing summer houses with them. She is forever leaving these houses in a huff or being forced out because of her demands. She wants to change her room because it is not as nice as someone else's, or the view depresses her; she wants to modify her share of the costs because other people eat more than she does; the boy friend of someone in the house rubs her the wrong way. Her list of complaints is endless and relentless and very few people can live with it.

Power Exploiters are takers, sometimes even in little ways and quite unconsciously. One Power Exploiter, always on a diet, had dinner with some acquaintances at a restaurant they all frequent. She refused to order dessert for herself, but when one of the men did, she asked if she could taste it. He said "yes" and bite by bite she proceeded to consume his entire portion by herself. He ordered a second portion for himself, and automatically, she did the same thing again.

Power Exploiters are selfish people with a mean view of the world. They see it divided between givers and takers, exploited and exploiters. Never do they want to be counted among the exploited.

The Mercenary Exploiter

Phyllis and Diane exemplify another kind of Exploiter.

Phyllis is a beautiful twenty-eight year old woman who goes out only with men who are able to take her to the most expensive restaurants in town and buy the best tickets for shows. She wears expensive clothing. Her accessories are pieces of costly jewelry from a collection of gifts men have given her over the years. Phyllis once had dreams of becoming a fashion model, but she wasn't successful at it. Today she has a small job in the personnel department of a multi-million dollar concern. She uses her position to make contact with many of the top executives in the company. She has had affairs with many of them. Most have been married. Whether they are married or not does not matter to Phyllis. What she cares about is whether they are generous with her. She belongs to a bridge club off New York's Madison Avenue whose members are wealthy. She uses the people she plays bridge with as contacts for meeting rich men.

Diane is a former starlet. Small and pretty with an appealing foreign accent, she often talks about her days in Hollywood. When she does, she carefully omits references to dates. Diane does not disclose her age, but she is a woman in her late forties. She is all too conscious of the way her face and body are beginning to sag. She worries about her ability to continue to attract men. Her most recent love affair among the many she has had over the years was with a wealthy manufacturer. This is her story of the relationship:

"He didn't tell me he was married until after he started sleeping with me. When he finally told me he had a wife, I just looked at him and said, 'Okay, so marriage is out. If you want to continue seeing me, you have to take care of me.' He said, 'What do you mean?' I said, 'Help me out. You know I'm having financial troubles, I need help in paying the rent.' We haggled a bit over how much. I wanted $450 a week. He refused to give me more than $250, and I finally had to accept that. We had good times together. He looked very distinguished, and he took me to the elegant restaurants I like. But we used to have fights. I didn't think he was giving me enough money, and I told him so. Sometimes I would refuse to sleep with him after one of those fights. Finally he got a divorce. I wanted him to marry me, but he found himself another girl friend—a divorced woman with two teenaged daughters. I was furious and devastated. I even called the other woman's house after they came back from Las Vegas together. I knew, because he told me, that they met another couple and had switched partners for the night. She wasn't home, but her sixteen-year-old daughter answered the phone. I decided to say something to her. 'Do you know,' I said, 'that your mother slept with somebody besides her boy friend when they were in Las Vegas?' I figured maybe that would cause trouble between them and he would come back to me. But do you know what that daughter said to me? 'So what?' ''

Diane, who has used men to "help her out" is very frantic. Her looks are going and she knows she has to earn some kind of living for herself. She recently took a typing course. She travels in a circle of men and women who are social climbers, women who are demimondaines like herself, or women who were lucky enough to have married and divorced well and have life-styles that Diane intensely envies. Recently, one of the wealthy women in Diane's crowd felt sorry for her and hired her to type some correspondence. While Diane was working in the woman's home, a gold bracelet disappeared from the bedroom dresser. Everyone assumes Diane took it, although she denies it. A wealthy man in this crowd explained where Diane now stands. "She's dead,'' he said. "No one will have her in their house anymore.''

Phyllis and Diane are Mercenary Exploiters. Mercenary Exploiters have the same feelings of worthlessness, insignificance and deprivation that Power Exploiters do and for the same reason. They, too, feel they were deprived in their early life because of lack of love or lack of material possessions.

One Mercenary Exploiter grew up in an impoverished family with a frequently absent, alcoholic father and a mother who worked as a maid for a rich family. The wealthy woman who employed her mother helped the child get a scholarship to a school where the other students were mostly the daughters of the rich. She felt inferior among them. She was quite conscious of not having what they had. Determined to redress this wrong, she did so over and over again when she grew up to be a beautiful young woman, by exploiting men in return for her sexual favor.

Occasionally, a Mercenary Exploiter learned her trade as a little girl when she was able to twist her daddy around her finger and get things from him.

Her success with her father gave her a feeling of power over both parents. Her father could be manipulated; and she felt superior to her mother because she could get her daddy to give her more than he gave her mother. Later in life, when the Mercenary Exploiter takes from men, she again feels superior to the man she has exploited and to other women as well. She can get things from men that other women can't.

For many Mercenary Exploiters it isn't only the expensive meals, the jewelry or other gifts that she receives which are important. It is the gesture of giving itself. Mercenary Exploiters equate the act of giving with love. The more they are given, the more they are valued and loved. Tenderness, caring, human qualities are discounted if a man doesn't regularly give material goods of value.

Some Mercenary Exploiters enjoy the feeling of taking a man for a ride. Others think of themselves as involved in a fair deal. They are trading their presence, their conversation, their sexual availability in return for gifts of one kind or another.

The ones who feel that they are involved in a con game are more hostile. They will try to extort even petty things from men. They may try to coerce or shame a man into taking them to a more expensive restaurant, for example. "I'm surprised a man of your stature would want to go to a place like that," said one Mercenary Exploiter to an escort who had suggested they go to a nice, moderately priced restaurant. Exploiters will deliberately order the most expensive thing on the menu even if they are not particularly hungry. One man told the story of a woman who, when faced with a choice between a large or a small steak on the menu chose the larger one. She ate only half, explained that she couldn't finish the rest, and instructed the waiter to put the rest of the steak in a doggie bag. That would provide her with another meal on the man the next day.

Mercenary Exploiters often will try to avoid sex as a repayment, but they are also prepared to jump into bed for a good movie, an excellent meal, an expensive charity ball, if they must.

Mercenary Exploiters frequently can't have orgasms because they are so hostile to men and because they find it hard to abandon themselves in general. Nevertheless, they may be interested in sex for its touching aspects. Some part of them wants to be held, babied and cared for.

The Mercenary Exploiter who thinks of herself as part of

the bargain with a man (prostitutes are among those who think of themselves as fair traders) is less sick than the one who thinks of herself as leading a man through hoops.

Mercenary Exploiters don't necessarily limit themselves to taking advantage of men. Some, if they find a woman who is willing to give to them, are capable of entering a lesbian relationship.

The Kind of Men Exploiters Attract

The kind of men who get involved with Exploiters are very often men who like playing the role of Daddy. They want to provide for and give to a woman. They think that's a man's role. It makes them feel powerful and masculine. They are often much older than the Exploiter.

Exploiters' men generally feel inadequate themselves. They think they don't measure up to other men. Showing off their relationship with a much younger or beautiful woman serves to enhance their stature in the eyes of other males. To many of these men, the ego boost is so important that being used and taken advantage of doesn't matter. It's a deal they can live with.

The more polished Mercenary Exploiters sometimes marry and when they do, it is always to a man with power, high status or money. Ordinary men aren't even in the running. Some Exploiters wait until marriage to show their true colors. It is then that the incessant demands for material things start.

For other Mercenary Exploiters, marriage is a continuation of the same game they have been playing all along. They got as much from a man as they could before marriage, and they continue to do so after marriage.

An Exploiter's marriage is frequently punctuated by arguments. Surliness, pouts, shouts, abusive language or general denigration of the man will come into play. An Exploiter is determined to get her way at all costs. Mercenary Exploiters frequently withhold sex to coerce and punish and grant sex to reward a man. They have frequent extramarital affairs which simultaneously serve to humiliate a man, express hostility toward him and make them feel they are putting something over on him. Exploiters rarely have problems with guilt. The only thing they worry about is being found out and losing their meal ticket.

Mercenary Exploiters often end up as mistresses rather than wives. Many of them prefer it, for they feel crowded in full relationships. As a mistress, they can be catered to and provided for, yet still retain their freedom and not be tied down with responsibilities to which they are allergic.

Although many Mercenary Exploiters hate men they also arrange their lives so that they have to be dependent on them since they refuse to make a living on their own. There is a neurotic reason behind the bind they put themselves into. Since Exploiters feel deficient, someone else has to make up for their deprivation in order for justice to be done.

How Exploiters End Up

If they don't marry rich men, Mercenary Exploiters often end up badly. The smarter Exploiters grab the best men they can find when they think they are losing their looks. Middle age is always difficult for women like this. Every wrinkle is a trauma, an erosion of their tradeable assets. Those who refuse to face the facts—and there are many—characteristically fail to provide for their own futures. They never think about tomorrow, never acknowledge that they, like everyone else, will someday grow old. The demise of their looks, and thus their bargaining power, as they see it, with men, often sneaks up on them.

As their choice of men dwindles, some of them resort to very old or handicapped men willing to provide for them.

A fair number of Mercenary Exploiters end up as suicides. Their looks are gone, they have no money, no one is ever going to give them things anymore. They feel they have no job or career options. They refuse to take what may be available to them, for example, a saleswoman's job in a department store, because it would be too humiliating. They feel nothing is left.

Power Exploiters often have a better fate. They may not end up with a man, but they do have their careers and a means of earning a living for themselves. If Exploiters marry, they generally choose not to have children. If they do, however, they turn out daughters who become users like themselves and sons who become givers to women.

The Exploiter mother is rarely able to see her child as a separate person with his or her own needs. The child is an extension of herself. Exploiters generally think of children as good-looking creatures who will stand next to them and present a pretty picture to the world.

Exploiters and Society

There is a little of the Exploiter in many women. How many of us don't feel more highly valued when we are presented with expensive gifts, wined and dined well? How many of us don't feel a touch of pride when we tell our friends about being taken to the fanciest French restaurant in town? How many of us would refuse a mink or sable coat as a gift?

Women have been trained to think they are unable to provide for themselves and so feel they are at the mercy of men for their economic well-being. The Exploiter simply carries this view of women in our society to the extreme. She extracts forcefully from men what other women simply expect from them. They want favors or gifts as well as economic support.

How an Exploiter Can Help Herself

Exploiters are women who, behind their tough, grabby, demanding exteriors are really terribly vulnerable women afraid of being hurt. For emotional protection, they have built an impenetrable fortress of apparent invulnerability around themselves. They are so afraid of letting anyone hurt them or get the better of them that they won't let anyone get too close. They are kept at bay with a series of demands.

If you are an Exploiter, you have probably seen relationship after relationship fail in your life up until now. You may want to change, but don't know how.

It may seem like the most frightening thing in the world to

you, but in order to effect change, you have to first recognize and acknowledge the terribly hurt person residing within you—the one whose existence you are denying by your tough exploitative behavior. This is the prelude to finding real strength rather than pseudo-strength.

You also have to recognize and vent some of the rage that you walk around with—a heritage from your unfortunate past.

One way to get in touch with your core of vulnerability and also to locate your rage is to take a chair and pretend it is your mother or father or whomever it was you feel wronged you as a child.

Tell the chair everything you remember feeling as you grew up. Accuse the chair of all the crimes against you. Don't control yourself. Really let go. You may be surprised at how much hurt and anger will suddenly show.

Once you are able to locate your anger and identify its source, you will find it easier to go on with your task. First, stop trying to force the rest of the world to make up for what was done to you a long time ago. Second, put to rest the vulnerable little girl—your guiding spirit—who is preventing you from becoming an adult with a chance at real happiness. Once you stop looking through that little girl's eyes and stop seeing the world as your enemy, you can meet people with friendly feelings instead of the vengeful ones which make you try to calculate what you can get from them. Only then can you get what you really crave—not power or possessions, but respect based on love.

CHAPTER 7

THE NURSE

What can Roberta possibly see in him, her friends want to know? Why does she stay with him? He is a chronic alcoholic, and suffers from depression that immobilizes him. He hasn't worked in years.

Roberta is a bright and lively woman with a pretty face and fantastic figure. One would think she could have the pick of functioning, attractive men. But the truth is, she has picked.

She's a Nurse who goes only for needy, incapacitated men. Nurses hook up with alcoholics, men who go in and out of mental institutions, those suffering from chronic diseases or impairments, severe depressives, drug addicts, men who can never hold onto a job, even prisoners.

One very religious Nurse started corresponding with a prisoner out of a sense of Christian charity. Without having met the man, she started to fall in love with him from his letters. When he was released from prison, he came to see her and a love affair ensued. He was frequently violent, and on more than one occasion, he threatened to kill her. Once he called to say he was coming to get her with a gun that night. He arrived to find her gone. She had taken refuge in a friend's house. Enraged, he then raped a neighbor. The Nurse turned him into the police, but continued to correspond with him in prison in hopes she could convert him to her religion and turn him into a better human being. Recently he told her he had become religious because of her and now she has promised to marry him when he is released from prison. She is sure that under her care he will stop being violent and turn

into a worthwhile man. Her chances of success are practically
zero, but Nurses are always eternal optimists.

While power is the magnet for some women, weakness is
the lure for a Nurse.

A Nurse may get involved every now and then with a
healthy, functioning man, but her heart isn't really in it. The
minute a basket case comes along, she will go to him.
Although she does get genuine pleasure from helping, her
role as Nurse also makes her feel powerful. She needs this
power to compensate for an inner sense of weakness and
inadequacy. Playing nurse can give her a sense of superiority
as well. No one could put up with him, but her.

The Nurse can be spotted early in a relationship. She is an
especially good listener. She listens patiently and sympathetically, then suggests practical solutions to problems. If one
solution is rejected or has already been tried or doesn't suit
the listener, she will then come up with other alternatives.

The Nurse's interest, her support, her helpful suggestions
are irresistible to the incapacitated man who is often so
overwhelmed by depression on top of his other problems that
he can't see any hope in his situation. The Nurse offers hope.
The man is ready to become her patient.

Once he falls into her hands, she takes control of his life,
and, in some ways, his problem becomes compounded. His
dependency needs come into full flower. He turns into her
total charge. She runs his life, tells him what to do for his
own good, puts up with his defects, his complaints, his
moods, sometimes his irresponsibility, with good cheer. She
is sure he will recover sooner or later—with her help, of
course.

She may covertly resist, however, any kind of cure that
would take him from her hands and deliver him into others.
For example, a Nurse may encourage a man to join Alcoholics Anonymous, but when he does, she undermines his faith
and his possible cure by saying to him, "I think you're
getting bad vibes from those meetings."

The Nurse wants to be head nurse. It is important to her to
be the most important person in a man's life. She feels
threatened by institutions, doctors, therapists who cut into her
job or threaten to take it away altogether.

Once the Nurse/patient relationship is well established, she can be counted on to be serene, no matter what goes on. She is able to put up with what might seem intolerable to other women—an infinite amount of excuses, foul ups, or even physical or psychological abuse from a lover or husband.

She may complain about his outrageous, provocative or abusive behavior, his surly, rude moods, his regular descent into torpor and depression, the financial strain because he can't find or keep a job, but she gets so much gratification out of her role as helper that it overrides all and keeps her in a good frame of mind. He makes her feel good about herself.

The man, however, inevitably comes to resent her. Not only is she aware of and constantly focusing on his emotional or physical handicap, but now he depends on her for survival as well. She also creates guilt in him because she is always so giving, good and caring while he by contrast is a no-good person. He becomes secretly hostile, which appears as passive resistance.

He tries to reassert his independence by not following her suggestions, by not complaining as much as he used to, by hiding his despair, by appearing to be less needy in general.

She is aware that his basic problem still isn't solved, so his sulky withholding and withdrawing actions, his new stoicism, his refusal to come to her doesn't upset her too much. "It's just rebellion. It's part of his problem. It's all right. He'll turn to me again," she thinks.

This kind of rebellion plays into her hands. The man who refuses help with problems is the best mate a Nurse can have. It insures the perpetuity of her job.

Often the man seesaws between healthy and sick periods. In his better periods, he can be overly nice to make up for his deficits. He'll help around the house, for example, buy her little gifts or a new plant to add to her collection. The homes of Nurses are often filled with beautiful, flourishing plants. Their basic wish to nurture is shown in the careful care of plants as well as people.

Often the patient/Nurse couple lives in relative isolation from the rest of the world. His problems may interfere with the couple's ability to socialize freely. If he isn't working, they often have no money to go anywhere. If he is a wreck, he often doesn't want to see anyone or be seen. He may be so moody with people or drink so much that it is better to stay home. Rather than resent it, she often enjoys the total intimacy and closeness that isolation provides. She discourages friends from becoming part of their inner life. A friend is liable to offer help or suggestions. The Nurse becomes envious and jealous if someone comes between her and her patient or interferes with her role.

Superficially, the Nurse/patient relationship looks one-sided. She seems to have all the power and control, and he seems dependent on her. But a closer look reveals that he wields equal power.

His inability to cope, his fears, his incapacity to do many things is what ties her to him and he knows it. He keeps her dependent on him by staying sick.

Generally, the minute a man starts to get better, the Nurse's interest tapers off. If he recovers and stops drinking, for example, or recovers from his depression, or his physical condition improves, or he suddenly gets himself a good job, then the relationship is all over. She splits. She may claim that there wasn't enough in common to hold them together, or that she doesn't have enough time to keep fussing over him, but the real reason for the break is that she no longer feels useful.

For this reason, if a man's interest in a Nurse goes beyond her ability to bind up his wounds and offer him support and encouragement, if he really appreciates her as a woman, he may hide the fact that he is feeling better. He may not be as depressed but continue to complain of his melancholia, for example or pretend that he is still doing battle with drink in order to hold her interest. One man went so far as to pour liquor down the sink and leave the empty bottles around for his Nurse to find, when she returned from work even though he hadn't touched a drop in months. Fear of losing a woman may also keep a man locked into his problems. He doesn't want to solve them because then he would lose her.

Sometimes if a man is only partially incapacitated, he will move out during a period when he is able to function better. He may find the relationship too stultifying or he may realize, finally, that she may be bad for him in certain ways.

In cases like this, the Nurse and her former patient often remain good friends. She will feel kindly toward him as long as he keeps reminding her of how wonderful she was to him and how grateful he feels for all she did.

Most often a man leaves a Nurse when he has actually recovered. She may try to get him back by switching attention from the cured problem to another defect. "It's terrific you're not acting crazy anymore," one Nurse said. "But now that you're better, you have to do something about your weight. Look how fat you are!" and she started to tell him how to lose weight. If a man is not really bothered by the new problem she has spotted, he finds that her tendency to point out his defects all the time is impossible. The Nurse won't let the matter drop. She keeps after the man, under the guise of trying to help him.

Nurses frequently take on cases that set them up for getting cruelly dumped. A copywriter at an advertising agency met a shifty, shiftless, good-looking young man who eventually disappeared with her check book. Bad checks with her forged signature kept coming in for months afterwards. Another Nurse took on a homosexual who said he wanted to switch from men to women. He finally ran off with another man.

Other Nurses may think they have a perfectly healthy man only to discover that their instincts are more accurate than their perceptions.

A young, attractive woman married the editor of a magazine in Los Angeles where she worked as an assistant in the production department. She was dazzled by his power, his sophistication, his wit, all in sharp contrast to the people she grew up with in the South. Although he was drinking heavily all through their courtship, she thought it was nothing more than what everyone else was doing in the sophisticated crowd he moved in. After a few years of marriage, she finally realized that he was an alcoholic. Eventually his drinking cost him his glamour job. He went into a funk, isolated himself and refused to look for another. She found herself playing Nurse, to his game of Wreck, the same role her mother had played with her alcoholic father.

A perfectly adequate man will not become interested in a Nurse. He will find her ability to see defects and make a man aware of them, the fact that she is always trying to tell him what to do and to control his life, totally unappetizing.

Nurses often marry the men who allow themselves to become their charges. Sometimes a Nurse is also a nurse by occupation. It is not uncommon for a real nurse to marry the chronic invalid she has been caring for. The locale changes from hospital to home, but the relationship remains the same.

Some Nurses are able to have a variety of interests and friendships outside of the home. Others concentrate on their mission to the exclusion of everything else.

They frequently have careers in which they are competent and successful. More often than not it's necessary because they have to take care of an incapacitated man financially as well as spiritually.

Nurses' cheerfulness and comforting quality make them popular. With co-workers and friends they will play Nurse at the drop of a hat. They have an instinct for sniffing out every depressed or emotional wreck in the office. They hang around until they find out what is wrong, then offer advice and help. As a friend, the Nurse will become much more involved when the other person is experiencing some difficulty or illness. Self-sufficient friends are only of superficial interest.

The Nurse as Mother

As a mother, a Nurse is adequate but only mildly interested in her child until disease strikes or her child is hurt. She snaps to attention the moment there is a scratch, a bleeding wound, a broken thumb, a cold, measles, pneumonia. As a result, she tends to create hypochondriacs, whiners, and complainers. Sons and daughters come to realize early in life that mother becomes totally absorbed in them only in times of illness or need.

The Nurse can help members of either sex, but she prefers being a Nurse to a man or a son. She feels that men are more powerful than women, so praise and admiration for her efforts have to come from a male to be really meaningful. This is an attitude that has been foisted on her by society. It is not an instinctual preference.

In the Nurse's home, everyone dances around her. Sons, daughters, husband realize that she is the only adult with competence in the family, and the only one who gives sensible advice.

Her house may be filled with blooming plants, but chances are good that it is also a little messy. Nurses are not good housekeepers. People are what count, not things.

Why a Nurse Is the Way She Is

Nurses think of themselves as deficient human beings. They often feel unattractive, or inferior for a variety of reasons that could range from being overweight to having been born in a lower class family. But Nurses know their own assets as well. They realize they are good, capable people with an ability to help others, and they emphasize these qualities as a way of compensating for their deficiencies and to achieve success in relationships.

It is surprising just how early Nurses exhibit their adaptive behavior. They can already be observed in elementary school. Nurses are the little girls who come around when a boy falls and hurts himself, or cries when he is punished by a teacher, or is sad because some other child has wounded his feelings. The Junior Nurse puts her arm around the little boy, tells him he will be all right, soothes his upset feelings. She is already gaining a sense of power from her kind actions.

A Nurse may have had a nurturing mother whom she admired and copied, or she may have had a mother who didn't give her enough nurturance so she is determined to be a better person. If mother wasn't her model, then the Nurse found another nurturing figure to emulate. It may have been an aunt, a teacher, or a character in a story, in a movie, or on television. Nurses see nurturance as the female role.

Because of their fancied inadequacies, Nurses are afraid of relationships with equals. They base their self-esteem on the approval of others. They increase their chances of getting approval by choosing a damaged person who will be grateful and beholden to them.

Nurses and Society

Nurturing is part of the traditional female role in our society. The Nurse is a nurturer gone haywire. She carries it to extremes.

But she isn't the only one who wants to put band-aids on men. Many women are attracted at some point in their lives to men who need to be fixed up in one way or another.

Difficult men with brilliant wits and drinking problems, incredibly talented composers with more than a taste for drugs, charming men with vicious tempers, sweet men who would rather be kind to animals and have nervous break-downs than look for steady jobs are part of the pasts of many women. They all thought in their innocence that they would be the one with enough magic to help these men conquer their life-threatening habits.

There is something romantic about the notion that you will be the one to change a person's life from bad to good. And there is plenty in the mythology of romance from songs, books, movies to support this notion—hell-raisers, bad men, tamed by the love of a woman, unhappy men brought out of their morbid shells by a patient, loving woman.

Most women learn the futility of the Florence Nightingale game after a couple of bad eggs turn their own lives into scrambled eggs. Only the Nurse hangs in there, trying her healing skills forever.

How a Nurse Can Help Herself

Okay, Nurse. You are ready to hand in your white uniform and try to find a guy who will take care of you as much as you take care of him. How can you give up your addiction?

The next time you meet a man you find attractive, use the following list:
1. Is he unable to make a living?
2. Is he an alcoholic, or does he drink too much?
3. Is he a heavy user of drugs?
4. Is he considered "difficult"?

5. Does he have a history of depression or other incapacitating mental problems?
6. Does he seem eager for your advice?
7. Does he seem anxious for you to take control of his life?
8. Do you feel he needs you?
9. Are you already fantasizing about how much you can help him and how he is going to change with your tender, loving care?
10. Does he seem much more interesting to you than the guy without any obvious problems you met a couple of weeks ago?

If you have answered yes to any of these questions, stop and ask yourself what you are doing. Now is the time to stop the relationship before it starts—you are about to play Florence Nightingale again.

Work on other ways to make yourself feel important than taking on a man with insoluble problems. Work toward a graduate degree in the field you work in. Look for a job that will lead to advancement. Take classes that will give you a sense of mastery whether it is a mastery of finances or mastery of your body through exercise. You have to learn to feel significant on your own instead of on the back of some poor twisted, broken man.

And remember—the next time a man looks good to you, go down that check list. It will remind you if you are about to slip.

CHAPTER 8

THE BIG MOMMY

Another giver is Big Mommy.

Nurses are very selective about whom they dedicate themselves to—it has to be someone who is incapacitated or in trouble. Big Mommy is not nearly so selective. She gives and gives and gives to anyone at any time whether they are in trouble or not. She gives for happy reasons—for example, she will volunteer to help out when someone is giving a big party to celebrate a daughter's engagement—as well as in times of need and sorrow. She's the first one to show up when someone's wife has been taken to the hospital. She will take the kids to stay with her own, prepare a hot dinner for the husband of the sick woman, and run to the hospital with flowers to cheer up the patient.

Big Mommy may attract the schleps, the unsuccessful, the wounded and the insecure just as the Nurse does, but she doesn't specialize in them.

Friends, children, husband, co-workers all come to Big Mommy for little things as well as big and she tends to them all with warmth and graciousness. However, she creates chaos in her own life because of the demands placed upon her. Unable to say no, she often finds herself overextended.

One woman described walking into the office of a Big Mommy co-worker to have a short discussion with her. What was intended to be a fifteen minute discussion stretched to over an hour, not because of the business at hand, but because of continual interruptions. The phone rang incessantly. Big Mommy would not let her secretary hold the calls. She answered each and every one, patiently dispensing advice and encouragement to at least a dozen people. The door to her office was open, as always, and workers kept wandering in to ask for advice, help, orders. Big Mommy took time out to deal with each one. Her two children and her maid at home called at separate times.

"How can you stand it? How can you survive in this chaotic atmosphere?" the co-worker finally asked. "Oh," said Big Mommy with great sincerity, "if the phones stopped ringing and nobody came in, it would be disaster for me. I wouldn't feel needed."

And that is the key to the character of Big Mommy. She gives so cheerfully and unselfishly to others in order to feel wanted. When she is needed, she feels loved. When she isn't, she feels unloved. If someone firmly refuses to accept her help, she can suddenly turn on them. She generally shows her anger by icily staying away from the offending person. Her posture is one of defiance. She is saying, in effect, "You refused my offer of help, so now I'm not going to extend myself anymore for you." She gives a person more than one chance to accept her gracious offer, however, before she turns bitchy. She will return to her normal, warm self if and when her help is welcomed.

In the eyes of her friends, there is no one more marvelous than Big Mommy. They can and do call her at all hours of the day and night; she is never too tired, never too busy to be available to them. A Big Mommy was awakened at two in the morning not long ago by a tearful friend whose business was failing. Big Mommy listened patiently and offered her encouragement and support while the woman explained her worries to her.

Big Mommy's kitchen is constantly filled with friends wandering in and out. They confide in her while she gives them something to nibble on. The kitchen is the natural habitat of many Big Mommies. Giving food is giving love and Big Mommy likes to make delicious dishes to feed others—and herself. Big Mommy is often overweight as a result, but it doesn't bother her too much. Big Mommy enjoys giving to herself as well as to others. She feels she deserves that piece of chocolate cake, a new dress or a microwave oven if that is what she wants. She may not represent chic, but she is a reasonably well-dressed woman because she does not stint on clothing for herself.

Big Mommy's home is a magnet for her children's friends and the kids in the neighborhood. She treats them all like one of her own, and they respond to her like a second mother.

Big Mommies may not be physically attractive by conventional standards, but they are, nevertheless, attractive to men, especially those who are looking for a mother they never had, for example, a man whose mother died at an early age. Big Mommies also are irresistible to men unconsciously looking for duplicates of their own mothers.

Tom, an accountant in Minneapolis, had a mother who always told him what to do while he was growing up. She never let him do anything by himself. She made his bed until he left home; she chose and paid for all his clothes. When he met Maureen at a friend's house, he felt immediately that she was the woman for him. His instincts were very good. When they got married, she took over where his mother left off. She did everything. She decided which neighborhood they would live in, how many kids they should have. She took his clothing to the cleaners, paid the bills, drove him to the station each morning, made sure he took his vitamins every day.

Tom was able to remain a little boy with Maureen and that is always the danger with Big Mommies. If a man doesn't start out wanting a mother, he ends up with one anyway.

Big Mommies turn grown men into helpless children and children into complete dependents by not allowing them to do for themselves. Big Mommy achieves power and dominance in her relationships by making others depend on her, but she never looks at it this way. She sees her actions simply as responding to others and helping them when they need her.

Big Mommy chooses the role of protector and motherly provider because she feels inadequate and worthless underneath her very strong exterior. By letting others lean on her, she makes herself feel important. She also chooses the nurturing role because she often fears a competitive one. She is afraid to go out and do battle with the world or climb a corporate ladder, so she concentrates on one-to-one relationships where she can shine.

A husband soon grows accustomed to Big Mommy's ministrations. After awhile, he finds he cannot function without her; he comes to her for every little thing. The husbands of Big Mommies often call their wives "Mom."

Sometimes Big Mommy finds her modus vivendi creates a problem for herself within the family. The system breaks down in her absence. One Big Mommy had to go out of town. She returned to find three days' dishes piled up in the sink, her children's clothing scattered around their rooms, her husband's shirts in a neat pile waiting for her to take to the Chinese laundry.

"Why didn't you do the dishes or take your shirts to the laundry?" she asked her husband. He could only reply, "Well, you always do that."

Big Mommy feels frustrated by the fact that nothing gets done if she isn't there to do it, but she rarely complains about it. Instinctively, she is protecting her preserve. If her family actually started doing things for themselves, then they wouldn't need her anymore.

The Kinds of Men Big Mommies Attract

As a single woman, Big Mommy is very discriminating about whom she will go out with for any length of time. For example, Ruth, a twenty-seven year old social worker, rejected three men this year. One was always making cutting remarks about her weight, another only called her at the last minute for dates, the third tried to keep her dangling while he saw an old girl friend.

Ruth, like all Big Mommies, feels she has the right to be treated well. Big Mommy will not accept abuse of any kind from a man. "I deserve better" is a phrase you will commonly hear from a Big Mommy, explaining why she dropped a man.

During courtship, Big Mommy qualities appear right away. If a man has to go on a business trip or wants to take a vacation, for example, Big Mommy will volunteer to make all the arrangements for him because he is so busy. Or when a date invites her out to dinner, she will frequently respond by saying, "Why should we go out when I can cook a nice meal for the two of us?" Big Mommy will offer to return books to the library for a man, pick up his shoes at his shoemaker. She will drop everything and run to him if he receives a piece of bad news.

Big Mommy rarely lacks for boy friends even if she is not a beauty. A pharmacist's comment about his Big Mommy is a typical one. "I like her because she's so good-natured."

The kind of man who will not take to a Big Mommy is a self-sufficient one who responds to her continuing efforts to do things for him with irritation. "She's a nice lady," said one, "but for Christ's sake, I've spent all these years learning to do things for myself, and now she wants to take them over. I am an adult. I don't need a mother; I already have one."

Another kind of man to whom Big Mommy is poison is a tyrant or a sadist who likes to give women a hard time. After giving him every chance in the world, Big Mommy will put her foot down. If she doesn't leave him first, he will surely leave her in search of a more willing victim.

Big Mommies don't look primarily for good looks, power or success in a man. If they get one or the other, they regard it as a bonus. One rather fat Big Mommy who married a handsome Italian exchange student continually marvels at the fact that she has such a gorgeous husband.

What is important to a Big Mommy is a man's human qualities. She is impressed by generosity, thoughtfulness, caring, sentiment. It would be typical of a Big Mommy to say, "I finally decided to marry him when I saw how good he was to his mother." Generally, Big Mommies marry men who are basically nice though they have great dependency needs.

When Big Mommy commits herself to a man, it is with the most profound sincerity and for life. Her man has as much invested in the relationship as she does. Her husband truly loves her for her caring, warmth and dedication. He treats her with respect and deference, with consideration and kindness. She flourishes in his love and attention and in the home she now has. A home is important to a Big Mommy. It is a base from which to dispense her nurturing.

Although she may be responsive, sex is not a primary issue with a Big Mommy, which is just as well. Sex often turns out to be a scarce item in her marriage. Because Big Mommy's husband identifies her with his mother, he often loses interest in her sexually. Making love to one's mother is taboo.

Sometimes, Big Mommy's husband has affairs because of his lack of sexual interest in Big Mommy. But if he does, it is always with the clear-cut understanding that he often expresses to the other woman, that he may not be fired up by his wife sexually, but she is a wonderful woman, he loves and needs her, and he will never ever leave her. Big Mommy's tendency to overlook things that she might find upsetting helps her to remain unaware of her husband's infidelity.

Big Mommy is basically very generous in spirit, a truly giving person, but she does want gestures of affection in return for her nurturing. She never asks, but she expects that her birthdays and anniversaries will be remembered with gifts. Presents don't have to be expensive—a single flower will do—but unless she is remembered, she will be very hurt.

If her husband dies before she does, and she wants to date or marry again, she has no fears about finding other men. She is generally right. There are a lot of men in need of mothering in our world. Some Big Mommies are professional widows. They marry three, four and five times.

A good number of Big Mommies, however, are not interested in remarrying after the death of a husband. They feel their husbands are a part of them for life whether they are around or not. Widowed, they never get over a secret feeling of being incomplete.

Opportunities may present themselves to Big Mommy, but she chooses to remain faithful to the memory of her husband. She feels she will never be able to give as much again to any man, and besides, there are so many other ways to express her warmth. She turns to her friends, her children and grandchildren. She keeps herself busy knitting, babysitting, perhaps doing volunteer work. She comforts other women as they become widows. Big Mommies are women who are able to be cheerful and active throughout their lives.

Big Mommy seldom gets divorced because she tends to overlook negative things, no matter what. A man may occasionally leave her though, if he decides to stop being a little boy and grow up. She may leave him at this point, if he stops needing her in the same way.

Occasionally, a man will get fed up with the messiness of Big Mommy's life. She ends up fragmented and disorganized because there are so many people leaning on her, making demands on her time, and there are constant crises to which she responds by running to help.

Big Mommy at Work

Most people like Big Mommy and with good reason. She is always ready to go out of her way for them. She doesn't have to be asked. She sees a situation where she can be helpful, and she jumps in. As a result, she has many devoted friends. There are, however, those who hate her. These people feel themselves to be in competition with everyone else for her attention. They become spiteful when they cannot monopolize her time.

If Big Mommy works, she is popular; she also will assume the Big Mommy role with co-workers. There are her detractors in an office, too. These are usually the highly organized ones who react with aversion to Big Mommy's fragmented, emotional, occasionally frantic style. They deplore the fact that she allows herself to become overextended, that she is pulled in too many directions at once.

Big Mommy often feels that her job is secondary to her family role, but she may advance in her career despite herself. Superiors who like her personally may help her and will overlook her defects.

For the most part though, the same things that are assets in Big Mommy's interactions with people will work against her in a business setting. Her willingness to give so readily without questioning motives, to always try to see good in people is regarded as naive. The fact that she can't stand aggression and is unable to be competitive would leave her clinging to the bottom rung of the corporate ladder forever. Her style is regarded as the quintessence of femininity and is derided by many men in business.

Big Mommy as Mother

Big Mommy can be a supermom, always taking her children places, always baking cookies and cakes for them, always making big parties for their birthdays, always allowing hordes of other children in her home. But Big Mommy can also be smothering and a bit of a nag. If she works, she repeatedly calls her children to find out if they return from school on time, to see if they did their homework, to remind them to dress warmly if they are going out to play. Her kids telephone her regularly at work, because they cannot make the slightest decision without her.

If Big Mommy is a housewife, she is always after her kids, too. "Do you want milk and some cookies? Mommy just baked them; are you sure you don't want any? Do you need your gym shorts washed? Did you have a bowel movement today?"

Big Mommies' daughters generally turn out to be Big Mommies themselves, while Big Mommies' sons grow up to be complete male chauvinists. They simply expect that all women will cater to them the way Big Mommy did. They want women to act as nurturers without expecting much in return. That's the role of women. They are surprised and disappointed when a woman is more assertive about her own needs, or isn't a tower of strength to lean on, or expects him to help with the dishes or do his own laundry.

Why Big Mommy Is the Way She Is

Big Mommies generally have a fixation about their own mothers. They think of them in positive and idealized terms. Often early memories of a wonderful mother are all they have. A good number of Big Mommies lost their mothers when they were children. Other Big Mommies, fortunate enough to have had mothers who didn't die, had very close maternal relationships. Even if her mother had defects, Big Mommy overlooked or ignored them, and thought of her as the most terrific person in the world. They are not even ambivalent; they really admired their mothers.

They incorporate the positive and glowing picture that they have of their mothers into their own images. They themselves become the good mother of their fantasies.

Big Mommies often yearn for the kind of mothering they give to others, yet they are not able to accept it from anyone but their own mothers. There is no substitute for a real mother's love. Because Big Mommy has absorbed her mother within herself, she is able to be generous to herself. She will take a nap when she is sleepy, eat whenever and whatever she wants, hire help if she needs to, buy herself a brand new freezer if she so desires.

You will often hear a Big Mommy talk about how much she has missed her mother since her death.

In a few instances, a woman learned her way of interacting from her relationship with her father. Felice found that the best way to gain her father's favor was to do things for him around the house and to bake cookies for him. She played junior Mom. Her father was not pleased with her appearance—she was plump—but he was pleased with her attentions.

Felice as a grown up woman simply repeated this early pattern with other men.

The Pseudo Big Mommy

There are women who can be confused with real Big Mommies. Pseudo Big Mommies have the same warm, caring, nurturing manner when you are with them. They seem genuinely interested in you and your problems, but the minute you are out of sight they forget about you. A genuine Big Mommy keeps in contact with her friends and follows up on their problems. Sometimes Pseudo Big Mommies are Big Mommies to the rest of the world but not to their families.

Pseudo Big Mommies are nurturing only in order to be liked. It's an act. They are basically very self-centered people. Somewhere in their past they learned that people responded if they appeared to be generous and giving, and they use this knowledge to their own gain. They are Pseudo Big Mommies for personal reward and the instant gratification of being liked on the spot, as opposed to a real Big Mommy who has a genuinely giving personality and is not a calculating woman. People catch on to the essential phoniness of Pseudo Big Mommies fairly quickly. Despite their efforts, they are not always popular people.

Big Mommies and Society

The current climate for women is inhospitable to Big Mommies. A young woman who indiscriminately goes about trying to be helpful, who sees only the good in people is often regarded as naive these days by her peers. Also, the skills needed by women who want careers for themselves are not the skills that Big Mommy possesses. What she is good at is detrimental to her in the business world. Therefore, being a Big Mommy may prove less gratifying and be less attractive to young women today. This may be better because in being a Big Mommy a woman denies herself her full humanity—the right to be weak sometimes, the right to depend on others occasionally, the right to lose control every now and then. Nevertheless, if Big Mommy goes, it will be a loss for the world. How many genuinely giving people have there ever been?

How a Big Mommy Can Help Herself

If you are a Big Mommy you are a woman with many wonderful qualities. You are warm and generous and can be counted on by family and friends alike. You appear strong— everyone is able to lean on you and you give them comfort and support.

The problem is that you are not as strong as you look. You have developed a facade of strength to hide an inner person who feels a lot more helpless and inadequate.

To change, you must realize you have been shortchanging yourself by your strong act. You never allow yourself to express the weakness you feel internally. You can never lean on anyone else or ask others for help in any way.

You have to get in touch with the person hiding within yourself, the one who wants so desperately to be loved that she made a bargain with the world—to give and never receive.

One thing you as a Big Mommy can do is to realize there are really two parts to your personality—the strong Big Mommy that everyone knows and the weak little girl underneath the Big Mommy persona. Awareness is an important route to change. Once the less adequate person hiding inside the strong Big Mommy is acknowledged, you can have a dialogue with her. You as the strong Big Mommy should ask the little one you harbor what she wants out of life. You may find out that the little girl inside yourself is angry because she wants to be taken care of sometimes but you as Big Mommy refuse to let this happen. The little one is afraid or vulnerable, but you as Big Mommy refuse to let her express this. Big Mommy should incorporate the needs of the little one into her personality.

You can learn to lean on others and to ask for things for yourself by starting slowly. You can ask for help once a day, for example, until you get used to requesting things for yourself. What you ask for can be simple—someone to drive the car for you because you are feeling tired, or the chance to eat in a restaurant because you don't feel like cooking.

A Big Mommy's task is to become a more well-rounded person, able to depend on others as well as have others depend on you. In doing so, you will find that the people close to you will become stronger themselves. Leaning on you makes them overly dependent and stunts their emotional growth. In a more interdependent relationship, you will have the privilege of being both weak and strong. Thus, you can experience the full range of your humanity instead of cutting out one portion of it.

CHAPTER 9

THE MARRIED MAN MAGNET

It is Friday night and Marcia is feeling blue. She takes a walk and sees couples walking together, holding hands and it accentuates her loneliness. She tries to call a girl friend, but no one is at home. Finally, Marcia decides she wants to go out for dinner, so she drags herself to a hamburger place around the corner from where she lives, then goes off to see a movie by herself.

Marcia feels blue every Friday night and Saturday night, and all day Sunday as well.

But Monday, her world comes alive again. She will be able to talk to her lover on the telephone and she will see him sometime during the week before deadly Friday, Saturday and Sunday roll around once more.

By now you've probably guessed it. Marcia's boy friend is a married man.

Lots of single women get mixed up with married men once or even twice in their lifetimes, but they learn better. They find that not being able to see him on weekends and holidays, not being able to telephone him whenever they want, hiding out when they are with him, and being the second woman in a man's life, is unrewarding. They run like hell the next time a married man approaches them, and concentrate on single men, instead.

Not so for Marcia. Her current love is the sixth married man she's been involved with. "I just can't find single men who are nice. I guess all the best ones are married," she sighs.

But Marcia is fooling herself. She's a woman who prefers married men. Married men *are* better but only for Marcia and women like her. A guy already taken serves a purpose.

Married Man Magnets are struggling with an unconscious fear of commitment. By going around with a married man, they can dupe themselves into believing they really want an intimate relationship—it's just that there is this wife at home, see?

Very often the fear of commitment is a result of their relationship with their fathers. Married Man Magnets often had a father whom they adored, whose attention they yearned for, but whose love they never could have because their mother was there first. Married Man Magnets never separated emotionally from their fathers. In their adult relationships with married men, they are duplicating their original family romance. Their married man belongs to someone else just as Daddy did. They are the second woman in his life, just as they were second to Mommy.

They are terrified of being the primary woman in a man's life, because it requires responsibility and commitment. Married Man Magnets also are afraid that by becoming the primary woman they are displacing their mother and they will inevitably be punished for it.

Sometimes Married Man Magnets are afraid of commitment for another reason. If they saw their mother as a captive in a poor marriage, one filled with hatred, disappointment, and fights, unconsciously they may fear that all relationships end up that way and they don't want to take the chance.

Rarely, however, does the Married Man Magnet realize the dynamics behind her predilection. Speak to her and she's just a girl in love. So it happens to be with the wrong guy. So it happens to be with a series of wrong guys, one after the other. She doesn't connect her affinity for married men to the fact that she herself is not married yet. She may even say that marriage isn't important as long as she is able to be with a guy she likes—even if it's only sometimes.

But no matter what she says, hidden away in the psyche of a Married Man Magnet is a fantasy. In her dream, her married man is going to leave his wife for her someday.

This fantasy serves the purpose of keeping her illusions

about herself alive. It makes her feel that she does want a deep and committed relationship just as other women do. Her optimistic dream makes her feel okay and keeps her from having to come to grips with her basic anxieties about intimacy.

Her fantasy also serves the purpose of aggrandizement. The Married Man Magnet often feels inferior to other women, but by imagining that he is going to leave another woman for her, she proves how terrific she really is. She also manages to make herself feel superior in the relationship because she is in the position of being the "good" and giving one in comparison to him, the rat, juggling two women. She sits home waiting for him while he goes out and has a good time with his wife.

Of course, this fantasy of living happily ever after rarely comes true, but Married Man Magnets are able to hang onto the slim chance that it could. After all, some married men do leave their wives and marry their mistresses. They read about them—eagerly—all the time in newspapers and magazines. They may even be able to rattle off a list of husbands who have defected. If a Married Man Magnet gets her wish and her boy friend divorces his wife and marries her, she will almost always destroy the marriage.

This is the kind of thing that generally happens. She has come on during their relationship as an independent woman, while the wife at home has been a clinging vine with no interests of her own beyond the family. The married man decides that life with this strong, brilliant woman would be more fun and interesting. So he ditches the clinging vine in the suburbs.

Within a few years, the Married Man Magnet who has been privy to the husband's complaints about his former wife slowly starts to become just like her. Gradually, she gives up her interests, concentrates on only him, and starts to cling just like his ex-wife. He either divorces her at this point or he handles it by assuming, with a sigh, that all women are like this and so gets himself involved in other interests that keep him from home, or he may buy a new love nest for his wife in a faraway place so it takes hours for him to commute.

The Married Man Magnet will take on whatever the characteristics of the ex-wife were that drove the man to divorce the first time.

Most Married Man Magnets, though, don't marry. They spend their life going from married man to married man, getting from each a little friendship, a little closeness, a little sex but not true intimacy. What they get is a lot of freedom and time for themselves, something they need more than they will admit.

Married Man Magnets are often very sincere in their emotions about their married man. They care about him. They think about him when he isn't able to be with them. They imagine themselves to be unhappy because their time together is so limited. They talk to their friends about their bittersweet love affair.

For the married man, however, the girl friend is generally a little icing on their cake. She is a plaything without much significance in their lives, a nice little pastime once or twice a week or during lunch times.

If they happen to get caught, they are quite correct when they explain to an irate, grieving wife, "She never meant anything to me." One philandering husband explained his affairs. "I always like to keep a little something on the side. I'm deeply attached to my wife and my kids, but sometimes I just like to play without the heavy emotional involvement."

By contrast, look at this statement from a Married Man Magnet. "I know Dan is sincere. We have such fun together. He tells me he wishes we could be together all the time. I know he loves me."

Very often, the men involved in these extramarital affairs have a more realistic perspective of what is going on than the women do.

Sometimes the Married Man Magnet accepts her lot gracefully. She takes whatever crumbs she can get, waits around for more crumbs and tries to create a life of her own apart from the relationship. Some Married Man Magnets are faithful to the married man of the moment, others go out with more eligible men in their free time but they never get emotionally entangled with them. Their deep interest and involvement is always with the married man.

The Professional Home Wrecker

Some Married Man Magnets pressure the man. They try to get him to actually leave his wife. This version of the Married Man Magnet is a Professional Home Wrecker.

The Professional Home Wrecker works long and hard on a man to break up his marriage and she is often quite good at her work. She gets the man sufficiently enmeshed with her so that he decides he wants to spend the rest of his life with her. He leaves his wife and kids, but the minute he does, it's all over. The Professional Home Wrecker suddenly sees faults she hadn't noticed before. She gets bored or turned off for one reason or another. It isn't his charm that suddenly evaporates. It's her innate fear of commitment that overtakes her when there is a real chance to make a relationship into something more solid and permanent. Time and time again, Professional Home Wreckers go through the whole process of luring a man away from his wife, then dumping him.

The Married Man Magnet as Friend

Married Man Magnets need a good, ongoing life apart from their married man in order to survive. Most of them have good female friends. They enjoy going out to dinner with them, going to the movies or plays they will never see with their boy friend since he sees his movies and plays with his wife. They also use their friends as sympathetic ears to listen to the ups and downs of their current impossible romance. They are excellent at disregarding or discounting the advice of friends who don't see much glamour or profit in playing house with a series of married men.

Many Married Man Magnets have successful careers. They have to support themselves and they have plenty of time to devote to work.

How a Married Man Magnet Can Help Herself

If you recognize yourself as a Married Man Magnet, you must become aware that you choose married men because you fear commitment. It is no crime if you decide you really prefer not to get married. Women can choose to live alone and still lead satisfying lives. But if you really do want a committed relationship, you must give up the illusion that the only thing standing in your way is the fact that the men you like are married. Forget your fantasies of the man leaving his wife, and instead, try to find out what makes you want to avoid long-term intimacy.

You will have to look into your past life. Was your parents' marriage so filled with strife or pain that you don't want to take the chance that yours might turn out the same? Does intimacy mean to you being smothered or swallowed up as a person? Were your parents cold and distant with one another and with you, so that you have no model for intimacy? Does the thought of real closeness frighten you? Were you an orphan shifted from foster home to foster home so that feelings of closeness bring with it fear of separation?

Analyze your feelings when you start to become close to someone. Does anxiety suddenly start to creep in? Do you suddenly feel stifled or crowded or panicky?

Insight into your inner life will help you realize that married men are merely figures that help you maintain the illusion that you are really after the same thing as most other women.

Once you gain insight into your repetitive pattern of behavior, you will be able to change and make choices that exclude married men.

CHAPTER 10

THE FAG HAG

Fag Hags are very similar to Married Man Magnets. They, too, are afraid of intimacy and commitment, and their anxiety makes them choose unavailable men. For the Fag Hags, the safe choice is the male homosexual. Fag Hags are women who have a history of going around with gay men.

By choosing a man who is interested in them only as a friend, they take care of yet another deep fear. Very often they are afraid of sex, as well as men.

Some Fag Hags are fixated on their fathers just as Married Man Magnets are. The results are the same. They recreate a situation in which they cannot get their man, just as they originally could not get their father's love, attention or enduring affection.

Other Fag Hags had brutal or insensitive fathers who made them afraid of being hurt by men. Still others associate aggression with sexuality and are therefore afraid of being hurt in sex.

Some Fag Hags saw their mother constantly rejecting their father's physical attention and got the message that sex was something to be avoided.

Since sex with a gay man is out of the question, they are more comfortable with a homosexual than with a heterosexual.

Despite their deep rooted fears of men and sex, it is quite common for Fag Hags to hang onto a dimly perceived fantasy that someday a homosexual companion will turn "straight" for them. This fantasy serves two purposes for the Fag Hag. It makes her feel that she is really interested in a full relationship with a man, and therefore she is like other women. The fantasy also serves to make the Fag Hag feel superior. If the man were to become a heterosexual for her, then she is better than other women in whom he is not interested.

Fag Hags actually feel inferior to other women. Fag Hags are sometimes overweight or they are too tall or too short and think of it as a terrible handicap. They have some real or imagined defect which makes them feel not up to snuff. By choosing to hang around with gay men, they take themselves out of what they feel would be a losing competition with other women for heterosexual men.

Because Fag Hags crave male companionship yet also fear it, the homosexual male is the ideal solution to these two conflicting emotions. They don't have to be afraid of him yet they also have a man for an escort, confidante, and protector. If they have to come home late, they feel safer if he is with them. If they are feeling frightened about something, they can call him.

Another great attraction of the relationship with the gay male is the fact that it is quite free of tension for the Fag Hag.

Fag Hags don't have many female friends. They don't have many heterosexual boy friends either. The gay man is a replacement for both. He is easier to cope with. She doesn't feel the sense of competition she would if she were with a woman whom she might envy for being more attractive. She also doesn't have to worry about whether she will be able to keep a heterosexual male from other women. Finally, she doesn't have to worry about sex.

Generally, the relationship between a Fag Hag and her homosexual male friends is a very positive, mutually supportive one. She can be motherly and giving, warm and understanding with them and they can be kind, understanding, helpful and accepting of her. Fag Hags only associate with gay men who are relatively well adjusted to their homosexuality. There can be hugs and embraces and tenderness without the sexual overtones that might be present with another kind of man.

Sometimes the relationship is based on the feeling that they are outcasts clinging together and shoring each other up. He feels like an outcast because of his homosexuality; she feels like an outcast because she doesn't think she is as desirable as other women.

The Fag Hag as Mother

Some Fag Hags have been married and divorced and they have children from their marriage.

They are reasonably good mothers, but they behave differently with daughters than with sons. Daughters are seen as competitors, so the relationship is a cooler one than with a son. The Fag Hag lets her daughter have a good amount of freedom which is healthy for her. It allows her to develop, generally, into a fairly normal, independent human being.

The relationship with her son is much more intense. She uses her full powers to try and turn her son into the kind of male she feels comfortable with. She is afraid of an authoritarian man, and so she may train her son to be the opposite—soft spoken and sensitive. She may try to fill his life with artistic interests, and frequently discourages his physical skills.

She does not realize it on a conscious level, but she would prefer it if her son turned out to be a homosexual. Then she would not have to compete with future girl friends, and he would be hers forever.

Many women have one or two homosexual friends and maintain warm and comfortable friendships with them. On a purely practical level, it can be very convenient for a gay man to have a female friend to take to functions or places where he must be accompanied by a woman. She finds it handy to be able to call her homosexual male friend if she needs an escort to a party, a charity event, or because she has a couple of tickets to the theater.

Women who are Fag Hags, however, concentrate on gay men almost to the exclusion of heterosexual relationships or friendships with women. Gays are not just one part of a larger circle of friends and acquaintances; they are the entire circle.

The Fag Hag's friendships are based as much on her own fears as on the individual qualities of the gay men she associates with. In this sense, these associations are not freely chosen ones. Like most relationships of neurotic origin, there is a compulsive quality about them. The Fag Hag must be with gay men to avoid facing her own anxieties.

How a Fag Hag Can Help Herself

Many women have sweet and caring relationships with their homosexual friends that they may not want to give up. And why should they? No one wants to lose good friends. However, if you recognize yourself as a Fag Hag, then you need to realize how you have limited your life. Although you may be fearful of them, you probably want relationships with a different flavor, or with sex, or with a future.

First, recognize that your preference for male homosexuals is because of your own lack of self-confidence as a woman. Perhaps you fear sexuality and competition with other women.

Next, you have to work on your poor self-image. You are not inferior to other women. Heterosexual men will find you attractive enough, if you only give them a chance. If you are overweight or too tall or too short or you think you have some other physical defect, you must admit that it makes you feel terrible about yourself. You should remember that however awful your defect appears to you, it never seems as bad to the outside world. You almost certainly are exaggerating its importance and its impact on others. Most tall, short and overweight women have their share of romance.

Next, if you have a real fear of sex itself, psychotherapy is recommended. Your fears can be dealt with and overcome most effectively with therapy.

You need not give up all your male homosexual friends. But you can learn to choose homosexual friends because you truly enjoy them, rather than for the negative reasons that are operating unconsciously now—the fear of having relationships that include sex and heterosexual love, relationships you crave, but are afraid to try for.

CHAPTER 11

THE MARTYR

There is a joke that succinctly explains what a martyr is: How does a martyr change a lightbulb? She doesn't. She says, "Don't worry about me. I'll just sit here in the dark."

The Martyr is that long-suffering wife and mother, the woman whose motto is: Everything for the family; nothing for myself.

There is a legend in one family about a woman of the last generation who slaved for her family. She arose very early, cooked and cleaned all day, and sewed clothing for the children until the wee hours of the morning so that they would look good when they went to school. She wore old clothing that would practically fall off her back before she would make a replacement for herself. This same woman would skip dinners so that the children would have more to eat. She is described by her daughter as a saint. When you delve further into the family history, you discover that this saint had an iron fist. She and she alone decided when and for how long the children could leave the house, when they could eat or not eat, when they could sleep and get up. She decided which of the clothes she sewed for them could be worn. She interfered in every part of their lives, but all her children remember is how unselfish she was and how she never asked for anything for herself.

Like this woman, the image Martyrs want to project is one of unselfish saintliness. Yet if you take a closer look at Martyrs, you find that self-seeking rather than selflessness is at the root of their character. Their suffering always has a price tag attached, and the cost can be high to husband and children alike.

The Martyr expects absolute control in return for her devotion. She wants everyone to do exactly what she wants, and when and how she wants it. She will never give an order, direction, or indication of what's on her mind, however If everyone really loved her, they would be able to know what she wants without her having to ask. If she has to ask, it spoils it. Since minds are hard to read, whatever anyone does turns out to be not quite right or altogether wrong. As a result, the Martyr is constantly in the winter, spring, summer and autumn of her discontent. She treats those around her to lethal doses of small criticisms.

One woman regularly reduces her children to tears on her birthday when they present her with gifts they have taken great care to pick out. The present is always something she can't use, or it's ugly, or she would be ashamed to show it to anyone. She does everything for them and they can't even pick out a decent present for her. Martyrs always manage to turn things around so that they feel dumped on.

Another Martyr is a mistress of the unspoken criticism. She graciously accepts her presents and then puts them away in closets and drawers still in their original boxes, where they remain gathering dust for years. If the gift isn't used—well, you guessed wrong again. She has one deadly refinement on this gambit. Sometimes, a couple of years later, she will pull out the gift, and ask the giver if he can use it.

The Martyr's attitude that her needs should be known instinctively is a throwback to her infancy. Babies feel themselves to be powerful creatures in control of the universe because their mothers always know when they are hungry or thirsty or uncomfortable. Everything is done for them automatically. The Martyr's view of love is a primitive one of giving automatically and unceasingly like her mother. She feels that is what she does for you, and she expects the same in return.

Despite the Martyr's refusal to let you know directly what's on her mind, she is very good at indirect hints. She may point to the newspaper and admire a dress that's advertised, or she'll mention the fact that Mrs. Green just got a new fur coat. She will never simply say, ''I want a new dress,'' or, ''I'd love a fur coat.''

The Martyr is also an expert at presenting her desires disguised as yours. ''Wouldn't you like to . . .'' is an opening phrase that commonly falls from the Martyr's lips.

What the Martyr does best in life, however, is generate guilt. She uses it like a virtuoso. It's her most powerful weapon to keep the family in line. Her very presence is a reproach. She bustles about unceasingly, taking care of everyone but herself, often in old clothing maybe with a sad look on her face, or with sighs periodically escaping from her pinched or downturned mouth. The family should feel terrible because she suffers so for them. And, just in case they don't get the message, Martyrs have ways of reinforcing it.

One middle-aged lawyer remembers how his mother, a housewife, always managed to do the heavy cleaning on weekends when the whole family was sure to be home to witness how hard she worked. This man still feels a little nauseous when he recalls Sunday lunches on those weekends. There was an old-fashioned dryer hanging from the ceiling in the kitchen, just above the table at which the family ate. Lunch was always preceded by his mother doing the wash by hand with a scrubbing board. By the time food was served, there were always dripping socks, underwear, pajamas, blouses, shirts hanging on the overhead dryer above like silent accusations. The wash cut off light from the window so that the table was enclosed in a gloom that matched the mood of everyone in the kitchen.

Another Martyr never sits down to a meal with her family. She spends hours cooking breakfasts, lunches, dinners, but never partakes of any meal herself. She prefers to wait until the meal is over, the dishes are washed (by hand, of course), and everyone is tucked away in front of the television set or doing homework. Only then will she eat. Leftovers, of course.

The Martyr's way of handling immediate displeasure is by remote control. She doesn't get angry. She gets hurt. She makes it known, not by screams and yells, but by the silent torture treatment. She lapses into a long period when she doesn't talk. She looks through the person or brushes past as if he weren't there. She weeps by herself, but loud enough for her sobs to be heard. Some Martyrs with particularly well-trained husbands, can count on their spouses to speak for them. "Look what you are doing to your mother! You're killing her. You know your mother is not well; why are you aggravating her?"

Many Martyrs use illness and the threat of dying as part of their control-through-guilt program. A suburban housewife remembers getting angry at her mother when she was about five years old. After she kicked her heels on the floor and shouted obscenities she had picked up in the schoolyard, her mother managed a stricken look, placed one hand over her heart, lay down on the couch and announced that she was having a heart attack and was going to die, a statement that brought her husband running and scared the living daylights out of the child.

On the other hand, a Martyr may have little patience with an illness of her husband if it competes with her own image of being the one who can suffer the most. One Martyr, consumed by grief after the death of a child, would not talk to her husband much less help him when he came down with a nervous skin disorder and a high fever. She was suffering too much to bother about him. When this same poor man went to the movies to forget his sorrow for a little while, she had nothing but contempt for his wish to ease his suffering. Martyrs very often continue mourning long past the time when others have made their adjustment and gone on with the business of living.

One Martyr's daughter remembers how guilty her mother made her feel for months after the death of her father if she saw friends or even occasionally laughed. "It was as if we all had to stop living, too, and that any return to normalcy was a betrayal not only of him, but of her."

Why a Martyr Is the Way She Is

Some women become Martyrs by accident. Once they discover that the suffering stance gets them what they want, they keep on using it. Others saw their mother abused by a father and accepting it. They figured that suffering was what women did. Some women with a natural bent toward martyrdom are helped along by a religion which equates self-sacrifice and suffering with holiness.

But most often a Martyr is created by a long-suffering mother like herself. Manipulated by guilt from an early age, allowed to do only what her mother wants, always tiptoeing around her mother with the rest of the family, afraid of incurring her displeasure, the young Martyr becomes enraged at her mother. She is never allowed to express her anger, however.

She also has been turned into a complete dependent. Martyrs characteristically try to bind all their children to them. Martyrs make it extremely difficult for their offspring to break away and establish their own identities. Since the Martyr knows what is best for the children, any attempt at independence is treated as a betrayal.

The young Martyr finds herself struggling with a thorny problem—she is in a double bind. She is furious at her mother, but she is also very dependent upon her. She wants her mother out of the picture, but at the same time she fears her mother will abandon her for having such thoughts or will actually fulfill her secret wish and die. Racked by guilt, the little girl has nowhere to go with her hostility. Her solution is to turn the anger inward. Aggression, thus suppressed, creates both self-hatred and depression. Although she is not aware of it consciously—she's too busy thinking of herself as "poor little me"— the Martyr is basically a depressed, guilt-ridden, and hostile woman.

In later life if the Martyr becomes a wife, she transfers her dependency from her mother to her husband and her innate rage to everyone in the family. She must have her husband to feel protected. She needs to suffer for her family and thereby expiate her underlying feelings of guilt, but she hates her family because of the very things she needs them for. Her constant criticisms and eternal dissatisfaction are, in part, her hostility seeping out. She is unhappy, too, because her basic aim is not being accomplished. Her suffering is her way of trying to win love. Since her efforts are not being appreciated enough, she feels she has failed. In truth, very often she has failed. Martyrs manage to infuriate, create rebellion, and often alienate their children. They make their husbands anxious and angry. They give their whole family a burden of guilt to carry with them for the rest of their lives. As one psychiatrist told his patient, the daughter of a Martyr, "If somebody left a bag of guilt in the street, you would pick it up and take it home."

The Kinds of Men Martyrs Attract

The Martyr appeals to a tyrannical, domineering man. She is his perfect victim. These men can get the picture very early in a courtship and start cashing in on it. For example, he arrives a little late once and she is very sweet and says nothing. The next time he arrives a little later, and she still doesn't complain. Soon he is coming late all the time and perhaps being inconsiderate of her in other ways as well, but she still keeps quiet. Of course she is seething, but she never shows it. Domineering men and Martyrs are a match made in heaven. Sometimes the Martyr admires a tyrant's aggressive style. He does and says things in a way she would like to emulate, but can't. The tyrant continues to be inconsiderate once he marries the Martyr; she continues to put up with all of it. Little does he know, however, that she is carefully recording each and every one of the indignities she has suffered, and at the proper moment she will reel off her dazzling list of detailed sins. One woman waited until she had been married fifty years. Her husband had become totally crippled by arthritis and was at her mercy. Only then did she tell him how much she had done for him over the years, and exactly when and how often he had been miserable to her.

Very often domineering husbands make the Martyr's pressures upon the children even greater. The Martyr may expect her kids to make up for their father's sins. One man of fifty-two, looking back said, "My mother always insisted that my brother and I had to be perfect little gentlemen and do the right thing in any situation, because my father was so insensitive and inconsiderate. What horribly repressed kids we were!"

Another kind of man Martyrs end up with are men who

need to be controlled. Their own mother always told them what to do and the Martyr is a replacement. Although the Martyr's game of power is not out in the open, and she appears to be the opposite of mother—submissive—these men's instincts are good guides to the type of women they are seeking.

The Martyr's subtle tactics can be spotted during courtship, but only if you are alert. For example, a man will ask the Martyr where she would like to have dinner. She will say sweetly, "Anywhere you like, any place is fine." So he picks a Chinese restaurant, and they go to it. In the middle of the meal, he notices she is only picking at her food. "What's the matter?" he asks. "Well," she answers, "I don't like Chinese food very much."

Although a Martyr may act submissive and compliant and seems eager to please, there are moments when she suddenly is sulking and her man doesn't understand why. When he pokes around for the reason, she will finally say accusingly, "Well, you should know."

Another typical way for a Martyr to show displeasure is to simply say, "I'm tired. You can drop me off at my place." He knows something is wrong, but he doesn't know what, and she isn't telling.

A Martyr may be the kind of woman who teases a man and doesn't follow through, or leaves a man dangling. One woman has had a man calling her for two years now. She has no intention of ever going out with him, but she keeps on making up excuses why she can't see him instead of letting him know that she really isn't interested.

Sometimes the Martyr ends up married to a good-natured schnook, a dutiful husband who spends his life trying to please his wife, but never succeeds. He finds himself under stress a good deal of the time because of the ongoing guessing game of figuring out what she wants. Constantly failing to please her makes him feel inadequate and insecure. He tries and tries, bends over backward, but what he does is never enough or never right. Eventually he ends up a frustrated and furious man. Sex is not too great either. Most Martyrs over the age of thirty regard sex as just another duty;

besides, why should they take pleasure from sex when they don't take pleasure from anything else.

There is not even the relief of a good argument with a Martyr to clear away the underlying tension in the marriage. She just chips away at him about little things and he finds it difficult to have a real fight with a woman who can't assert herself, who only whines or cries instead. Martyrs find tears a very useful tool in putting a stop to arguments and rebellion, and in getting their way in general. One man marveled, "I can't believe I succumb to tears time and time again, but I do."

Many husbands of Martyrs stay because they are passive, or unconsciously enjoy the control. They manage to flee the oppressive atmosphere in their homes by spending long hours at work, and pursuing their own interests as much as possible. This, of course, makes the Martyr feel all the more unloved, unappreciated and burdened.

The Martyr who can't make demands on her own behalf, is often able to insist that her husband help with the kids. In her scheme of things, this is okay because it is for the children, not herself. After all, children should know their father. If she can possibly arrange it, the Martyr wants her husband to suffer as much as she does for the sake of the children. A Martyr is not happy, for instance, if she discovers that the father had a wonderful time with his kids. Many husbands of Martyrs learn to keep quiet about the fact that they enjoyed being out with their sons and daughters.

Children of Martyrs often rebel and defy their mother who frustrates them so, but after all is said and done, the fight with Mom may leave them feeling worse than before. She leaves them to contend with the bitterness of great guilt.

Families of Martyrs often become divided into camps—those for her and those against. When brothers and sisters don't have much to do with one another in later life, they often feel it is because they are so different and don't have much in common. If the origins of the schism or animosity were investigated, however, one would find that it was the Martyr who originally created warring camps based on loyalty and submission to her.

While Martyrs are able to be affectionate with their

children—that is part of what a good mother does—they are often cold and unaffectionate with their husbands and others because they wait for the other person to come after them.

One Martyr lost a friend of twenty-six years because in all that time the friend had to call her. The Martyr would never initiate a telephone call. Finally the friend warned the Martyr that it was her turn to call. The Martyr could not bring herself to call and the friend, exasperated, disappeared. Another reason Martyrs neglect friends is that they feel themselves swamped by their duties for the family.

Husbands sometimes leave, also. Ruptures in marriage occur most often when the Martyr's husband is involved in his own mid-life crisis. Typically, he asks himself, "Is this the way I want to live in the years left to me?" When the answer is no, he splits. His action is often looked upon as villainous by the Martyr and her friends. Often the Martyr has worked to put her husband through school. She has worked hard all her life to provide him with a beautiful home, wonderful children. After all she has done for him, how could he do this to her, friends and relatives wonder.

Daughters of Martyrs often end up like their mothers or at least display some traits and attitudes of the Martyr in their interactions. Martyrs' sons often become men who have trouble relating to women. The son feels that all relationships with women will become like that with his mother, and if so, who needs the unspoken demands, the criticism, the inability to please, the sense of inadequacy, the guilt? If sons do enter into a relationship, they often end up trying to second-guess their partner as they did their mother. Inevitably, they feel controlled; they feel that their partner is demanding, although in reality she may not be.

The grown sons of Martyrs maintain a close relationship with their mother. Unless they break with her emotionally, they are liable to be "good" sons who call their mothers every day and stop by to see her every evening after work. The Martyr is often stingy about going to see her children. They have to come to her.

A Martyr's daughter may be in for a rude shock if she expects her mother to be an active grandmother. The first words out of one Martyr's mouth right after her first grand-child was born was, "Don't expect me to baby-sit."

The Martyr is giving out a double message by refusing to baby-sit. She is saying, "I have done so much for you I have no more energy left to help." And vindictively, she is also saying, "I suffered. Now it's your turn to suffer, too."

The Career Martyr

Traditional Martyrs existed in greater numbers in the past than they do today. However, the suffering style among women has not disappeared. After all, Martyrs breed Martyrs. Vintage self-styled saints still exist among young women, but they are being replaced by a newer, zippier and much more deceptive model, the Career Martyr.

The Martyr of the eighties doesn't suffer for her family's sins alone. Today she suffers on the job as well. A Career Martyr never complains, no matter how much work is piled on her desk. She skips lunch hours; she works late. She makes sure everyone knows how hard she is working, but she says with a cheerful little smile, "I really don't mind."

Unfortunately, the Career Martyr nets the same result as the Martyr at home—she doesn't feel appreciated. True success rarely comes to the Career Martyr. She gets in her own way. In the working world, it is necessary to be more assertive and independent than the Career Martyr can allow herself to be. Co-workers and bosses tend to look on the Career Martyr as Mary, the Grind. They always depend on the Career Martyr, but also overlook her when it's time for promotions to be handed out.

The fanciest version of the new Career Martyr has had her basic philosophy altered a bit by the women's liberation movement. Today she is apt to believe that a woman should have more than a job; she should have a career. So she plunges into a profession energetically but with the same old Martyr ways. She juggles a very demanding career with a household that needs lots of upkeep. She also has a couple of kids to whom she is determined to give her "all" when she is home. She cooks elaborate meals for the family, refuses household help, and then complains that she doesn't have room to breathe. Her mother and friends tell her she's getting thin as a stick. Aunts, uncles, friends marvel, "How can she do it?" She does it by suffering, by making her husband feel sorry for her, by making him feel guilty that she has to work so hard.

One new Career Martyr gets up at four in the morning to do housework because she says she can't find any other time to do it. Her sympathetic husband feels he has to get up with her and help. She thinks of herself as a brave new woman. They see themselves together as a modern two-career couple, but their interaction can be traced back for generations in the Career Martyr's family.

Another new Career Martyr drags herself up at six every morning in order to cook the family's meals for the whole day before she goes to work. She serves elaborate breakfasts, leaves behind wonderful hot lunches for the kids and sits down every night to a fancy dinner with her husband and children. A Career Martyr never thinks in terms of easing her burden by eating dinner out more often or eating simpler meals or using prepared foods. Such a solution would not even cross a Martyr's mind. Only bad mothers and wives do that.

A psychiatrist described one of her patients, a young professional whose job required her to take work home often at night. Her husband's job was less demanding, and he loved to go to the theater. Rather than say no on those nights when she had work to do and he wanted to see a play, she would go but take a small flashlight along with her and work on her papers in the dark. When her husband would demand, "Why didn't you tell me you had too much work to do?" she would simply smile. "Oh, it's all right. I really don't mind." She's an example of the new superwoman, but as this Career Martyr's psychiatrist said, "She's not so super."

Many Career Martyrs don't get enough help from their husbands but it's not malevolence on the husband's part. The Career Martyr feels he has to offer help on his own. It is self-defeating to expect a man to volunteer if he was raised in a household where his mother did all the household chores.

Such a man has to be asked, but if he is, he will generally
help.

Many of the new Career Martyrs wind up frazzled. They
begin to think they are falling apart from all the stress they
are under. Often, at this point, they go to see therapists,
complaining of depression. They want to know what went
wrong. Only in therapy do they come to realize how much
they have contributed to their own burned-out state.

It is interesting that married Career Martyrs sometimes start
to improve only after a divorce. They may be depressed and
angry at a husband who has left them, but if they get help in the
form of therapy, they learn to enjoy themselves now that they
are alone. They learn to live for themselves as well as for
others. Two men who wanted to return to their Career Martyr
wives after a fling with younger women were appalled to learn
that their wives were no longer waiting for them to return.
The Career Martyrs decided they didn't want to return to their
same old marriages although their husbands did. The Martyrs
had learned to live for themselves for the first time in their
lives, they liked it, and they weren't about to give it up.

It can be predicted that as more women work, there will be
fewer Martyrs. Women in the marketplace soon discover that
being a Career Martyr doesn't bring them power at work,
although it may in their private lives. Martyrs have always
had a lot of underlying strength, but they had no place to
exercise their aggression except on their hapless families.
Todays potential Martyrs have more personally satisfying and
less destructive outlets to achieve power. They can achieve it
in careers rather than on the backs of their families.

It is interesting that many Martyrs are encouraging their
own daughters in this direction today. They feel that they
couldn't be successful in their own right, in their own times
but they want their daughters to be, now that women can.

How a Martyr Can Help Herself

The Martyr genuinely means well. She has no notion that she
is doing anything that is not for the good of her family.

If you see yourself in this chapter as a Martyr and feel you want to change, you must develop a clear picture in your mind of what you are doing in reality rather than what you think you are doing. You are suffering to expiate guilt. You are throwing off anger on your family that comes from your own past.

First, make a secret sign and put it into a drawer you use frequently so that no one will see it but yourself. It should read: I have a right to happiness. I don't need to suffer anymore.

Then write down all the good things you can think about yourself. Do not include anything that has to do with all the things you do for others. Just put down things you like about yourself apart from other people. Are you intelligent? Creative? Do you have good taste? Do you like your hands, your feet, the color of your eyes? Make an inventory of qualities you admire in yourself. This will help to enhance your feelings of worthiness. As a worthy person, you have a right to do positive, good things for yourself instead of always having to suffer for others.

Next, decide that each day you will do one thing for yourself and yourself alone, and that you will also each day neglect to do something for the good of the family. For example, don't get up early in the morning to make everyone a hot breakfast. Stay in bed and sleep, leave out cold cereals and let everyone shift for themselves. Your family may be shocked, but I'll bet they won't mind it.

You must also recognize the rage you have bottled up inside you. This rage comes out indirectly when you try to make everyone around you feel guilty for your sacrifices.

One way to learn about your inward anger and help redirect it to its rightful target is to use a technique mentioned in other chapters. Take a chair and pretend it is your mother or whomever it was who criticized you, overcontrolled you, or made you feel totally guilty in the past. Your mother may be dead and you may remember her as a saint, but just pretend she is sitting there and that you are a child again. What do you feel? What do you remember? Tell her. If you feel angry, shout. Let out any hostility that arises. You'll feel much better if you can do this.

Finally, get involved in activities outside of your home—a

job, classes, charity work—activities that you do for yourself and that will make you feel like an individual apart from your services to your family.

All of this will help you lessen your need to control by using guilt. If you change your behavior with members of your family, they will be less resentful toward you and more loving in a less ambivalent way.

CHAPTER 12

THE ELUSIVE OR ABUSIVE MAN SPECIALIST

Veronica is currently in love with Lester, the head of a medium-sized advertising agency. She has known him for almost a year. When they first met, they were attracted to each other instantly, and Lester asked her out. At the end of their first date, he told Veronica he would call her again. He didn't say when. Veronica waited five days and then she called him. She suggested they have lunch since they both worked near each other. Lester agreed. He called her two weeks later to ask her out again. Veronica, who had been sitting by the telephone waiting for his call, was delighted. They had a very pleasant time, but Lester left early. He had to return to his home in the suburbs where he lived with his two teenaged daughters. Lester was a widower. Veronica decided she really liked him, and pursued him vigorously. She called him regularly at his office just to chat. He was always cordial. He asked her out sporadically and she kept after him in the interim. She invited him to the movies, to dinner, for more lunches. Sometimes Lester accepted, and sometimes he didn't. By now they were sleeping together. Veronica pressed him to stay over at her apartment but Lester always refused, using one excuse or another. Finally he gave in, but left early the next morning. Veronica was crazy about Lester, but their affair was certainly not taking up all her time, so she continued to date other men. There was Bill, a nice young engineer who seemed to like her and wanted to see her more often. Veronica kept turning down Bill's invitations. She just wasn't that interested in him. Then there was

George, an editor at a large publishing house. He, too, was very interested in Veronica, but he just didn't turn her on. Even though he was eager to turn the relationship into something more serious, she discouraged him. She would see him now and then, but she told him she was seeing others. Her pursuit of Lester continued. Sometimes their relationship got better. He wanted to see her more often, and he seemed more interested. Veronica became more hopeful, but then he always backed off.

Veronica spends a lot of her time daydreaming about Lester. She sees herself living in his country home with his dog at her feet. She also spends a lot of time being miserable about him, and complains to her friends that he is so slippery, so uncommitted, so unenthusiastic and cool compared to herself, brimming over with craving and warmth. Veronica wants Lester with a passion that grows each day.

Last year Veronica was in love with Paul. She met him while she was going out with Ralph. Ralph was a business associate of Paul's, but that didn't prevent Paul from coming after her. Veronica immediately responded to him in a way that she couldn't with Ralph, although her friends could never understand why. To begin with, Paul was married, so he couldn't see Veronica very much. He carefully explained to Veronica that he hadn't slept with his wife in years, but he would never leave her. When Veronica began to indicate to Paul how much she liked him and press him to see her more often, he started treating her badly. He would break dates that she had been eagerly looking forward to. He would forget to return her phone calls. He treated her as a sexual object. By this time Veronica had dropped Ralph, but continued to date other men, some of whom seemed genuinely interested in her. They presented the possibility of a real relationship, but she couldn't get interested in anyone but Paul. She was obsessed by him. Her friends would sit through hours of conversations devoted to his antics. Many of them tried to point out that he was no good for her, but Veronica didn't want to hear. In her mind, she was convinced she had to have him. She kept chasing him, and the more she pursued, the less available he became to her. Finally Paul stopped calling her altogether. He refused to answer her many frantic phone calls to his office. Veronica never got over Paul until she met Lester, a man who in his own way is just as emotionally unobtainable.

Harriet was married for eighteen years to a man who was cruel and tyrannical. He continually criticized her, was hostile, cold and rejecting. He withheld sex and money when it suited him. Finally, Harriet gathered up the courage to leave her husband. Ever since her divorce, she has been seeing just one man. Her boyfriend seems the opposite of her husband. He is kind and supportive, friendly and generous. But he is married and lives in another city, so Harriet doesn't get to see him as much as she would like. When he is in town, he refuses to sleep over in Harriet's lovely suburban home. There is a common denominator between Harriet's ex-husband and her current lover, one important in understanding Harriet— both men were not fully available to Harriet. Her husband withheld his affection. Her lover is never around enough and belongs to another woman.

Veronica and Harriet are two in an army of women who are Elusive or Abusive Man Specialists. They attach themselves only to lovers and husbands who give them a hard time in one way or another.

Many of these women spend a lifetime at their game. One woman, a biologist of fifty-five, has been going with a man for five years who will see her only on Wednesdays and Saturdays. The rest of the week he insists he must be free for his other pursuits. He refuses to marry her, or have a more intimate relationship. Her last relationship lasted ten years with a man who continually rejected her, told her he didn't love her, and yet, when she periodically left him, he would come running after her. When she became pregnant once in an effort to snare him, he insisted she get an abortion, told her it was her fault, and refused to give her any money to help with the abortion costs. This affair ended only when he found a job in another part of the country and moved. Since her adolescence this woman has been involved with a series of men who either treated her badly or didn't want to get too involved, but still wanted to see her regularly. There have always been a lot of men in her life. She is very intelligent and beautiful. But she would have no part of the men who wanted full and committed relationships. The only men who could capture her attention were the men who didn't want her. This woman still believes that the reason she has never married is because the right man has not come along.

All women who are Elusive or Abusive Man Specialists feel the same way. They refuse to see their own role in the failure of their romances. They blame all their woes on the male rat of the moment.

Women who are Elusive or Abusive Man Specialists actually choose the man whom they will later feel victimized by. They have an uncanny instinct for picking up immediate signals that foretell the future of the relationship.

For example, Veronica met one of her men at a large party. They chatted for awhile and were obviously responding to one another, when suddenly he wandered off. Veronica watched him go with dismay. When he had not returned twenty minutes later, she went in search of him. When she found him, they chatted and flirted again, but once more he wandered off. Veronica sought him out again. At the end of the evening, it was Veronica who asked if they were going to see one another again. He answered, "Of course," and asked for her card.

Whether she realized it or not, Veronica already had a clear picture of what the relationship was going to be like—she pursues him, he rejects her, she runs after him even more.

A woman who always finds herself entangled with physically abusive men might find someone who when they meet for the first time is rude and insulting. She finds this intriguing, challenging, and exciting rather than a turn-off. Or, she accepts without protest the fact that a man grabs her by the arm roughly enough to leave a sizable black and blue mark, or that he pushes her against the wall a little too forcefully to kiss her for the first time. The man is getting the message at the same time about where their relationship is going.

Elusive or Abusive Man Specialists reject men who like and want them, men who treat them with thoughtfulness. These women favor unavailable men and men who treat them badly. It is quite common for these women to treat the nice guys in their lives as badly as they are treated by the elusive or abusive men they complain about.

The woman who always ends up with a man who gives her a hard time is more often than not the more active partner. She chooses the specific man, and then pursues him. It is the woman who gets the romance off the ground. The woman often is the one, also, who finally ends the affair after a suitable period of misery either because she feels it's hopeless or because she has driven the man away by her sometimes frantic and desperate actions.

While the affair goes on, the woman continually yearns for her man. His actions frustrate her; she feels rejected, angry, bad about herself. She feels that something must be wrong with her or he would respond more. She sometimes hates herself for putting up with his elusive or abusive behavior. She thinks obsessively about him and drives her friends crazy by talking and complaining about him to the exclusion of almost anything else.

By obsessing about her recalcitrant lover, she is actually trying to accomplish a magical goal. She feels unconsciously that if she thinks about him, he is really with her. She is a woman who fears being lonely or alone. Sometimes on a more conscious level, a woman may feel that if she thinks hard enough about her man, then he will think about her, too.

For the Elusive or Abusive Man Specialist, a relationship is a union in which two become one. Being overwhelmed by love is what she yearns for. Without her chosen man, she feels incomplete.

She thinks to herself, "If only I could have him," or "If only he would change, then all of my problems would be solved, and I would be happy." Elusive and Abusive Man Specialists ward off anxieties about their own inadequacies or failures by blaming all their troubles on a man.

Women who go for elusive or abusive men give out signals that say, "I am warm, I am wonderful," which is what they really are as long as the man is not available to them.

The men they attract and to whom they are attracted give out their own signals which say, "Come here, come a little closer, honey." But when the woman does try to get close, she gets pushed away.

A woman in therapy gave a perfect analogy. "I had an older brother who, when we were kids, would stand at the top of the stairs and say, 'Come here.' When I refused, he would say, 'If you come here, I'll give you a kiss.' Then, when I went to him and offered my cheek to be kissed, he would slap it instead."

The behavior of women with their elusive or abusive men is generally very clingy, aggressive and manipulative. They try to force the man to give them what they want. They are always after him to see them more, to give them more in the way of commitment or love. They may try coaxing, pregnancy, use threats of suicide, or go out with other men to create jealousy. They'll do whatever they feel will work. As one psychologist said, "If you think you are going to die without the man, how can you worry about ethics?"

The more these women cling, the more they push the man, the more they incur his wrath, and the more he withdraws and rejects them. The more he rejects and hurts them, the more desperate they become, and the more they try to force him to love them.

The man imagines he is protecting his autonomy. He reacts to her behavior by feeling she is possessive, demanding, and wants to trap him. When he thinks he has pushed her away enough to preserve his autonomy, then he may give her some crumbs. He will call her, ask her out a little more often. This, of course, is just enough to give her hope, and so she starts hammering at him once more.

If she starts to withdraw and becomes more aloof, you can count on the fact that he will then start to chase her.

Sometimes these women actually get their man. The couple marries. But a license doesn't mean that the essential nature of the relationship changes. He remains elusive or abusive as a husband, spending a lot of time away from home, being uncommunicative or withdrawing into his own shell when he is at home. She continues to be miserable, still blaming her unhappiness entirely on him. She keeps running after him, while he keeps sprinting away, resenting her attempts to get him into her emotional clutches.

Both are opposite sides of the same emotional coin. She is someone who, on a conscious level, thinks she desperately wants a relationship, but who, on an unconscious level, is terrified of one. He is someone who thinks, on a conscious level, that he doesn't want a close relationship but who, unconsciously, yearns for one.

Both need yet fear love, and they act out their ambivalences successfully together. He manages to have an intense relationship, but also to keep his distance. She manages to get intensely involved, but does not have a true relationship because he remains, finally, unavailable. If by some miracle he did become available, she would suddenly start to run away. She would experience it as losing interest in him, rather than the surfacing of her fear of intimacy. Love for her means engulfment, and she is terrified of it. Her man shares the same fear. They just approach it from opposite corners.

Nevertheless, if the Elusive and Abusive Man Specialists feel that the pain is too much for such a scant return and they must break off the relationship, or if they are finally abandoned by the man, they feel intense pain and depression.

Depression is part of their life. They go into funks when an affair ends, but they were often depressed while the affair was continuing. They are miserable when they aren't with him, and they are miserable when they are with him and he is rejecting or abusive.

Throughout the relationship, they have an ongoing fantasy that he is going to change, and then everything will be wonderful.

When the Elusive or Abusive Man Specialist is rotten to the other men in her life, it is a displacement of the anger she feels at her beloved. She is always in a rage at him, but she dare not express it to him directly. He might become even more elusive or abusive. So she is hostile to the nice guy instead.

A good example of this is a woman who had a passionate sexual attachment to her elusive man. He started to withhold sex, something that often occurs in marriages or affairs with elusive men. She had been seeing another man intermittently, and he invited her to the movies one night. In the middle of the movie, she told him she was tired and wanted to go straight home. This was her way of saying she didn't want to

sleep with him. The man was as hurt as she was when her
lover pulled the same thing on her.

Sex can often be fantastic for women trapped in these
hot-and-cold relationships. They build up such a desire while
they are waiting around for their man to call or give them a
crumb of affection that when they finally get what they
want, firecrackers go off.

Elusive or Abusive Man Specialists have a desperation
about them. They compulsively man hunt, spending their
entire lives looking for something they forbid themselves to
have. Their desperation is compounded by the fact that they
feel worthless as women unless they have a man of their own,
a common sentiment among women in our society.

Elusive or Abusive Man Specialists age miserably. They
feel like men's victims when they find themselves in middle
age, still without a man, and losing their looks.

Women who have been married to elusive or abusive men
sometimes come into their own for the first time only when a
husband dies. It is not until their man is gone that they realize
what a rotten, stultifying relationship it has been. As widows,
they finally are able to live for themselves, instead of in the
shadow of a rejecting man.

If they remain locked into the marriage, then they may
become like the protagonists in *Who's Afraid of Virginia
Woolf?* In their own way, they torture each other. If the
woman has a husband who beats her, she finds she cannot put
a stop to his physical abuse. When a woman feels as if she
can't live without a man, it is hard for her to say, "Don't
touch me!" Playing into this, of course, is the fact that
women in our society feel helpless and terrified to be on their
own. No matter how badly a man treats them, they at least
feel economically provided for.

Occasionally, an Elusive or Abusive Man Specialist plays
the game of chasing unavailable men as a defense against
homosexual leanings. As long as she is yearning for a man,
she can define herself as heterosexual. As long as she doesn't
have him, she doesn't have to confront the fact that she really
isn't interested in men. Once in a while, deeply buried homosexual tastes come to the surface. One woman trapped her
elusive boy friend into marriage by getting pregnant. Every

time he threatened to leave her, she became pregnant again. She had three children before he walked out on her for good. After that she discovered what she really wanted. She began a long term homosexual relationship—with an elusive woman.

Elusive or Abusive Man Specialists at Work

Elusive or Abusive Man Specialists usually have one ear cocked at the office for that telephone call from him, or they spend a good amount of time daydreaming about their lover. In spite of this, some Elusive or Abusive Man Specialists are able to maintain successful careers. Others are too distracted by their affairs. They go through their tasks mechanically and reluctantly with their minds on their man.

There are groups of brilliant, capable wives who continue to sit home waiting for crumbs from their elusive husbands, instead of carving out lives of their own.

The less that these women sit around waiting for favorable attention, and the more they busy themselves with other things, the better they are able to function well in the business world.

Why the Elusive or Abusive Man Specialist Is the Way She Is

Many Elusive or Abusive Man Specialists are the daughters of mothers who, after an initial period of closeness, disappeared through death or illness, or they became emotionally withdrawn. Sometimes this shift of interest on the mother's part occurred after the birth of another child.

When the Elusive or Abusive Man Specialist is yearning for her lover, she is also longing for her mother. Her original desperate need for her mother's love gets translated into the vital need she feels for her man. It's a very primitive feeling, and it's very strong because of it.

The inability to accept love, which draws these women continually to impossible men, is based on the fact that these women from an early age thought of themselves as having been abandoned, and their personalities evolved on the basis of being alone. They feel that if they stopped being alone, they would no longer know how to cope. They would disintegrate. By choosing relationships in which they can never achieve the fusion they long for, they are warding off the possibility of annihilation.

The rage and sense of frustration that these women feel towards the elusive or abusive men whom they choose as love objects is particularly powerful because it's a reenactment of the rage and frustration they felt when their original love object, their mother, was not there for them emotionally at a crucial stage in life.

For some of these women, it was their father rather than their mother who became unavailable to them emotionally, but with the same result. They yearn for love, but cannot accept it because it would be too threatening.

The Magnificent Obsessor

An important variation of the Elusive or Abusive Man Specialist is the woman who has had a series of more normal relationships in her past, but who at some time in her life gets obsessed by one particular elusive or abusive man.

Two good examples of Magnificent Obsessors are Jean Harris, who was consumed by her love for Dr. Herman Tarnower for fourteen years, and the heroine of *Adele H.*, the movie based on the life of Victor Hugo's daughter. Adele H. trailed a lover who had rejected her across continents, eventually going mad. Jean Harris finally killed the object of her obsession, and ended up splashed across newspapers around the world.

Magnificent Obsessors carry on their obsession with a particular man long past the time when the affair has ended and in the face of reality which tells them what they don't want to believe—that they really are not wanted. Irrationally and stubbornly, they cling to someone who is often long gone from their lives. They may write, telephone or attempt to see a man who by this time regards them as either a pest or a bit loony.

In a paper, "Obsession with the Rejecting Beloved," published in the *Psychoanalytic Review,* Dr. Elizabeth E. Mintz, a New York psychologist, gave five examples of women of more than ordinary intelligence, each with a successful career who were insanely attached to men who had dumped them. They thought and fantasized about their ex-lovers, found it hard to believe that they were no longer loved, and in one case the obsessed woman went so far as to travel to the city where her ex-lover lived, and camp on his doorstep until the police removed her.

Dr. Mintz feels that irrational obsessions have their roots in inconsistent parenting. A mother was once warm and close, but subsequently became cold and unavailable, or she alternated between being attentive or self-absorbed. Perhaps one parent was aloof while the other provided more nourishment. On one level, the obsessed woman yearns for her lover as she originally yearned for her mother—with a desperate need and a sense that she will not be able to survive without that all-important love. The obsessed lover may also be trying to reunite with the more nourishing parent and may be, according to Dr. Mintz, even trying to elicit belated affection from the more rejecting parent as symbolized by the lover.

Some of the obsessed patients described by Dr. Mintz were able to carry on their demanding careers and function in the world despite their crazed, all-engrossing absorption in a man who didn't want them anymore.

Obsessions about one man are not rare among women in our culture, but they vary in degrees. Some women get hooked to the point of insanity. They can't pick up the pieces and go on. Other women can step ahead. They have other affairs but they never forget the object of their obsession, staying attached to him, for example, by finding out from friends what he is doing, by telephoning him every now and then to hear his voice. One woman even searched out another woman who had an affair later on with the same man. She has, on occasion called this woman just to talk about how terrible their ex-lover is. She also calls the man to harangue him for having messed up her life. For years she didn't return money she had borrowed from him, even though she could well afford to, because it kept some tie between them.

Obsessed lovers go out of their way to pass the street where their ex-love lives and gaze up into his windows. They hope against all odds for chance meetings. They think they recognize him on the street, but it turns out to be somebody else.

Most obsessions are fueled by a feeling of love for the lost partner, but there are also women who cling to the memory of a man through an all-absorbing hatred for him. These women often have fantasies of revenge.

As with Elusive and Abusive Man Specialists, Magnificent Obsessors feel that there is a magic attached to their compulsive thoughts: If they continue to think about their love, he will continue to think about them.

Elusive or Abusive Man Specialists and Society

Many women, at one time or another, have had an unrequited love affair in which both their love and their misery knew no bounds. Knowing the feelings involved, it is easy to sympathize with Elusive or Abusive Man Specialists and Magnificent Obsessors. Sympathy quickly turns to frustration, however, when dealing with some women. They are both illogical and blind, preferring to suffer over a man rather than recognize the primitive force that compels them to carry on a romance long beyond the time when it's sane to do so.

The feeling of these women—that they cannot live without a certain man—is given support by a whole body of sentimental material from popular culture. Unrequited love is an old and recurring theme in folk songs, popular songs, operas, novels and movies. Such cultural backup lends a legitimacy and romantic flavor to mooning over a man and allows the obsessed woman to feel that she is just doing what other people do when they're in love.

How an Elusive or Abusive Man Specialist Can Help Herself

If this chapter gave you a hint that perhaps you are an Elusive or Abusive Man Specialist, but you are still not sure, ask yourself the following two questions: What were my last four relationships like? and, Who were the men who got me the most steamed up in my life?

Consider yourself an Elusive or Abusive Man Specialist if the following statements apply to you. In three out of your last four serious relationships you were always chasing the man and wanting more than he could give, or the relationships seesawed back and forth, with one running and the other withdrawing. The only men who have really grabbed you in your life were those who were unavailable or rotten to you. The men you could never respond to were those who were kinder or more accessible.

You are already on your way to change if you can recognize your pattern and accept it as your own problem, not made by those wretched men who always seemed just out of your grasp.

First, you must shift your focus. Stop putting your energy into agonizing over the man in question and put it into pondering about yourself. Instead of spending your time wondering how you can get him to love you or want you more, think about what it is that makes you so drawn to him. He may be handsome or sexy or exciting, but is this the real reason? Your friends may already have told you that he seems like a terrible man and it's a mystery to them why you want him. What is it that is so compelling about the relationship? Is it the angst he creates or your actual love for him? Do you love him because you can't have him? Try to be honest with yourself.

The ultimate question you must begin to think about is why you are afraid of intimacy. That's the reason you always attach yourself to people you can't have in any consistent, loving way. The answer is hidden in your past.

Did you have the feeling that your mother or father didn't

really love you or pay enough attention to you? Was there a parent who seemed to abandon you through illness, alcoholism, death, or emotional withdrawal? Did your mother's attention shift from you to a new brother or sister? Does intimacy in a relationship mean that you will lose yourself and not know who you are anymore? Does this make you fearful? Do you feel, deep down, inadequate? Are you afraid if someone got really close they would recognize how terrible you are?

Perhaps you can't reconstruct what it was that originally made you afraid of intimacy, and therefore makes you chase after men you can't have. What you can do is simply recognize the fact that this is what keeps you in bad relationships and prevents you from getting involved in good ones.

If there is a man currently in your life who is either continually elusive or abusive to you, now is the moment to put your plan for change into effect. Tell him you don't want to see him anymore. This may cause a change in his behavior that will tempt or confuse you. When you tell him the bad news, he is very likely to come running after you. It will be hard, but don't give into the temptation to stay when this happens. It won't last. He will become elusive again the moment you are once more enmeshed in the relationship. Just tell him it's all over with, no matter how much he calls you and protests.

Next, when you are looking for a replacement, keep in mind your predilection for the elusive or abusive man and watch for early warning signs. If you find yourself having to chase him from the beginning, it's a danger signal. If he is doing insulting, humiliating or abusive things early on, and you keep putting up with them—that's another danger signal. If the old familiar feelings of frustration and deep yearning appear, remove yourself from this new relationship as fast as possible.

When an available man comes along, before you dismiss him as too boring or uninteresting or unexciting, figure out why he is so unappealing to you. Maybe it's because he doesn't present the challenge and the angst of the chase.

Learn to give nice guys a chance. Keep yourself open to

them emotionally instead of mentally comparing them to the passionate attachments you had to the rats in your past. If you stay out of the way of any more elusive or abusive men, and accustom yourself to nicer, more available men, you may eventually find yourself getting used to better treatment and settling down into a possible relationship rather than an impossible one.

CHAPTER 13

THE ENSLAVER

When you walk into the apartment of Ken, a forty-five year old photographer, you are struck immediately by its atmosphere. There are old family photographs, beautifully framed, interesting objects everywhere. The walls are covered with paintings. Dominating one wall is a large portrait of an attractive young woman with flaming red hair and large green eyes. Ken points to it with pride and tells you that it is his mother as a young girl. He adds a little anecdote about his mother, one of the many anecdotes about her that will sprinkle his conversation. He tells you that when she was a little girl, his grandmother used to dye his mother's hair because red hair was not considered ladylike. It wasn't until she became a young woman that red hair became the rage of Europe, and suddenly his mother became a fabled beauty because of it.

As Ken shows you around his apartment, he points out other artifacts that belonged to his mother. He takes you into a bedroom, preserved as a shrine. There is his mother's bed, just as it used to look while she was still alive. There are her brushes. A charming chest of drawers that she brought with her from Europe is full of family memorabilia.

As you settle into a chair in the living room, you notice a stillness in the atmosphere. It is as if you have walked into the past. Everything in the room has a history. Although Ken lives here alone, you know you are in an apartment that belongs more to the woman whose green eyes stare down at you from the wall.

Ken has never married. He never will.

His mother died five years ago. He tended to her until the end with devotion and tenderness. Ken misses his mother. She was the center of his existence which is now empty and formless.

Ken's mother was an Enslaver. An Enslaver ties an emotional noose around one of her children at an early age. She never unties it. This child is bound to his mother for life. The child picked by his mother is also, of course, the one who allows himself to be chosen. The Enslaver may try to enslave her other children as well, but soon concentrates on the one who is more vulnerable to her guile, charm and manipulations. She is a woman who will use anything and everything that works to get her way, including charm, illness, guilt, and martyrdom.

You can spot the Enslaver's victim early. He is the child she takes everywhere. He never has playmates he would rather be with, or things that he wants to do more than be with his mommy. The Enslaver often uses her son as a junior escort and sometimes she dresses him accordingly. One woman remembers a visit from an Enslaver relative who had her five-year-old son trailing along, dressed in an impeccable white linen suit with long pants. His hair was slicked back. He already looked like a young gentleman.

The slave is a child who keeps his room clean. He puts his dirty clothes in the hamper. He is a good boy who never creates major problems for his mother. She creates a sense of vulnerability in him which serves to keep her in command as his protector. He is often a hypochondriac, afraid of getting hurt or falling ill. As a teen, he worries about catching VD. Because he is concerned about not getting enough sleep, he keeps regular hours. A slave is often conscious of nutrition; he may exercise regularly for health.

Generally, the Enslaver's victim is a son, rather than a daughter. However, if an Enslaver has no sons, she will settle for a daughter.

The Enslaver's victim can never leave home, either literally or emotionally. The slave often lives with his mother until she dies. Her needs and wishes give form and meaning to his life, a life that is otherwise impoverished. It is common in the world of Enslavers to find men in their forties and fifties who spend all of their free time fussing endlessly over their mother, taking her out to dinner, running little errands for her, buying little gifts for her, entertaining her friends.

The Enslaver discourages any show of independence on her son's part. She denigrates any choices that would make him a person in his own right. One man who wanted to become a doctor was told by his mother that he was a heartless beast for not wanting to go into his father's business instead.

Often success itself is discouraged. Some Enslavers feel that work is somewhat vulgar. Most also sense unconsciously that a son who is not successful is more dependent on them. Many sons of Enslavers are only marginally successful in their life's work.

An Enslaver in her late seventies who now takes a nap in the afternoon to conserve her strength has been trying to persuade her son to take naps when she does, at a time when he should really be attending to his ailing free-lance business.

Some enslaved sons are able to leave home eventually and live elsewhere. If they do leave, it is generally at a much later age than most other children leave home and only after a great internal and external struggle.

Although they bed down elsewhere, these sons often remain at home psychologically. They visit their mother all the time, they worry about her, they phone her continually. If something is the least little bit wrong, their mother is sure to tell them and they go racing over.

Some sons of Enslavers become homosexuals; others are neuters. Those who have an interest in heterosexual relations find it hard to carry on an affair because their mother demands so much of their time and attention. They find it even more difficult to marry because their mother is so critical of any woman they bring home. The mother is sure to point out to her son that his girl friend wears too much makeup, her nose is too long, she looks like a tart, she had a run in her stockings, and her nail polish was chipped.

Enslavers even run interference in the affairs of homosexual sons. An Enslaver managed to drive away one of her son's few male lovers by shouting to her son in the next room, "Gilbert, there's some spic on the phone for you."

She left the telephone uncovered so that the Cuban heard what she said each time he called.

When their sons don't marry, these women rationalize it by saying there was no one good enough for them.

If a man does take a wife, despite his mother's best efforts to prevent it, then he finds himself caught between two women, straddling a fine line with his mother on one side, his wife on the other. The Enslaver can be counted on to be hostile to her enslaved son's spouse. She will make cutting, nasty remarks, criticizing everything the wife does from the way she cooks to the way she dresses or raises her children. In addition to his mother's hostility, a slave's wife has to put up with the inordinate amount of time her husband spends with his mother, doing her biddings. Rivalry between the women is intense, and there is much mutual resentment and hatred.

At best, life for the enslaved son is bittersweet. Although he devotes his life to his mother, taking the very best care of her, trying to please her, he finds himself dealing with a very difficult woman.

The Enslaver can be charming. She has a sense of humor. Often she has an aristocratic demeanor, but she is also a critical and demanding woman, quick to show her disapproval and discontent. The Enslaver has a vision of the way things should be, and she cannot accept any deviation from her stifling set of rules and regulations. The appearances and behavior of everyone around her must match her own standards. If they don't, she will most certainly let you know. Nothing escapes her critical eye. She is a rigid perfectionist, what psychiatrists call an obsessive-compulsive. A piece of dust can drive her to fits.

The son who attends to her is subject to criticism to which he is particularly vulnerable because his mother is his high priestess and the love of his life, but everyone else gets it, too. Neighbors, friends, her other children, servants—no one escapes her evil eye and malicious tongue. Her husband is criticized, too, but sometimes to a lesser degree. After all, the Enslaver picked her husband and therefore she must maintain the semblance that he is right and good. The glorification of dead husbands after a lifetime of carping at them is quite common to Enslavers. He is brought to the saintly perfection he should have had all along.

The Enslaver's tastes are exquisite and conservative. She considers herself to be a connoisseur of the finer things in life. She may not have much money, but whatever she owns must be the finest. If she can't buy much clothing, then she purchases just two designer dresses each year. She takes excellent care of her clothing, and her purchases add up to a whole wardrobe over the years. An Enslaver won't wear perfume or drink wine unless it's French. She recognizes good china. Her furniture generally consists of antiques or excellent reproductions. Everything is chosen to last. Her objects become part of her legend and the family heritage. Her collections create an ambience that makes her seem so special to her son and her husband. Her housekeeping standards are stringent. Everything has a place and must be kept there.

The Enslaver helps convince her family of her uniqueness by her constant criticism of the way other people do things. Mrs. Jones uses only frozen foods, for example, while the Enslaver only uses fresh vegetables because she cares about the health of her loved ones. Mrs. Smith's house is so tacky with all that plastic and all that orange and olive green in her color scheme. Quite, refined pastels create a more serene environment and show that the Enslaver's family has class. If a member of her family buys something without consulting her, it is often criticized as lacking in taste. "What she chooses is right. What I choose is wrong," complained one daughter-in-law of an Enslaver.

Finally, the Enslaver's son and husband come to believe her, that only she has the best taste and knows what is right. They consider themselves lucky to be in her orbit.

Despite her critical and demanding ways, the Enslaver generally has a long-lasting marriage.

An Enslaver usually looks for a man who is a hard worker as well as someone who will meet her physical standards. Good looks and a future count. If a man doesn't have one, he should at least have the other; hopefully, he has both. She also values neatness in men.

As a young woman, the Enslaver is able to attract a lot of beaus. Her perfectionism is already apparent in the way she dresses and conducts herself. Her clothing and her gestures are always precise. An Enslaver is generally vivacious and attractive, the possessor of a biting wit that can be one of her assets, but which she also uses to slay her enemies. People often don't realize just how critical an Enslaver is, especially when she is young, because her attacks are often disguised in humor. Her essential nastiness creeps up on one slowly.

There are several ways the basic character of an Enslaver comes through during courtship. To begin with, she is preoccupied with externals—manner and dress are scrutinized and important to her. Her vision of relationships is all-encompassing. She demands absolute exclusivity from a man. This doesn't mean only other women. It means he has to give up his family, friends, bridge, tennis and any other diversions that might take time and attention away from her. The future Enslaver is demanding. She wants to be fussed over, and expects little gifts as a sign of devotion. She expects regular phone calls. Although the Enslaver-to-be is smiling and cheerful most of the time, she can also be explosive and unpredictable. She is apt to lapse into moodiness and is capable of tantrums if she doesn't have her way.

The man who marries the Enslaver tends to be passive and a little bit vague. He needs someone to create order and discipline for him, and it is a relief to have a woman who will set his standards, decide what is right and wrong, tell him how things should be done. The Enslaver's husband is happy to leave the details of his life to his wife. Some husbands of Enslavers even let their wives pick out the clothing they will wear the next day. The Enslaver's aim is to make everyone a dependent, which in turn gives her power and control.

An Enslaver is not very interested in sex. She is too constricted, guarded, and rigid to be able to enjoy it. Sex becomes one of her duties.

This creates another relief for the husband of the Enslaver. He is happy to have at least one less thing to be insecure about; he can count on the fact that his wife will be faithful.

Despite the fact that the Enslaver's husband continues to admire his wife, he is not happy. She is still critical and tyrannical, and he is not immune from her anger or scorn.

Why does he stay with her? Because he starts to believe in

the legend of her perfection, and because he is a dependent who can't break away. Enslavers' husbands learn to handle their situation. They stay out of the Enslaver's way as much as possible by choosing interests or jobs that take them away from home a lot. They go on long camping or hunting trips alone, or they choose golf over tennis because it takes more hours to play. They may take courses to improve themselves, or simply work late.

The Enslaver is quite capable of twisting her husband's absences to her own advantage. One Enslaver, whose husband goes on long fishing trips, brags to her friends about the wonderful fish he brings home. She cooks marvelous dishes using his catches. His escape trips become a source of gratification for her.

Another salesman who has to travel for six and eight weeks at a time refuses to retire even though he is now eighty-one years old. He knows he may drop on the road, but he isn't going to stay home. His wife has turned his refusal to retire into something to be proud of. She boasts about what terrific mental and physical shape her husband is in.

Some husbands of Enslavers have affairs, but if a husband is reasonably discreet, the Enslaver, who deals with unfavorable things by denying them, never finds out about it. If she does, she is able to rationalize the affair as not being important. "It doesn't matter," said one Enslaver about her philandering husband. "He's just playing with garbage." She draws upon her superiority over her rivals to discount the affair's significance.

Enslavers feel that women essentially are better than men. They think men are dirty, have questionable taste, get involved with women without class, and are driven by lowly desires. Basically, Enslavers are hostile to men.

The Enslaver's hostility to her enslaved son is virulent not only because he fails to live up to her standards, but also because she is aware, either consciously or unconsciously, that he is unable to break away or assert himself. She sees him as weak, and despises him for it. She is also in a subliminal rage because she has become her son's dependent. She, of course, has turned him into her caretaker, but on an unconscious level she hates him for it.

The son is also hostile to his mother whether he shows it or not, because of his total dependency on her, and his anxiety provoked by her whims and moods. No matter what he does, it is never good enough. They are locked into a love-hate relationship.

The Enslaver is in continual subliminal fear of losing her slave. Every time he is late, every time he takes a trip, every time he leaves the house, there is a crisis. The Enslaver is afraid he will never return, he will have an accident, or he will be magically snatched away. This is why Enslavers are so loathe to let their sons out of their sight.

Although there is mutual dependency, if the Enslaver's worst fears come true and her son dies first, she fares much better than he does when the situation is reversed. Upon her death, he is doomed to loneliness and misery. He feels empty and incomplete without the focal point that his mother provided. He is unable to establish another relationship with the same intensity and intimacy.

The Enslaver has more to draw upon. The center of her universe is, after all, herself. Enslavers have a lot of basic strength that their sons lack. They are survivors.

The Enslaver also has a coterie of female friends to fall back upon. She is able to have cordial relations with women who are admirers and followers. She tends to attract women who admire her taste and culture, her sense of humor, or enjoy the atmosphere of her home.

The Unmarried Enslaver

If an Enslaver never marries, she manages to find other victims to do her bidding. She often hones in on a young female co-worker. The Enslaver, who is able to be quite charming when it suits her, carefully disarms a co-worker in order to hook her. She remembers birthdays, sends cards, flatters. When she feels the chosen one has succumbed, she begins to run her ragged getting coffee, running little errands, helping out in a thousand and one ways. She has found her slave. The Enslaver is a woman who needs a victim and if she can't have one at home, then she will unerringly find one elsewhere.

Why the Enslaver Is the Way She Is

The Enslaver often came from a disorganized parental home and her perfectionism, compulsive neatness, and rigid rules originated as an attempt to create order out of chaos. By concentrating on details, she was able to allay the anxiety that overwhelmed her.

The Enslaver's father was usually a weak man whom she felt she could never count on. At the same time, her mother may have been overwhelming and overly critical, always pointing out the faults of others. The Enslaver determined at an early age to become better than those whom her mother criticized. Thus, she was set on the rocky road to her adult perfectionism based on what she regarded as higher standards than ordinary.

Sometimes an Enslaver had an overly close relationship with her father whom she overidealized and from whom she never separated emotionally. The Enslaver projects the overblown fantasy of her father onto her son. She expects her son to give her the attention and provide her with the same gratifications that her father did. When the son doesn't live up to his mother's unrealistic expectations, she becomes critical of him.

Occasionally the Enslaver has been overcontrolled by her parents, and she only knows control and counter-control as a means of relating to others.

The Enslaver craves a closeness in relationships that does not leave room for the other person to have separate desires or interests. It is a romanticized, one-sided view of love. She is the recipient; he is always the giver.

As a young girl, the Enslaver generally displays an enormous and indiscriminate need for approval, love, and closeness from everyone. She is always trying to achieve it rather pathetically by giving playmates little gifts, or making drawings for adults. The later enslavement of their sons is a distortion of their early desire for closeness.

The Religious Enslaver

Another kind of Enslaver uses religion to terrorize her children and husband into submission. She relies on God and the local priest as her allies in pointing out to everyone around her how bad they are. If they don't do what she says, or if there is dirt on the carpet they may roast in hell. She justifies her desire to control as a desire to get everyone into heaven.

The Future of Enslavers

Enslavers are an endangered species. Although there are plenty of them still around with their rigid codes of genteel and proper behavior, they are simply becoming outdated.

An even more important factor in the extinction of Enslavers is the fact that their children do not tend to propagate. Daughters, with the image of their own horrible childhood in mind, refuse to have children of their own. Or they rebel and refuse to act like their mother, even though they may share some of her tendencies. Sons often turn out to be homosexuals or neuters, or if they are heterosexual, they often don't marry. They fear a wife will turn out to be bossy, tyrannical and critical like Mom.

Sociologically, new roles for women will mitigate against the destructive behavior of Enslavers with their families. Enslavers are women with a strong drive for power. Up until recent times, the only place they could exercise it was in the home.

Today, a potential Enslaver can go out into the world and use her innate strength and drive to establish a career for herself. If she receives gratification from her work, she is much less likely to concentrate her efforts on enslaving those around her. Of course, she may be a ruthless boss, but at least employees can return to their own lives after work, something that is not possible for the families of Enslavers.

How an Enslaver Can Help Herself

Enslavers are not all bad—they are often women with a great deal of charm and strength. An Enslaver has to learn to change her definition of love from possession and control to giving and sharing.

If you recognize yourself as an Enslaver, you must learn to let a loved one have interests of his own and time for himself. You must allow him a life of his own. The only way you can do this is by using your power to create a life of your own, apart from your family relationships.

Find a job that can provide an outlet for your strong power needs. Volunteer to be in charge of fund raising or membership for a local charity. Outside interests will provide you with a way to express yourself so that your focus won't be exclusively on your relationships at home.

It would also be enormously beneficial to you to examine what love means to you. Right now it means possession, control, suffocating closeness. Try to find out why. Are you afraid no one would return to you, if you gave them the freedom to roam? Did you have a model for such a distortion of love in your own parents? Did they rule you the way you rule your family? Are you really inwardly frightened? Can you feel safe only by keeping a tight rein on things?

Next, you should try to get in touch with the anger hidden in your personality which makes you so critical of others. Look back into your own life. Remember yourself as a little girl. Who made you afraid or angry in your memories? Mother? Father?

Put a chair opposite you and imagine this person sitting in it. Talk to this person and spit out your anger at them. Tell them, even if they are no longer alive, what they did that made you so angry at them. Don't think this is silly. It will help you. Let all your resentments come out without stopping them.

Finally, insight into how destructive you are with your family can be of help now. Try not to order them around or be so critical. Set short-term goals for yourself as you try to change. Go through one whole day without asking for anything from your children; expand it to two days and so on until you begin to feel you can really get along without constantly issuing orders.

Start to ask those around you what they think. Again, start slowly. Once a day ask your son or daughter their opinion about something; listen respectfully when they talk. At first they may be surprised by your new behavior, but they will be grateful. You will find the love you are looking for if you are more respectful of others. Your relationships will be warmer and closer in the end than the ambivalent love-hatred you now get by ordering your loved ones around.

CHAPTER 14

THE WIDOW

More than thirteen percent of the women in this country are widows. Although widows are generally assumed to be older, a study by the Census Bureau revealed that the majority of widows lose their first husband before the age of fifty.

No matter at what age a woman becomes a Widow, her bereavement and the problems she faces as a Widow are largely predictable.

The Widow in our society is a woman who quite suddenly finds herself without a role. She discovers that not only has she lost a husband, but her main function in life and her self-identity are gone as well. The emergence of the career woman in our society may change this in the future, but at present, most Widows are women who defined themselves primarily as wives and mothers.

Lynn Caine, in her book *Widow,* explains the sudden bewilderment that Widows feel:

" 'Widow' is a harsh and hurtful word. It comes from the Sanskirt and means empty. . . .

"After my husband died, I felt like one of those spiraled shells washed up on the beach. Poke a straw through the twisting tunnel, around and around, and there is nothing there. No flesh. No life. Whatever lived there is dried up and gone.

"Our society is set up so that most women lose their identities when their husbands die. Marriage is a symbiotic relationship for most of us. We draw our identities from our husbands. We add ourselves to our men, pour ourselves into

them and their lives. We exist in their reflection. And then
. . .? If they die . . .? What is left? It's wrenching enough
to lose the man who is your lover, your companion, your best
friend, the father of your children, without losing yourself as
well.''

One of the tasks of a Widow is to forge a new identity for
herself. She also has to readjust her relationships with her
children, with in-laws, her own relatives and friends.

But before she can even begin to tackle that she has to deal
with her grief, the time when she mourns for her lost husband
and lets go of the emotional ties that bind her to him.

Normal bereavement is composed of five stages:

1. *A state of shock and disbelief.* The initial tendency is for
   a widow to deny the death. "He can't really be gone. He'll
   walk in the door any minute now." The Widow in this period
   has to come to grips with the fact that her husband is gone
   forever. A sense of numbness is often felt for several weeks
   after the funeral.

2. *Guilt.* It is common for a new Widow to feel she erred.
   "If only I had taken him to the doctor sooner. If only I
   had paid attention to him when he complained of being
   tired. If only he had been treated by a better doctor."
   Widows blame themselves for what they feel are recent or
   even past sins against their husbands. Tears are copious in
   this stage.

3. *Anger.* This stage often comes as a surprise to Widows.
   Suddenly they are in a fury at their deceased spouse.
   "How dare he leave me alone? How dare he leave me
   with all these responsibilities to shoulder by myself?"
   Feelings of anger may be directed against fate ("Why
   me?") or against the medical profession ("That doctor
   killed him!").

4. *Sadness and loneliness.* Depression is overwhelming at
   this stage. It may almost paralyze her. She feels she may
   not be able to go on living by herself. A Widow may
   withdraw into herself.

5. *Resolution.* Only after having gone through shock, guilt,
   anger and sadness will a Widow be able to successfully
   build a new life for herself. In this final stage, she says

good-bye to her husband and begins to think of herself as an individual rather than her husband's wife. She now will be ready for a new romance or at least male companionship.

The mourning period can last anywhere from nine months to three years. Mourning is frequently accompanied by various psychosomatic symptoms—headaches, insomnia, apathy, digestive disturbances, agitation. The Widow tends to over-idealize her husband, remembering only the good parts of his personality and their relationship together, and striking out anything negative.

There are many Widows who get stuck in the mourning period for the rest of their lives. They continue to think obsessively about their dead husband. They stay in the apartment or house they shared and refuse to move one chair or one picture. They keep his clothing in a closet. His pipe continues to sit by the television set.

A grave error that some Widows make is to go to the other extreme. They try to pull themselves together too quickly. They throw themselves into activities; they stop talking about their mate because they don't want to depress children or relatives; they put away their mate's picture because it makes them sad to look at it. In an effort to present a more cheerful picture to the world, often in response to well meaning relatives who have been urging them not to brood so much, they try to start a new life before they are ready to. By denying to themselves as well as to those around them just how badly they feel, they may appear to be getting over the loss, but in reality they have made it worse.

Creating silence about the dead husband and obliterating his traces from her life makes the Widow feel inwardly guilty. "After 25 years together, how could I forget him so quickly?" Despite her cheerful exterior, grief continues, but now it is lived out in secret.

Her submerged feelings can make the Widow react with uncharacteristic irritability to others. An invitation out can make her accuse others of being unfeeling, which takes them by surprise because she has been acting as if she has recovered. Repressing memories and forcing cheerfulness merely prolongs the period of mourning.

Grief is more powerful and lasts longer, according to studies, when the death of a husband was sudden—a heart attack, for example, or a brief terminal illness. Long illnesses at least prepare a wife for the inevitable. An unrelated life crisis preceding his death, such as the discovery of a husband's infidelity or a financial crisis, tends to prolong the mourning period as well.

Studies have found that if the marriage was a troubled one, the Widow grieves more than if she were happy. The Widow, who was an unhappy wife, becomes consumed by debilitating guilt. Secretly she feels that she wished for her husband's death.

In general, Widows find themselves in a period of great strain and upheaval. They have to take on responsibilities they shared or that their husband handled alone. They may have children at home, and have to deal with them without advice or support. The Widow's income may be severely reduced. She may have to find new housing. She may have to find a job, readjust her relationships with friends and relatives. So many changes all at once lead to great emotional stress and even to physical illness. Studies reveal an unusually high rate of illness among Widows.

Many Widows feel socially awkward after the death of a husband. If most of their friends still have their husbands, the Widow feels strange, for example, being the only woman at a gathering without an escort. Some Widows find that married friends gradually drop them.

Many Widows develop a sense of social isolation. They feel lonely and left out a good deal of the time.

Some Widows become too dependent on their children, visiting them frequently, calling on a son or daughter to handle financial matters, run errands, and provide them with company. This often creates resentment eventually on the part of children who have families and lives of their own. They feel burdened by their mother's new needs.

Sometimes the Widow becomes resentful if she feels the children have not rallied round her enough. Ruptures with the in-laws occur if the Widow feels they have not been sympathetic or supportive enough to her.

If children still live at home, the Widow may have to cope with their problems which are connected to her husband's death.

There is a feeling among Widows that they are the ones who suffer the most compared to other single women. And, indeed, compared to divorced women, they may. For one thing, when separation occurs because of death, it was not willed, and Widows feel singled out by fate. They are also able to idealize their marriage more than divorced women who know there were plenty of problems.

The successful Widow is the one who allows herself a proper period of mourning, and then with determination forges an identity of her own that is not dependent on a man. Instead of hunting frantically for a replacement for her husband, the successful Widow joins clubs, takes classes, develops hobbies, does volunteer work, finds herself a job—anything that will help her feel more competent as a person alone.

As I mentioned, some women try to shift their dependence from husband to children. Others become dependent on doctors for a variety of psychosomatic ailments.

The Widow also has to be wary of children who try to turn her into a dependent, reversing roles and acting like wise parents, telling their mother how to run her life. Listening too much to children will not help a Widow establish the competence to live on her own that she needs in order to feel good about herself and her new circumstances.

If and when she is ready to date the Widow has to learn to accept the fact that the world has changed. Many older women prefer to wait for marriage or at least some commitment before sleeping with a man. Today, however, they may be considered old fashioned or uptight because of their attitudes. One woman was told by a man pressuring her for sex that she needed to see a psychiatrist because she wanted to wait.

By accepting the change in sexual mores, the Widow will not become embittered about men. This doesn't mean that the Widow should do anything she feels is wrong for her. On the contrary, a Widow should realize she has a right to her own set of values. A decent man will allow a woman to act according to her beliefs, even if he doesn't share the same values.

The chance of a woman becoming a Widow is very great—men die at younger ages than women, and women tend to marry men a few years older than themselves. Widowhood is a state all women should consider and plan for, grim as such a thought may be.

CHAPTER 15

THE DIVORCED WOMAN

Divorced Women, like Widows, find themselves stripped of the role of wife which leaves them uncertain about their identity if they aren't attached to somebody. They may suddenly be in reduced financial circumstances. A woman may have to look for a job or a new place to live. She may have to adjust to coping with children by herself. All of this may be happening at the same time that she is adjusting emotionally to separation and divorce.

The mourning process for a marriage is similar to that for a mate. The divorcée goes through a period of shock, and an air of unreality prevails. One subject in a study of divorced women done by sociologists Janet Cohen, Carol Brown and Roslyn Feldberg expressed it very clearly. "It was like I was asleep for two years." Another said, "Your whole life drops out."

Divorced Women grieve for their marriages. They feel terrible that this relationship which started out with such hope ended in disaster. They feel sorry for their children. They feel the world, in general, is a crummy place since this happened.

Many Divorced Women feel guilty. Perhaps the marriage would have survived if they had been better wives or had acted differently, or they feel guilty that they have deprived their children of a live-in father.

A period of anger is normal. It can, however, be much greater and last much longer than the period of rage that Widows go through. The Divorced Woman may be furious with her husband whom she blames either for leaving her or for being the cause of her having to leave him.

She may be angry at the amount of child support or alimony she is receiving or the settlement she was awarded. She is often angry at finding herself a single woman again with what she sees as added liabilities—increased age and children.

Divorced Women sometimes get angry at in-laws for not calling or visiting anymore. They are angry at having given up careers for a marriage that didn't last. Some are angry because they worked to put a husband through school, but now that they can reap the financial benefits, they are suddenly divorced.

Having gone through shock, grief, anger, and guilt, the Divorced Woman should be able to come to terms with what has happened to her, make her husband part of the past, and go on with her future.

Unfortunately this doesn't always happen. There are many Embittered Divorcées around, women stuck in stages of anger or grief or both.

The Embittered Divorcée

The Embittered Divorcée is permanently dislocated by her divorce. Frequently she has been abandoned by her husband, sometimes for another woman. She is sad because she often remembers her marriage fondly as a time of happiness or fulfillment for her—as opposed to her current life as a single woman which she doesn't like. She is also in a fury at the man who did this to her. Intense anger at an ex-husband can last for many years, if not for a lifetime.

One woman in Houston whose husband left her for another woman fourteen years ago still talks compulsively about him and his perfidy, as if it all happened yesterday. She regards all married men as possible Judases and warns her friends to watch their husbands carefully and to prepare themselves so that if they are dumped they will be able to survive. She means survive better than she has. Many years after the fact this woman still carries around with her fury at friends who knew about her husband's affair but never told her while it was going on.

This divorcée is bright, still marvelously attractive, funny. Basically she is a terrific lady. But she thinks of herself as old, and washed up. Her image matches her internal feelings. Inwardly she is a frightened, furious woman and she drives men and even potential women friends away by her belligerent, frantic personality.

Another Embittered Divorcée, in Florida, also talks about her "bastard" husband compulsively. She has even made friends with a woman who went out with him after the breakup, and now they both are able to talk about what a rotten man he is together.

This woman hates to accept money from her ex, but she also refuses to get a job which would allow her to refuse his money and get out from under his financial clutches.

There are a whole group of Very Embittered Divorcées around who, in their behavior are almost indistinguishable from The Bitch (see Chapter 16). They not only talk badly about their ex-husbands, they act out their fury with all men. They are nasty, insulting, and/or demanding of men, even those they barely know.

One 50 year old woman whose husband deserted her acts insultingly and rejectingly toward men who call her for a date at the suggestion of friends. She is really afraid of being hurt again which gets converted into pickiness about men and hostility towards them, but the men will never know that. They just think she's a Bitch.

Most of the Very Embittered Divorcées are middle-aged to old women who were left by husbands for younger women. They allow their sense of anger and injustice to poison their whole life and all their relationships with men.

Very often anger for divorcées, is a way of not letting go. Their rage keeps them tied to a husband.

Some Embittered Wives take out their fury on the man directly. They are pointedly cold if he calls or comes over to take the children out; they use visitation days to fight with him about a variety of things. They bundle a child with barely a sniffle off to bed, so her ex-husband won't be able to see him that week.

Some Embittered Divorcées use children as their pawns. They may encourage a child, for example, to ask his father for something expensive, not because the child needs or wants it but simply to hurt the father in his pocketbook if they can't hurt him in any other way.

The Pathetic Divorcée

The Pathetic Divorcée is a woman whose life becomes a shambles after her divorce and she can't reconstruct it. A good example of this is a woman who had moved to Los Angeles from New York right after her divorce. She arrived without any plan about how she was going to support herself or her disturbed adolescent child who needed psychiatric care. She also knew, because he had warned her, that her husband would not send her the money he had agreed to if she moved to California. Nine months later, she was still living hand-to-mouth. She was job hunting frantically in a field where there were few opportunities, although there were plenty in New York. She lived in a rough neighborhood and was frightened most of the time. She used to live on Park Avenue in New York. She kept meeting men who preyed upon her pathetic, desperate state. One man thought he had the answer to her problems. "He told me," she said, trembling with tears, "that what I needed was just some good sex."

The Divorced Mother

Divorcées with children are an important new subgroup in our culture. They have many problems, the worst of which are often financial. Two-thirds of divorced fathers do not pay court-awarded child support payments. They simply stop paying and Divorced Mothers find it hard to get them to comply.

This leaves the Divorced Mother struggling to make a living for herself and her children. She may have to do it anyway, even if she is receiving support payments, because the money does not cover everything. Often the Divorced Mother is not prepared to do very much, since she has spent most of her adult life as a homemaker.

In order to hold nine-to-five jobs, divorcées have to provide child care for young children while they are at work. This immediately puts a dent into their salaries. They also have to give their children attention and love when they get home. They have to cook and find time—generally evenings

and weekends—for housecleaning. They try to maintain some
kind of social life, as well. Divorced Mothers find there
is never enough time.

Love lives become a problem for women with children.
Sometimes children, from toddler stage to adolescence, act
hostilely to the men who come to take mother out. Children
may fear that their father is going to be replaced, or that
Mommy will be taken away from them. On the opposite side
of the coin, Mothers sometimes fear that young children will
become too attached to a man they know is not going to be
around for very long.

Many mothers prefer to meet men outside of the home
when they go out with them, in order not to run into problems
with their children. A divorcée recently told me she waits for
her children to go to sleep before leaving. "My love life is
conducted between eleven at night and three or four in the
morning. I leave after they go to sleep and get back before
they wake up. I tried once to have a man pick me up at home
but my child said to him, 'I know why you're taking Mommy
out. You want to sleep with her.' That's what my husband
had been telling him I was doing."

Another woman told me about her solution to children and
relationships with men. "I let my children meet a man only
after I've been seeing him for awhile, and I think it's a stable,
good relationship. At that point, I even let them know that I
stay at his house on weekends when they see their father. I
feel it's okay because it's a relationship that they know has
been going on for years. But," she added, "I don't invite
casual dates home, and I would never invite this man to sleep
over at my house. I think that would be too heavy for my
children to handle." Many women make the same distinction
between casual or more serious relationships.

Other Divorced Mothers parade a string of lovers through
the house. They rationalize it by saying their children should
know the facts of life. This creates problems for children who
may act out their troubled feelings by becoming hostile to
their mothers. These mothers are in the minority.

Apart from problems connected with dating, divorcées find
themselves faced with a variety of indignities from the outside world simply because there is no longer a man around.

Some women report that schools and hospitals sometimes ignore requests from them that they wouldn't if the request had come from a husband. Landlords sometimes refuse to rent to divorced women. They consider them to be financially or morally irresponsible. Their own parents often start to interfere in their lives once a husband has left. Home repairs become a problem, especially, as is often the case, when there is no extra money to pay someone to fix things.

Divorced Women frequently learn to do simple repairs themselves. They plaster, they paint walls, they tighten screws. Whatever they find too difficult to fix themselves often simply goes unrepaired permanently or until a kindly, handy relative or boy friend offers to tinker with the tv set, the leaky sink, the toilet that doesn't flush properly.

Newly divorced women, whether they have children or not, commonly share one emotion—fear. They are afraid of living alone and of being alone for the rest of their lives. They are afraid of the unknown.

The sudden loss of an attachment after years of living with someone causes stress to many divorced people, according to Robert S. Weiss in a study called, "The Emotional Impact of Marital Separation". Separation anxiety results in periodic illogical wishes on the part of a divorced woman to make contact with an ex-husband either by telephone or in person. This yearning for contact occurs even in women who genuinely dislike or no longer have respect for their husbands. Women sometimes establish contact by fabricating excuses connected with the children, by calling to ask some question about finances or the home, or by harassing him about something. Fights about child support, alimony, and other matters have kept bonds between ex-marital partners going for years.

Sometimes separation anxiety makes a woman read signs into her ex-husband's actions that he may be thinking of a reconciliation. One woman, divorced from a tyrant and glad to be rid of him, told her friends she thought he was showing signs of wanting to come back, for he had suggested they have a drink together. When they met for the drink, he spent the whole time bragging about his affairs with other women. This kind of speculation about reconciliation, generally with little basis in reality, is common among new divorcées. The desire to make contact passes gradually for most women.

The desire to maintain the old contact fluctuates with feelings of euphoria where the Divorced Woman feels good about her new freedom.

Despite the stress, financial problems, and ambivalence they may feel toward ex-husbands, many Divorced Women thrive as single women. They begin to feel more competent about themselves as human beings, are proud of their ability to make it on their own. They relish not having to account for money or time to anyone. They find they have more self-respect than they had as wives.

Others continue to be miserable about their state, or alternate between liking and not liking it. They tend to pin their hopes on meeting the right man, so they can stop being a Divorced Woman and become a Wife again. For them, being a Wife means becoming whole once more.

Going Out Again for the Divorcée

Most women begin their post-divorce dating with the desire, often on an unconscious level, to prove that they are still attractive and desirable. The dissolution of a marriage is generally a blow to a woman's ego, even if it was she who initiated the divorce. She feels she has failed, time has passed, and men won't find her attractive any more. If a woman's husband left her, her ego has been dealt an even bigger blow, and she will need proof of her desirability even more than other divorcées.

Because of this need for reassurance, many women go through a period of promiscuity soon after the divorce. They sleep with practically any man who comes along, and the more men there are, the more attractive they feel.

At first, a lot of dating and sexual experimentation may seem like fun. It's exciting as well as a balm to a damaged ego. But the sense of excitement and fun is short-lived. Most women find that sleeping around begins to pall. They become disappointed in the quality of their relationships with men. They start to want a more steady and meaningful relationship with a man.

Occasionally one finds a woman, generally one whose husband has left her, who goes the opposite way. After the divorce she feels she is through with men, and she remains celibate, choosing to build her life around her children, friends, and job. Often this is as temporary a state as the promiscuity of other divorced women. It lasts until the post-divorce period of anger is over. There are cases of celibacy, however, that are permanent. The Divorced Woman simply no longer looks at men in a romantic way, and as a result, she may miss the clues that indicate a man's interest.

An example of this is a woman in her late forties who was left by her husband for a younger woman. No longer interested in a romantic attachment of any kind, she assumed that a male neighbor was simply being a friend to her when he came to her home to sit and talk. She didn't notice that increasingly he came over when the children were not at home. When he finally made a pass, after months of sitting around, she was both surprised and offended, since she thought of him as only a friend.

How a woman who has been left will react and adjust to her divorce depends largely on her individual past. If she had supportive parents who were accepting of her throughout childhood, she will stand a better chance of picking up the pieces and starting a new life successfully than the woman who felt that one or both of her parents had rejected her in some way as a child and now relives the old trauma when a husband leaves.

Some women who have been left maintain a suspicious, negative attitude toward men. If they find the phone rings a lot with calls from men, they will turn all suitors down. For such women, the calls alone serve as an ego boost so they do not have to resort to promiscuity to prove their desirability.

Suspicious, hurt women often look for what is wrong with a man rather than what is right with him.

Divorced Women of all kinds commonly fall into the trap of looking for traits in new men opposite to those they found objectionable in their husbands. For example, if a woman was married to a belligerent tyrant, she will search for a more meek, compliant man. If the husband was lazy, she will look for someone more ambitious.

The pitfall in zeroing in on opposite qualities is that the divorcée in the process forgets to look at the whole man. As a result, she can find herself involved with men who are basically incompatible with her in other important ways. Relationships based only on the fact that the new man has characteristics diametrically opposed to those of the ex-husband rarely work out in the long run.

Many Divorced Women get involved too quickly and want commitment too fast in their early post-divorce relationships. When commitment isn't forthcoming, women like this try to force it, in which case the man starts to run away or the relationship experiences such strains that it falls apart. A breakup as a result of a woman pushing too hard often serves as a catalyst for her. She is able to see for the first time what it is she is really doing—she is so in need of a secure, committed relationship that she is grabbing at practically anyone. Explained one woman, "I was so desperate after Harry left me, I just wanted somebody—anybody. This guy came along. He was a lawyer. He was successful and looked presentable and that made him seem like the right man to me. The fact that he was a womanizer and drank too much was overlooked. All I felt was that I wanted him to be mine. When he wouldn't commit himself in three months, I kept pressuring him until he stopped seeing me altogether. It was then that I sat down and realized that it wasn't him I wanted—it was any man."

Although Divorced Women tend to start searching for a committed relationship soon after the divorce, they rarely are able to achieve anything approaching a sane, stable relationship until after they have worked through their period of anger and grief which can take up to three years. Women who have been the ones to leave their husbands tend to regain their stability sooner than women who have been left. Their egos are less wounded, and they generally divorced after a long period of considering what was wrong with the marriage and what it was they weren't getting out of it.

After the period of grief and rage has passed, women start to look for a new relationship in a more realistic way. Often a new practicality creeps into the divorcée's approach to men. She is no longer looking for the same sense of romance she searched for before her marriage or even perhaps in her early post-divorce relationships.

Grand passion would be nice, but down-to-earth matters are equally important to her. Does he have a good job? Is he presentable? Is his health good? What are the ages of his children? A very attractive man may seem less attractive when the divorceé begins to consider the fact that he has young children and she has teenagers, a sentiment expressed by a woman in therapy. "He is terrific, but he has a two-year-old and a five-year-old. I can't go back to diapers again. He's very attractive, but I can't start raising children over again. I'm tired of it."

Because men tend to be judged in a more realistic way by many divorcées, second marriages frequently turn out to be better than first ones. First ones are often based on romance and illusions. Second ones based on practical considerations are grounded in reality, and therefore are less subject to disillusionment.

When, as happens often in today's world, a divorcée keeps meeting men who are unable to commit themselves to anyone or men who have lots of other personal problems—the "rats and crazies" as one divorcée calls them—she often begins to think longingly of her marriage. A divorcée may tend to forget the rotten parts and remember only the good things; even if she remembers what was bad in the marriage, she nevertheless begins to think it was better than her present life. She yearns for the stability marriage provided. After a few years of not being able to find a suitable relationship, she begins to think, "At least he was committed to me. He was there, and we were married, and my life was in a state of less upheaval and uncertainty."

The longing for stability that overcomes many divorced women sometimes leads them to settle into less than perfect relationships, affairs to which they are not totally committed emotionally. These affairs may go on for years just because they are steady and provide some sense of security. Generally these relationships are with men who have a certain decency and who are kind, if not exciting. But there are other divorcées who maintain an ongoing affair with a rat, because it is a steady relationship even though it has misery built into it.

They would rather put up with the misery than face the uncertainty of life without a man again.

Many divorcées start out their new lives rather naive about men. They have only their premarital experiences to draw upon, and if they married young, these experiences were often limited. When they start dating once more, they find things are different than before. Men turn out to be elusive, or they only want sex. Divorcées tend to get hurt when they are naive, but they quickly learn a lot more about life and men, and divorce becomes a growth process for them.

Unless a divorcée is careful, the man she settles down with may be a psychological duplicate of her husband. It happens time and time again. For example, a woman, previously married to a passive man, will end up with a passive man the second time around, even though he may appear, on the surface, to be different. Or, a woman married to a domineering man will pick another authoritarian man, and so on. Unless a woman learns a lot about herself through introspection or therapy, the chances of her repeating the pattern of her first marriage are very strong. Most people tend to pick those who in some way will provide them with a replay of a past relationship, generally with a parent—as other chapters in this book have pointed out.

The Divorced Woman and Careers

A woman who is already launched on a meaningful career at the time of her divorce, has an easier time of it than the woman who has to scramble to find work to help support herself and perhaps her children.

A woman with a career has confidence that she can take care of herself. She also has something apart from her relationships with men which provides her with pride and satisfaction.

For women who have to settle for low income, low prestige jobs, however, they often see the jobs as tangible proof of the failure of their relationships. If they weren't divorced they wouldn't have to work at such an unsatisfactory job, or if they did, the job would be unimportant—the real spotlight would be on marriage and family.

Women in less than satisfying jobs are frequently angry at their work. The job, of course, is important to them because it brings in a paycheck, but it is looked on with scorn and as a secondary issue. These women are prepared to drop their jobs in a moment if a suitable man shows up who is willing to marry and support them.

There are women, however, who first become serious and ambitious about their work after they are divorced. Without a man to support them, they suddenly take a new interest in work and gain a new respect for their jobs. They begin to buck for promotions, higher salaries and even may attempt to change their careers for other ones that will bring in more income and provide them with a better future.

Other divorcées find themselves frightened and paralyzed. They know they have to find a job, but feel they are unqualified to do anything. Others feel they are too old or too proud to take the kind of beginner's jobs they might get. Programs for displaced homemakers are helping confused, depressed, terrified women assess their talents so that they can sell themselves on the job market and deal with debilitating fears. One woman kept sleeping until noon when she should have been out looking for a job. Another woman spent six months trying to write a resume. Both were using delaying tactics. They really were too frightened to go out and look for a job in earnest.

The marketplace today is full of divorcées. Most of them, unless they have been given large amounts of money in divorce settlements, are hard-working employees. Their work is necessary for their economic survival as well as their emotional well-being.

The Divorced Woman's Relationship With Her Children

The basic nature of a woman's relationship with her children often changes after a divorce. Suddenly, a woman's own needs may come into conflict with those of her children.

A new job may seem more demanding now that she must support her children, and because she is newly determined to make something of herself.

Sometimes she comes home to the children tired, irritable, wishing for just a little time to herself before the children pounce on her with requests, complaints, and demands that they have saved up all day. She may find herself distracted or perfunctory with the children when in the past she gave them her full attention.

Dating once more, the Divorced Woman sometimes feels that the children get in her way. She is always scrambling around for baby-sitters. She finds it hard, sometimes impossible, to accept last minute dates. She can't sleep at a boy friend's at will, and she won't let him sleep over because of the children. Dating is not as she remembers it. She is now encumbered by children and when she is feeling low, the children seem like big encumbrances, even though she is quick to add that she loves her children dearly and wouldn't give them up for anything.

A divorced mother is often full of ambivalences and guilt toward her children. She loves them. She doesn't know what she would do without them, but sometimes she wishes they weren't there so she wouldn't have to work so hard or so she could be freer to live her own life.

The Divorced Woman often feels guilty, because now she must sometimes put her own needs above those of her children. She worries and feels she isn't doing right by them if she goes out a lot, or if she works full time or overtime, or if she has to travel on business.

Generally though, divorced mothers manage to reconcile the pull between their own interests and needs and those of their children by finding rationalizations that make their actions more acceptable. "The children need a father. By going out, I am trying to find one for them." Or, "I am working so that the children can have everything they need."

On the whole, the divorced mother's new preoccupation with herself often works out to the benefit of all. It keeps a woman from being an overinvolved mother.

Older children may try to play a parental role with a divorced mother. They pass judgments. They may openly disapprove of the man their mother is currently seeing. Or, if a child is about to leave for college, the child may approve of any man on the scene at the time. Children at the stage of departure often feel guilty about leaving a divorced mother alone, and they will try to push any man who is around at the time on their mother to alleviate their own guilt. Often younger children will disapprove of any man, no matter who he is. They feel he is taking their mother away from them, or he will replace their father whom they still love.

Divorced mothers too often take what their children have to say about suitors to heart. Many serious romances have never blossomed into marriage because a child openly disapproved of his mother's choice.

It is important for a divorced mother to realize that when children either approve or disapprove of a man, they generally have only their own interests at heart. Mothers should give their children time to air an opinion and listen to them, but a child's opinion should never be a deciding factor in making a final decision about a man—unless there is something obvious that seems to justify the opinion, for example, a man abuses the child psychologically or physically. Certainly it is easier if a child likes a man, but since the child is always seeking to personally benefit in one way or another from his stated judgment, his mother must detach herself, try to see what the child is trying to gain, and then make up her own mind about a man based on his character, his actions, the interaction between them and, of course, the man's willingness to become a stepparent if marriage is being considered.

Divorce is often thought of only in negative terms—as a failure for all concerned. Today many therapists take a more positive approach. They look upon divorce as an expression of growth on a woman's part—she is able to recognize and give up a relationship that is no longer good for her and go on to seek a more rewarding life. It is seen as a step forward.

CHAPTER 16

THE BITCH

Jane is an attractive woman of fifty-three. She has been married to Tim for thirty years. For most of those thirty years, Tim has been miserable. Jane and Tim met through a mutual friend in their home town of Atlanta. Tim thought that Jane was beautiful and bright, and she also seemed nice. Jane married Tim because she knew she was supposed to get married, and he met all her requirements—he came from a well-to-do family, and he had a solid profession. They had a whirlwind courtship. Within four months after their initial meeting, they were married.

Very soon after the marriage, Tim wondered where the sweet girl he had courted had gone. Jane became progressively more critical of everything he did. She flew into violent rages at the least little thing. Despite his growing misgivings, Tim never thought of divorce. Marriage to him was sacred, and he wanted a family more than anything in the world. He felt that maybe with children, Jane would be happier. They had three sons. Jane was fine with the children until they grew to an age when they began to have minds, wishes, and personalities of their own. Then she started to find fault with them, too. As soon as the children reached adolescence, the scenes with Jane became horrendous. They rebelled at her constant criticism, her domination. By the time the eldest child was 16, he became so unruly that he was sent to live with an aunt in New Orleans. The boy refused to return home. Now a young man in his early 30's, he barely talks to his mother. He hangs up on her regularly on the telephone whenever she starts to criticize his lifestyle or the fact that he never comes home. The second son became a drug addict and now lives in a different state. He refuses to see his mother at all. The youngest son is still home but it is open warfare. He and Jane alternate between fighting and not talking to one another for months on end.

Tim feels, rightly, that Jane has driven two sons away from the family forever. He welcomes the presence of the third child at home because he provides some relief to the atmosphere. Tim finds being alone with Jane a poisonous experience. Their home is a torture chamber for him. She is forever pointing out to him his shortcomings, the things he does and has done wrong, and how inept and stupid he is in her eyes.

Jane is clearly a Bitch.

So is Miranda. Miranda has never been married. At 38 she has been through a series of relationships that have all ended badly. Her last boyfriend walked out on her a short while ago when he discovered that she had been sleeping with an old boy friend throughout their relationship. She had flaunted other affairs before he found out about this one. It wasn't only her sexual infidelity that drove him away. Miranda was arrogant and contemptuous of him, and she had a temper that would flare up with little provocation. When she felt she wasn't getting her way, there were angry confrontations and accusations. When arguing, she was abusive. On those occasions when she felt like having sex and he didn't, she flew into uncontrollable rages and told him he wasn't a real man. In addition, she was always trying to teach him how to live properly, to train him to be a better person. Her attitude was that she was superior to him and everyone else.

Bitches such as these women have been portrayed in the arts. Mildred in Somerset Maugham's *Of Human Bondage* was a Bitch. So was Marlene Dietrich in *The Blue Angel* and Kate in Shakespeare's *The Taming of the Shrew*.

Bitches are the stuff of which bad dreams are made. They are hostile, vindictive women always intent on proving themselves right and everyone else wrong. They bully, threaten, explode, attack, humiliate, criticize, blame, judge, punish. It's ongoing. One never knows what will set them off.

Some Bitches are miserable to everybody, but more often,

a Bitch is hostile only to men. She is able to remain cordial and friendly with women. Some Bitches, like Jane, don't show their true colors until they become wives. Others, like Miranda, are bitchy with their men as soon as the relationship begins.

The Bitch's basic attitude is one of suspicion. She regards the world as a hostile place full of potential enemies out to prove that she's a fool or to do her in. She is continually misinterpreting things that people say or do to fit her view of the world. She is always distorting and seeing slights, rejections, affronts, bad intentions or attacks. She defends herself by counterattacking, or even attacking first.

Her temper is vicious and unbridled. Nothing can stop her once she gets started. Hell hath no fury like the Bitch who always feels the threat of scorn. She is never repentant, never admits that she could be the slightest bit wrong. Her aim is to win whatever way she can, to always prove herself better than others, to put people in their places, to never allow herself to be taken advantage of, to never be the underdog or loser. She is a professional blamer. Anything that goes wrong is someone else's fault. She can criticize others with impunity, but others can't criticize her. She is maddening to deal with.

A Bitch is annoyed when anyone else enjoys himself. Without being conscious of it, she envies happiness, joy, and fun in others. It's a personal rebuke to her, because she can't feel these things herself and, therefore, she does her best to spoil it for others.

Inwardly she is a very frightened, extremely vulnerable, helpless woman and her way of dealing with this is to make herself invulnerable to others and to always appear strong. Hostility to her is a show of strength. She hates herself and so she finds fault, things to hate in others. She also feels unloved and unlovable and because of this she feels she does not have to cater to others. They hate her anyway so why should she worry about how they will react to her? She secretly hankers after love but is afraid of tenderness and dependence. Relationships for her are fraught with terror and so she keeps those close to her at fist's length.

Why a Bitch Is the Way She Is

Bitches almost always have come from very emotionally deprived backgrounds. Physical brutality and verbal fights were often everyday occurrences in their homes. Parents were often selfish or insensitive, unable to give the child love, tenderness, respect, attention.

Laura and Stella are two typical cases.

Laura, an only child, grew up with an alcoholic father who frequently became violent and beat both her and her mother whenever he was drunk. She learned in this environment to view men as brutal, abusive, unpredictable. Today, as an adult, she is totally suspicious and frightened of men. Hostility is her defense against the threat she feels they pose.

Stella, an attractive woman of twenty-nine, grew up in a very impoverished household with a violent father and an angry, rejecting mother. There were continual fights between her parents. When she was young, she found out from her mother that she had been an "accident." Her mother had only married her father because she had been pregnant. From this, Stella deduced that her mother really hated her, and because of Stella, her mother remained a prisoner to her abusive husband. She felt rejected and unloved by her mother, and afraid of her father who would become unpredictably angry or violent. Nevertheless, Stella felt dependent on her mother. She was the only one Stella could count on.

At the age of sixteen, Stella became pregnant by a man who disappeared on hearing the news. She was determined to have her baby anyway. Lonely, unloved Stella felt the child would be someone she could love and who would love her in return. Unfortunately her baby died at birth, and she felt this to be yet another abandonment. From that time on, Stella was a seething mass of hostility. Now she reads into the most innocent remark or circumstance, threats of being rejected, hurt or abandoned, threats which she defends herself against by attacking the offenders. Although she is suspicious and hostile at all times, her full bitchiness with men doesn't come out until she gets into a close relationship. Then the threat of abandonment and rejection becomes unbearable. The moment she feels that she needs someone and is dependent upon him she becomes extremely hostile and punitive which, of course turns her relationships into self-fulfilling prophesies. She fears men will leave her and they do because of her mean personality.

Some Bitches developed their hatred and suspicion of men from being sexually abused as children. Gloria was continually molested by an uncle who lived with her widowed mother throughout her young life. She came to regard men as brutes and women as their victims. Her everpresent hostility is her way of guarding against becoming a man's victim.

Generally in the background of Bitches is the view of one parent as dominant—the attacker—the other as a victim. Generally the mother is seen as the abused one, but sometimes it will be the other way around.

One Bitch grew up as a poor little rich girl, in a wealthy home where she was totally disregarded by a very narcissistic, self-absorbed and hostile mother who was only interested in seeing that her little girl was well dressed. She left her in the care of maids. Her father was the only one who showed her any love or held her affectionately.

She witnessed her mother verbally abuse her father and saw that she was cold and unaffectionate towards him. She was aware, too, that her mother was having an affair with another man. She was angry that her father did not stop her mother from being so cruel, rejecting and selfish.

Today, her own behavior with men is a replica of her mother's treatment of her father, but she is also acting the way she feels her father should have acted with her mother. She disciplines men and puts them in their place. She identifies with her father. She would rather be a man than a woman.

Many Bitches are ambivalent about being females. Although they are often fearful of men, they also think of men as powerful in contrast to women, and they envy men as a result. In their assaults on men, they are in a sense trying to take their power from them.

Another way of understanding Bitches' behavior is to realize that they approach life with the feeling that they have been abused, and are entitled to retribution for the injuries done to them in the past.

The taunts, criticisms and provocations of the Bitch can also be viewed as a testing kind of behavior. Bitches are always trying to see how much they can get away with. This accounts for the fact that the Bitch's hostility escalates within a relationship. The more she is allowed to get away with, the more contempt she has for the man, and the more bitchy she becomes. It is as if she is testing her lover or husband to see if he will stand up to her and "be a man" and to see if he will continue to love her despite her terrible behavior.

If a man refuses to put up with her bitchiness, it is quite possible she will keep herself in check, finding outlets for her hostility elsewhere.

The Kinds of Men Bitches Attract

One can only react to Bitches in two ways. Either reject and run away from them, or attempt to pacify them. The kind of men who hang around with a Bitch for any length of time are often passive men, kind and gentle by nature. As husbands, they are generally unable to deal with their wife's hostility in a direct way. Instead of doing battle, or putting their foot down, they remove themselves from the battlefield. They spend long hours at work, they moonlight on a second job, they go into the office on weekends. These acts frequently infuriate the Bitch so she redoubles her attacks, which makes the husband stay away even more.

One man married to a Bitch makes sure their weekends are full of social engagements with other people because he knows his wife is on her best behavior with the rest of the world and is only a Bitch in the bosom of her family. This kind of dichotomy in behavior is common to Bitches.

Bitches' husbands are often very traditional men who regard marriage as something one enters into for life, for better or for worse.

Sometimes a Bitch's husband or boy friend is a masochist, who because of inner guilt likes the punishment she metes out.

Other men feel themselves to be so undesirable and have so many insecurities that they are afraid no other woman will find them attractive if they leave the Bitch. They want and need a relationship with a woman, and any relationship, even one with a Bitch, is better than none at all. They feel, too, that a family structure, even if it houses this vituperative woman, makes them look and feel more normal than they think they really are.

Sometimes the man involved with a Bitch has a similar kind of parent in his background. One man suffered under a despotic, nasty father as a child, and now he suffers again with his bitchy wife.

Not to be discounted when considering why the husbands of Bitches stay with them is what the late Eric Berne described as the IWFY game—If It Weren't for You. The Bitch's husband can avoid his own problems by concentrating on his difficult wife instead.

Throughout their relationship, the Bitch's man retains the fantasy that she is going to change someday and then everything will be fine.

It is interesting that as nasty as these women are, they don't turn their husbands off sexually, even though the Bitch will frequently use the withdrawal of sex or unreasonable sexual demands as part of her arsenal against her husband. The Bitch remains sexually attractive to her husband because he often thinks of the sexual act as an aggressive one. The only way to get at this Bitch is to "have" her.

Bitches and Friendships

Bitches are generally able to maintain friendships with women without the hostility invoked by men. Even if the Bitch had a mother she viewed as a victim, it is a sunnier image than she has of men as personified by an abusive father. Thus, if the Bitch had a more positive role model in her mother than her father, she will be more favorably inclined toward women. Women may also be valued more by Bitches simply because they are the opposite to men, those miserable, frightening, hurtful brutes.

The Bitch as Mother

Bitches who are bitchy only to men will be much more hostile and critical with their sons than their daughters. But Bitches who are universally hostile will spread their nastiness in equal measure to daughters as well as sons.

Later in life, her son will often try to find someone who is as unlike his mother as possible—a woman who will become the warm, supportive mother he never had. A fair number of Bitches' sons become homosexuals or never marry.

Daughters of Bitches often end up as women who were so appalled by their mother's behavior that they run into another kind of problem as adults. They find they are unable to express anger at anything, even when it is justified.

The Bitch at Work

If the Bitch has a career, she carries the feeling that she is abused into the office with her. Bitches generally resent having to work. They look down on work as something beneath them, and they are angry to have to be humiliated in this way. If they are working because of divorce or because a husband doesn't earn enough money, their anger increases, specifically at the man for putting them in such a position.

The Bitch's resentful attitude is felt by those around her in the office. If the Bitch ends up being a boss, she will be hated because she is critical, never expresses appreciation and is generally unpleasant to those who work under her. You will hear her described in this way: "She's a bitch!"

How a Bitch Can Help Herself

Bitches are really terrified, fragile, vulnerable women who hide their fear and weakness behind a show of strength.

If you recognize yourself as a Bitch, and are able to say, as one did recently to a therapist: "I am a dispenser of pain," you may be ready for growth and change that will make you into a more lovable and loving person. You must recognize the fears and rage from your emotionally deprived past and deal with them in a less destructive way than by always attacking or humiliating others.

Your basic problems are similar to those of the Exploiters discussed in Chapter 6. See page 97 for suggestions to help you move into a more satisfying way of life.

CHAPTER 17

THE TECHNICOLOR LADY

When Terry's three year romance ended, she got behind the wheel of her car and drove it straight into her lover's house.

When Debbie's boy friend didn't want her to take a shower with him, she went into his living room and smashed some windows. When he came running, in response to the sound of shattering glass, she stood in front of one of the broken windows in a draft of viciously cold air and threatened to throw herself through.

When Brenda and her husband started quarreling in the car while she was driving them back from a weekend in the country, she stopped the car with a screech, ordered her husband out and left him in the middle of a freeway, miles from home.

Terry, Debbie, and Brenda are three Technicolor Ladies, women who live by their emotions and act them out in moments of high drama.

Technicolor Ladies fly out of rooms, angrily opening and shutting doors so forcefully that the whole room shakes. They rush out of restaurants in the middle of dinner, furious with lover or husband. In reaction to something a man has said or done, they will suddenly turn to ice, yet a minute ago they were all warm and loving. They use telephones like umbilical cords, calling a man several times a day when all is going well, and every half hour all through the night with complaints and threats when they are in a stew.

Technicolor Ladies are all emotion—they blow hot, they blow cold, they hold nothing in, and they are at any moment liable to get angry or hurt and erupt into scenes of monumental proportions. High comedy, melodrama, tragedy—when Technicolor Ladies take to the stage, they are capable of anything, even if it causes embarrassment to themselves or their loved ones.

One striking-looking fashion model having a disagreement with her husband, became more and more agitated. Finally, she flung open the window and marched three stories down the fire escape into the crowded street below. This wouldn't have been so terrible except that at the time she was wearing only a pair of blue jeans and was otherwise topless. The furor caused by the sight of her beautiful breasts was enough to attract a policeman who covered her and escorted her home.

Cops are no strangers to the antics of Technicolor Ladies. On occasion these women are even capable of violence in their rages.

A children's book illustrator in Chicago was asked by her boy friend to leave his apartment after they had quarreled. She refused. He kept asking. Finally, he pushed her to the door and opened it, whereupon she swung her handbag and smashed him across the face with it. He slapped her face in return. She rushed out of the apartment screaming and sobbing.

Fifteen minutes later a policeman was on the telephone telling the man that a complaint had been sworn out against him, and would he please come down to the police station? When he arrived at the police station, she was kept in another room. He wasn't allowed to see her, the police sergeant explained, because she was afraid he would attack her again.

Since his lip was by now discolored and swollen from the handbag attack, he pointed to it and asked the sergeant if he had observed any wounds or bruises on her. The sergeant admitted he hadn't. The policeman spoke to the woman and finally she agreed to drop the charges. They both went home.

The man went to sleep. He was awakened by two telephone calls in the middle of the night from her. Annoyed, but joking, he told her that if he had known he was going to get arrested he would have given her a real reason and hit her harder.

She hung up in a fury. He went back to sleep. Soon the police were on the phone again, telling him that she had asked for protection because he had threatened her. The man explained his joking statement.

The policeman begged both of them, "Promise me you won't speak to each other any more—at least tonight."

What often triggers the liveliest scenes of Technicolor Ladies is rejection, real or fancied. They react strongly at the merest hint of it. One new romance was progressing splendidly, with the Technicolor Lady and her new love talking to each other five or six times a day from their respective offices. At the end of one afternoon call, she said, "I have to hang up, but I'll call you this evening." He explained he wasn't going to be home; he had something else to take care of. Immediately, she became icy and hung up abruptly. She felt rejected and suspected that he was going to see another woman. "The irony of it was," he explained, "that I was going to see another woman. It was someone I had been seeing before I met her and I was going to tell her, 'Good-bye'."

Technicolor Ladies are more sensitive than other people to rejection. So much so that two New York psychiatrists, Dr. Michael Liebowitz and Dr. Donald Klein, who describe them as hysteroid dysphorics, have called it the "hallmark of their personality." These women have an "extreme intolerance to personal rejection, with a particular vulnerability to loss of romantic attachment."

Technicolor Ladies are normally ebullient, dramatic, outgoing, and expansive. They flirt and act seductively with men. They are very attractive creatures to many people. But there is a hidden side to their personalities. They suffer from frequent bouts of depression. When they are happy, they are flying high, but when they get depressed, they go to the other extreme—they crash. This reaction can be to a real or fancied slight, or a clear-cut rejection. They feel worthless, sad, hopeless. This is frequently accompanied by a craving for sweets, general overeating, sense of paralytic inertia or fatigue. They also often take to their beds, shutting out the world by sleeping too much or just lying there with eyes shut. A Technicolor Lady explains that she simply pulls her red quilt, bought for that purpose, over her head until she feels better. Technicolor Ladies can in their depressions, sleep and eat. This same Technicolor Lady always keeps a stash of cookies to nibble on when bad times strike. Threats and minor attempts at suicide are common to Technicolor Ladies, but successful suicides are rare.

The depressions which occur periodically in Technicolor Ladies' lives can impair their normal functioning. Writers stop writing, office workers call in sick and take a day or two off from work, hair doesn't get washed, housework doesn't get done, valium or uppers get popped, pot is smoked. Self-medication with drugs or alcohol is common.

Luckily, depressed periods don't last long. They are repetitive and occur frequently but they are over within a matter of hours or days. Rarely do they last beyond a week. However, with continued rejection or if a husband or lover abandons them, the period of depression may persist.

A sudden, attractive invitation or a word of approval can generally coax a Technicolor Lady out of the blues, or at least cheer her up temporarily.

When Technicolor Ladies finally snap out of their depressions, and clean up the cookie crumbs and empty ice cream cartons from their eating binges, they are faced with what is often another chronic problem. They find they have put on a few pounds. Now they have to diet, because they are generally concerned about their appearances. An ongoing struggle to maintain a slim figure is an integral part of many Technicolor Ladies' lives.

Technicolor Ladies, actresses that they are, are also applause junkies. To shore up self-esteem that is at worst terrible and at best shaky, they need constant approval, attention, and praise from others. Some need it from everyone, others need it only from men. In their relationships they tend to be self-centered, manipulative, and demanding. They will try all means of coercion to get what they want, including threats of leaping from windows, repeated phone calls hammering at an issue, or frequent walkouts so the man will make the first move toward reconciliation. These women are active in their relationships. They are willing to call a man, issue invitations, invite themselves over, ask for whatever it is they crave.

Men find Technicolor Ladies to be intrusive, demanding,

and volatile, as well as colorful, warm, vibrant, fun, and
attractive.

Applause and approval can make a Technicolor Lady feel
so energized that she verges on giddiness or hyperactivity at
times. She is always preoccupied with romance; when the
possibility of love comes her way, she is extremely optimistic. The beginnings of her affairs are generally marked by
overidealization of the man involved and the high that
accompanies the first flush of romance. She wants to stay in
touch with her love with lots of phone contact, touching,
hand-holding, and love-making.

If a man really goes all out for a Technicolor Lady, caters
to her and displays unwavering approval and devotion, he
may be unaware for a while of the basic anger that is built
into her personality. He doesn't see the rage that comes out in
volatile arguments and scenes, because he has done nothing
yet to provoke it. A man can move in with a Technicolor
Lady, even marry her, and if he has had a smooth, adoring,
uninterrupted courtship, he will not be aware of the full
ramifications of her vivid personality style until later. He
may think of her as emotional and colorful but not as
someone who is demanding and hysterical. Sooner or later
though, her rage comes out when she doesn't get what she
wants. She usually wants exclusivity, respect, deference,
and to be kept on a pedestal. It can happen at any stage in
a relationship, whenever she begins to feel frustrated about
getting something she expected or hoped for. She also
smashes her idol at that moment. The man, initially so
overidealized in her fantasy of him, suddenly is seen as
a worm.

Why the Technicolor Lady
Is the Way She Is

There are several varieties of Technicolor Ladies—some
better, some worse. The worst ones, most disorganized in
their thinking, most demanding in their relationships, are
stuck at an early stage of fusion with their mothers. They
smother those around them with their exaggerated needs for

mothering and nurturing. They turn to both women and men to satisfy their needs.

One Technicolor Lady was extremely disoriented by the death of a cousin. Although she could manage to look up a friend's phone number, she could not manage to look up the phone number of an airline ticket office to make arrangements to go to the funeral. Her friend had to make the arrangements for her.

A sense of being overwhelmed and unable to focus often besets Technicolor Ladies who are never, even in their best moments, logical or clear-headed thinkers. They operate on intuition and emotion. They often have trouble concentrating, and do badly under stress. A woman applying for a job she desperately wanted, had to work in the office for a day as a tryout. She reported to a friend that she was sure she had blown the deal. "I couldn't think straight the whole time I was there."

Some Technicolor Ladies are hung up on their fathers rather than their mothers. Their fathers did not give them enough attention, love, or approval, and they expect the men in their lives to make up for their father's sins or live up to their image of the way their father should have been. This type of Technicolor Lady generally is attracted to father images—men who have status or power.

Since men never are able to live up to their expectations and fantasies, Technicolor Ladies have trouble in relationships. Sooner or later they become frustrated and angry at husbands or lovers for their failures.

The Kinds of Men
Technicolor Ladies Attract

Men who are bedazzled by Technicolor Ladies are often part of the theatrical profession—playwrights, directors, set designers, composers, actors. They are intrigued by the dramatic quality of these women. They are often Technicolor Men, the counterparts emotionally to Technicolor Women. The scenes that can ensue when a Technicolor Man gets together with a Technicolor Lady are worthy of Oscars.

They love about each other what others might hate or be embarrassed by. For example, one Technicolor Lady was told by her Technicolor Man that he didn't want to have dinner with her that night. He wanted to eat instead with some old friends. In a fury, she called another man and invited him out to dinner. Quite by accident she and her escort chose the same restaurant that her boy friend and his friends had chosen; they all arrived simultaneously. She swept by her boy friend without a glance, and ate without looking at him, even though he was only two tables away. He went by her table on his way to the men's room without acknowledging her. Instead of being embarrassed or annoyed at what had happened, they both enjoyed every minute of it. They called each other the next day and reconciled simply to be able to talk about the incident.

Rather than hook up with a Technicolor Man, a Technicolor Lady will often settle down with her opposite, a dour, logical, serious man with great control over his emotions. They are each initially attracted to the other because of what they lack in themselves. In these marriages the husband eventually feels that he is overshadowed by her more vivid, exuberant personality. He sees her histrionics, her need for attention and praise as a form of control. He appears to suffer her hysterical attacks stoically but resists passively. He fights back by withdrawing emotionally and withholding signs of affection, which, of course, drives her crazy. They often end up in a covert struggle for power.

The kind of man who quickly leaves a Technicolor Lady is the one who feels her histrionics and angry scenes are a reflection on himself. Not recognizing what her basic personality style is all about, he imagines himself to have failed the Technicolor Lady and he gets out. Other men are driven away by her constant, intrusive need for attention and admiration.

If the Technicolor Lady ends up getting a divorce, it will be a spectacular one with public accusations and counteraccusations. If there is enough money involved, famous lawyers will be hired and every lurid detail will be reported in the press.

No matter what caused the divorce, Technicolor Ladies

almost always feel as if they were the victims. They tend to think of their ex-husbands as bastards.

Technicolor Ladies go through many short-lived, tumultuous relationships. At the end of each one, they crash, coming out of their depression to frantically search for a new or additional relationship.

The Technicolor Lady at Work

There are many Technicolor Ladies who never live up to their potentials. They start projects and jobs enthusiastically, but then run out of steam, feeling that there hasn't been enough praise or recognition accorded them. They often become embroiled in office romances. Sometimes Technicolor Ladies suffer from chronic unemployment. They find it hard to search for a new job for fear of being rejected.

There are however, Technicolor Ladies with very successful careers. These women do well in jobs that allow them to use their talent for histrionics directly or they are in a field where their dramatic style will at least be accepted. There are Technicolor Ladies who are artists, writers, and women in the theater, film and tv industries.

The Technicolor Lady invariably wanted to be an actress as she was growing up.

The Technicolor Lady as Mother

Technicolor Ladies often are good mothers; they can be warm, open, and nurturing.

If they maintain a fantasy of a perfect father that all men must fit into, then, however, they may create problems for sons. They expect a son to fit into a preconceived image of male perfection and he eventually begins to feel that he has failed his mother. He hasn't lived up to her ideals.

Technicolor Ladies and Society

The style of Technicolor Ladies is encouraged, in part, by a society which sees women as immature, overly emotional, hysterical creatures and not only accepts, but expects such behavior from them.

As in the case of other personality syndromes, such as Nurses, Chameleons, Martyrs and others, the antics of Technicolor Ladies are exaggerated, out-of-control versions of what is considered "feminine" behavior in our world.

How a Technicolor Lady Can Help Herself

Technicolor Ladies can be bright, funny, quick and colorful creatures who are delightful to have as friends. They are effusive, with exaggerated opinions and reactions. They describe things dramatically—they love them or hate them. As a result they are never dull to have around. They add spice to life.

If you are a Technicolor Lady, you may want to change from an infantile, easily swayed, emotional female into a more mature woman, one who is less explosive, less at the mercy of passing whims, more in control of your own life. You need to have a stronger sense of your own persona than you sometimes feel now. To do this, you should concentrate on understanding how you think and react, and learn to modify your behavior.

As a Technicolor Lady, you think differently from many other people. Your world is not one of sharply observed facts, and well-developed judgments. It is a romanticized, sometimes sentimental world. You react and judge in terms of immediate impressions. Your attention is easily distracted. You are suggestible and easily carried away by things that momentarily strike a chord with you.

You must learn to reflect upon your diffused impressions and reactions. What is only a half-formed impression in someone else takes over your whole being. You react immediately to dimly perceived notions and initial emotions without the intermediate process of reflection that characterizes other people. Your ideas should be fully integrated into your thought processes before they are acted upon.

You must learn to think before you act. Imagine that in your head there is a little door that leads into your brain. When you feel rejected or enthusiastic or annoyed, make those emotions pass through the door into your brain where you can shape them and make them truly yours before acting upon them. In this way, you will feel that you can control your actions rather than feeling, as you often do now, that your actions frequently do not quite belong to you. You no longer need to feel you are "possessed" by your explosions. You can learn to mean everything you say or do.

Being in control a good deal of the time should make you feel more powerful and less helpless or overwhelmed than you do now. It will also make you an easier person to live with and love.

CHAPTER 18

THE SUPERWOMAN

Here is a typical day's schedule for Laura, a thirty-six year old career woman with two children:

4:00 A.M. Get up.

4:30-5:30 Jog for an hour with husband.

5:30 Shower and dress.

6:00 Prepare breakfast for family including freshly squeezed orange juice, homemade whole wheat pancakes, bacon, freshly brewed coffee.

7:15 Clean breakfast dishes. Select recipes to be used for dinner. Set table for dinner. Make homemade fruit juice Popsicles for children's after-school snack.

7:30 Put children into car pool to go to school.

7:45 Catch train to work. Use commuting time to work on report.

9:00 A.M.-5:00 P.M. Work non-stop with a fifteen minute break for a sandwich and coffee at desk.

5:30 Catch train back home. Use commuting time to read research papers.

5:45-6:00 Jog again.

6:30 Prepare dinner of homemade soup, homemade biscuits, chicken with cream sauce, baked potatoes, fresh peas and carrots, homemade applesauce, freshly brewed coffee and milk. While preparing dinner, help children with homework.

7:30 Clean dinner dishes, tidy up kitchen. Set out dishes for tomorrow's breakfast.

8:00 Read professional journals.

10:00 Bed time for the whole family.

On Saturday, Laura devotes the whole day to grocery shopping, household errands, house cleaning, taking children to soccer games or swimming lessons. On at least one Saturday every month she also prepares an elaborate dinner and invites friends over.

On Sunday, Laura teaches Sunday school.

There is not one minute, except when she is sleeping, that Laura is not doing something, and doing it well.

Laura is a Superwoman, one of a new breed of women who feel they must and can do everything from being successful career women, superior wives and mothers, to outstanding homemakers. Their aim is to do as much as they can with as little outside help as possible. They embrace all the roles of women. The only real problem that causes Superwoman to complain is that there are only twenty-four hours in the day.

A Superwoman's demands on herself are extraordinary and she makes everyone around her feel inferior and guilty because they aren't as efficient and get tired doing only half of what she packs into a day. Superwomen are a living reproach to the rest of the world. They are often resented by other women as a result.

The Machine

Although there is more than one type of Superwoman, the most super of the bunch is the Machine.

Laura is one of the Machines. She, like all Machines, is a perfectionist. Her reports at the corporation where she works are always on time, meticulously done, cogent, readable. Her research is scrupulous. She never falls behind in her correspondence. Her desk is always neat. She is in perpetual motion all day, answering phones, dictating, hurrying up and down hallways, going to and from conferences. Coffee breaks and lengthy lunch hours, unless they are for business purposes, are not for her. She wolfs down a sandwich because she needs nourishment to keep going, then hurries on to her next task. She generally arrives at work earlier than anyone else and at the end of the day, she is as perky as she was at the beginning of it.

The Machine's standards at home are as rigid as at the office. There is never an ash tray out of place, a dish in the sink. Her carpets are always vacuumed. If she sees dirt or a spot on anything, she attacks it immediately. No dust mars the surfaces of her furniture. Meals for her family are always full course affairs, well-balanced, delicious, and homemade. The Machine rarely uses convenience foods.

Her life is run according to a tight, carefully planned schedule. She makes lists for everything. She goes to sleep at the same time every night and wakes up at the same hour every day, even on weekends. A Machine has a tendency to underrate the value of sleep and she will occasionally get up earlier in order to accomplish more.

Anything that interrupts the regular schedule of the Machine, such as an illness, or something another person might regard as merely a nuisance, such as the breakdown of a washing machine, is regarded by her as a catastrophe. It throws the Machine off kilter.

A Machine can never be only wife or mother or worker. Her life seems in tune only if it encompasses every possible role for a woman today. To do it all and do it well is seen as one of her accomplishments.

Performance is the only thing the Machine really values. Achievement is her ongoing goal. But she rarely can enjoy any of her successes in life. One achievement is merely the springboard for another. Machines are never content. There is a restless quality about them. They are always searching for something else to do. Life for them is a constant struggle to prove to themselves and the world just how strong and capable they really are. They overcompensate for the fact that unconsciously they feel quite weak.

As they go through their paces, there is little feeling. The tasks in their routines are attended to automatically. If they ever feel tired, they regard it as a sign of failure. They are rather cold individuals with little empathy or psychological understanding of their co-workers, husbands, or children. Machines generally have little imagination and few of the skills to enable them to relate to people intimately or well. They are practical and efficient, and as a result, they are often wooden, blunt, untactful, and plodding. They can be boring.

The Machine's communications with her family deal with practical matters—not what one is feeling or thinking. Emotions are foreign territory to her. She is functional, rather than winning, charming or concerned. Machines are the doers of the world, not the feelers or interactors.

Their homes are a reflection of their basic values. They are yet another achievement in the sense that they are stylishly decorated with every detail perfect. They are immaculately kept. Not an ash tray is out of place, not a pillow sags. Diplomas, plaques, and awards are displayed on the walls. The homes of Machines may be impressive in terms of style, but they are also cold and uninviting, without a cozy corner anywhere. Visitors are afraid to crush a cigarette into an ash tray, or move a chair an inch closer to someone.

The Machine's career has to be one with high status. Money without prestige would not do. There are a lot of female doctors and scientists among the Machines.

One of the reasons the Machine is bogged down in tasks is that she finds it impossible to delegate authority. She must do everything herself whether it is cleaning the kitchen or preparing a report. Nobody can be trusted to do the job as well as she can. Besides, she takes enormous pride in being able to handle things on her own.

No matter how much the Machine does, she never feels overwhelmed. But she doesn't feel contented either.

Everything is approached as a duty. No matter how much she does, she never feels capable enough. Like Ole Man River, she just keeps rolling along.

A Machine chooses her profession in a cold and calculating way and not because she likes a certain line of work. A prestige career is a ruling criterion, or a career that runs in the family. Machines are not aware of it, but because their emotions are left out of their career choices, they often end up hating the work they do, even though they do it successfully.

The Kinds of Men Machines Attract

The Machine often marries very early in life. Her husband is one of her earliest achievements. Many Machines are married to men they met in high school or the early years of college. Their degrees were earned while married, their children born between exams; births are always carefully timed to create the least disruption of work.

Most Machines marry men like themselves, ambitious male Machines, very absorbed in their own careers.

Machine couples use their living quarters as service stations, places to eat, sleep, refuel for the next day's endeavors, rather than places to relax and enjoy each other's company.

Even if the Machine's husband didn't start out in life to be as obsessive, authoritarian, and performance-oriented as she is, he often is turned into another Machine.

One woman, now in her mid-thirties, met her husband in her sophomore year of college. He was a handsome, easygoing athlete—the star of the school's basketball team. Machines are determined women and once this woman made up her mind, she knew she would marry him, no matter what. Both fathers objected to the romance because they were business rivals. To overcome their objections to marriage, the Machine became pregnant. She was then allowed to marry. Within a few short years she managed to turn this easygoing boy into an opinionated, ruthlessly ambitious professional who joined her in making achievement their only god.

A man, to survive very long in a Machine's affections must be a hell-bent winner. Occasionally a Machine can guess wrong. She may marry an achiever in a field that requires more imagination than hers, for example, a creative field like advertising or television. A greater emotional connection to life might make a husband get fed up with the mechanical Machine sooner or later. He would like to laugh and relax a little. If he is unable to live with an automaton, he may leave her.

The Machine is rarely able to understand her role in destroying a relationship. The fact that she is cold, plodding, and quite inhuman escapes her. She doesn't see virtue in any other way of being. In her own mind, she goes down her list of accomplishments. She mentally checks off all her degrees, her titles, her efficiency as a housewife and mother, and she concludes that since she is so accomplished, the breakup must be his fault.

If the Machine is forced to look for a new husband, she

does so systematically. It's another chore to be approached in
an organized manner. She makes a list of all the possible
ways of meeting men—and goes through them one by one.
The men she meets are evaluated according to a checklist.
Are they tall enough? Is their career the right one? Do they
have a defect, like a stutter or a limp? Men are selected not
because they appeal to the Machine on a personal level but
because they have enough of the right qualities on her list of
requirements. Men get discarded for the same reason—they
don't have enough of the prescribed qualifications.

The Machine and Female Friends

When the Machine chooses women friends they must meet
certain requirements. They must be accomplished women.
Since she is dimly aware that she may be lacking in some of
the social graces, she may choose friends because they are
more gracious in a social setting, and therefore, will be assets
to her.

Her friendships are never composed of exchanged confidences. She issues communiqués from the front—what she is
doing on her job, what her children are doing.

The Machine as Mother

As a mother the Machine is a ruthless pusher. Her children
are given the insistent message that they too must be achiev-
ers. She insists on straight A's in school work, and extracur-
ricular activities that will get them admitted to Harvard,
Princeton, or Yale. Machines often try to channel their children into their own careers. Doctors for example, may want
their sons and daughters to become physicians also. Machines
often meet resistance on this score, however. Although they
generally do manage to turn out children who are success-
oriented, their sons and daughters often choose careers that
are different from the parent's. It's a way of preserving their
own sense of identity apart from these overdemanding,
overcontrolling parents.

Why the Machine
Is the Way She Is

A woman who is a Machine frequently had as model for her restless drive and ambition a father who was an outstanding success in his field and who expected his children to excel, too. This father was accorded respect for his accomplishments rather than for his human qualities, which were in short supply. He was cold, authoritarian, and demanding rather than kind, loving, or warm. Generally he treated his wife as an inferior whose purpose was to serve him and make his life comfortable. He was often critical of her performance as a housewife. As a result, the Machine learned to value those things that made others respect her father—his efficiency and productivity—and to turn them into her own goals. She found, too, that high achievements netted her the approval of her father whose attention she sought. Although her efforts to excel were always applauded, the young Machine found ultimately that she could never do enough to please her father. He demanded bigger and better successes, a pattern that she internalized in her adult life, making her reach for more and more but which also left her insecure about her abilities.

The Machine, as a child, found herself in competition with her mother who was also vying for the father's approval. The Machine became determined to be a better housewife than her mother, one with whom her father could find no fault. In this way she became the superprofessional, supermother, superhousekeeper who values only accomplishments. Happiness or other human qualities were not deemed important in her original family.

In her family, the Machine often was involved in a lot of sibling rivalry. The achieving parent would pit the children against one another to see who could accomplish more. This competition with brothers and sisters often persists into adult life.

While most Machines are supermothers, going to Little League games, accompanying their children to the doctor and dentist, attending school plays, sometimes you find one who will leave most of the tasks attached to parenthood to the father.

Such is the case of Glenda, a high-powered stockbroker. Her father was a well-known surgeon—an arrogant, demanding, brilliant man. During her childhood, Glenda's mother became an alcoholic. Glenda was left in the care of maids who would frequently depart because they couldn't stand Glenda's father. Because Glenda had no model for motherhood and the children grew up as best they could on their own, she now leaves most of the extra parental duties to her husband. He is the one who has to take days off to take them to the dentist. And he is the one who goes to see the daughter play in the school orchestra, or watches the son pitch for the baseball team. Glenda feels she has too many other career obligations.

When the System Fails

The Machine, always pushing herself, always aiming for greater heights, never resting, never content, faces one grave danger: Like all overworked machines, she may break down.

Women who are Machines frequently and without warning snap. One day they are bustling around, going about their various duties efficiently; the next they are in an almost catatonic depression, unable to rouse themselves from their beds.

They then invariably end up hospitalized or in the care of a psychiatrist. Doctors can generally bring them out of their paralyzing depressions with anti-depressant drugs, but the Machine rarely gains any lasting insight into her own behavior. Instead, she marvels at this period in her life as something strange but inexplicable. "It couldn't have been a breakdown!" she protests, and soon she is back to her usual unending round of activities.

Often a depressed state, which may be suicidal in nature, occurs in reaction to losing a job. One woman, the victim of a large-scale cutback in her industry, ended up in the hospital soon after losing her job. She kept explaining to the psychiatrist that she was upset because her husband would no longer love her if she couldn't bring home a paycheck. It wasn't true, but it was what she believed.

Machines equate their value as people with their abilities to produce. Without a job or a paycheck, the Machine feels lost, unlovable, worthless. Even though the unemployed Machine retains her other roles, being only wife and mother isn't enough to sustain her self-image. Being a housewife is a worthless role if it stands alone. It only becomes valuable as part of a package—in conjunction with her other role as career woman.

Although the Machine is the most extreme and the most driven of the superwomen, she is not the most common.

The Garden Variety Superwoman

The Garden Variety Superwomen are women who have internalized the new career goals for women, but they also carry within themselves old values. They feel their careers are in conflict with their roles as wives and mothers. These women would feel guilty and deficient if they left their children and households in the care of servants more often, or if they took too many shortcuts, so they try to be career women as well as traditional housewives and mothers. Although their standards are often high, they are not perfectionists like the Machine. There is a makeshift, frantic quality to their very busy lives. When their job gets very demanding, their housework may slide a little. When it eases up, their houses may be sparkling clean again. Little things continually slip through their fingers. For example, their refrigerator may be full of food and basically clean, but leftover food gets forgotten in the back of shelves and spoils.

A Garden Variety Superwoman will rarely ask her husband for help because doing a lot for him and the children makes her feel less guilty about not being a full-time housewife.

Some Superwomen would accept help from a husband if he offered it. They just don't feel right about asking. Some women feel that it's simply easier and faster to do things themselves than to try to teach their husbands how to do

household tasks. Others fear making waves and alienating
their husbands, so they just carry on alone.

Garden Variety Superwomen, by contrast to Machines,
frequently feel frazzled and overworked. Some feel resentful
and put upon.

Most Garden Variety Superwomen have set unrealistic goals
for themselves. They are trying valiantly to live up to these
goals, in response to what they feel is now required of them
by society.

Some Garden Variety Superwomen are products of households in which they were chosen from among brothers and
sisters as the child with the most promise. The expectations
they try to live up to are those imposed on them from a parent
who singled them out as special.

Sometimes a Superwoman operates out of a fear of poverty. She works hard now, as she has her whole life, to
overcome the poverty she was born into.

Sometimes Garden Variety Superwomen burn out. They
get too overworked, too frazzled, too resentful. They sink
into a depression, feeling they have failed in the role they
have assigned to themselves. Overwork generally doesn't
make Garden Variety Superwomen break down completely
like the Machines, who are more rigid in their standards and
personalities. Burned out Garden Variety Superwomen simply wilt. They may leave the work force for awhile and return
to it at a later date when demands from the children lessen, or
they may go into therapy and discover that if they don't do
everything by themselves they will not fail as women. They
may even discover that accepting help is not a deadly sin.
Garden Variety Superwomen can feel warning symptoms that
all is not well; this is what saves them from complete break-
downs. A Machine can't feel much of anything.

Of course, numerous Garden Variety Superwomen just
keep on going, accepting their hectic pace stoically, or in
some cases, enjoying it.

What all the Superwomen share is a sense of being special
in a world where women are just emerging from their purely
domestic roles. Unfortunately, they interpret special as having to be bigger than life.

How a Superwoman Can Help Herself

Superwomen can be extraordinarily accomplished women who have a right to take pride in themselves. However, if you recognize from the portrait in this chapter that you are trying to be a Superwoman, and you would like to slow down, here are some things you can do. If you are the Garden Variety Superwoman, recognize that it is guilt about not being a traditional housewife that is driving you to your excesses. Once you accept this fact, you should find it easier to get more help and relax your standards. Use some of your salary to hire someone to clean your home on a regular basis, so that you can have more time to enjoy yourself and your family. Ask your husband to pitch in more. He may need some direction, but he may be quite willing to learn. Use more convenience foods and eat out more often. The object is to do everything possible to make your life less work-oriented and more enjoyable for you and those around you. Get going! You may not be Superwoman any more, but you'll be a more terrific woman for it!

CHAPTER 19

OTHER FAMILIAR WOMEN
The Love Wrecker

Daphne met Jim through mutual friends while he was visiting San Francisco. It was instant mutual attraction. By the time Jim had to leave San Francisco two weeks later he felt he didn't want to leave Daphne behind. He asked her to come and live with him in Atlanta. Daphne agreed. She and Jim lived together peacefully for three months. Jim thought everything was fine. He came home one night to find Daphne in bed with another man. He was puzzled, surprised, and hurt.

Daphne is a Love Wrecker. Love Wreckers are women who will do something to destroy a relationship that is going along too well. They may start an affair with someone else, pick a fight, suddenly become sulky, irritable, unreasonable, bored or turned off.

Love Wreckers crave love, but can't accept it. To them, love means fusion with their beloved and a resulting annihilation of their own self. This perception is one from early infancy when the baby saw mother and self as one entity without separate boundaries.

Love Wreckers frequently had a mother who discouraged attempts by the child to establish a separate identity, as she grew. The fathers didn't interfere with the mother's stunting of the child's growth. As a result, the Love Wrecker remained tied to her mother in an overly dependent way which caused conscious or unconscious resentment. To the Love Wrecker there are only two alternatives in a relationship. Get enmeshed in confining ties, lose oneself entirely and become overly dependent. Or, cut those ties forcefully in order to survive as an individual person. Love Wreckers are people who don't know how to coexist.

Although they do everything to launch a successful love relationship, once in it, they begin to feel smothered, confined, overly dependent, and anxious, either consciously or unconsciously. When they fight, abruptly withdraw, start to dislike their beloved or do something impossible, it is a revolt at overdependence, it is an expression of the automatic resentment they feel being in that position, and it's a way of reestablishing a separate identity.

Most Love Wreckers create ruptures in the relationship as soon as it begins to get serious, but there are some who don't start their wrecking program until after marriage. Only then, do they feel really committed, and as a result, smothered, resentful, and anxious, which propels them into a kind of behavior sure to cause trouble in the marriage.

Love Wreckers don't recognize that ambivalence is part of every close relationship, that partners can hate temporarily as well as love. They fail to understand that disagreement and self-assertion can be expressed along with love and loyalty to the same person. When feelings of irritation or anger arise or even when they mildly disagree Love Wreckers feel it is fatal, and in one way or another they flee the relationship.

The Juggler

This week Wendy saw Bill for dinner on Friday. She went to the theater with Gregg on Saturday. On Sunday she went to a movie with Frank. Next week she will rotate these men again on separate nights. Bill, Gregg, and Frank don't know of each other's existences. Bill slept over Friday night and spent Saturday afternoon with Wendy, but she managed to get him out of the apartment before Gregg showed up on Saturday night.

Wendy is a female Juggler, a woman who habitually dates several men at once. A Juggler is a very insecure woman with profound doubts about her desirability. She is always ready to add a new man to her stable because she is afraid of being rejected by one or all of the men she is already seeing. She deeply fears being left alone. Sometimes women are open about their juggling, but most often Jugglers lie to the men in their lives because they are afraid they would lose them if they told the truth.

What commonly happens with a Juggler is the following sequence of events. She gets involved with one man who isn't quite right for her, but she is afraid to stop seeing him because she doesn't want to be alone and maybe he isn't so bad after all. Then a second man comes along who is interested in her and she starts to see him in case the first man disappears. Then a third man enters her life and the Juggler goes out with him because what if the other two men left? And so on.

Her worst fears frequently come true. Men often catch on to her game, and they drop out of her life. If the Juggler really liked the defector, she is apt to become depressed even if there are other men around. But if he was just one of the crowd, his disappearance is taken more lightly.

Female Jugglers are interested in commitment. They juggle men, because they are afraid of not getting it. This is in direct contrast to male jugglers who dislike commitment and juggle in order to avoid it.

When a woman confronts a male juggler about his woman habit and says, "Either you give up those other women or I'm taking off," the male juggler may try to turn her into a friend, but will let her go as a lover, even if he likes her a lot.

The opposite is likely to happen with the female Juggler. If one of her men says, "Listen, I know you are seeing other men and I don't like it. I want you to drop them and see me only," it will be music to her ears. If it appears that he is serious and she likes him, she will very likely drop her other men and stick with him. If he is not ready to commit himself, however, she will continue to see other men.

Many Jugglers tend to want commitment too fast in a relationship. The relationship may be going along very well, but if, within a month or two, a man hasn't said anything that sounds like the possibility of marriage or living together in the future, or if he isn't seeing her every single night, then she interprets this as a sign that the relationship is "going nowhere" and that she should start seeing other men.

It is usually the Juggler's own anxiety about commitment which makes her see the relationship as lacking a positive direction, rather than the reality of the situation. Jugglers are women with an above average need for commitment. A relationship is often built around the issue of whether he will or won't and a Juggler is frequently so focused on commitment that she forgets to evaluate the essentials—whether a man will be compatible or share the same values as she does.

The Defensive Juggler

Many women without such a strong commitment anxiety, but who do have a normal desire for a long-term relationship, nevertheless, are juggling these days, too. A quickly increasing segment of the female population is juggling as a defensive or even hostile position against the kind of men they keep meeting. These women are Defensive Jugglers.

There are a large number of women who have engaged in a series of fruitless one-to-one relationships with men who ultimately were not interested in commitment. They begin to feel that it is smarter not to tie themselves up to one man only or not to get too involved, so they start to see two or more men at the same time. These are women who have become almost hopeless about ever finding the kind of relationship they really want, and in lieu of a committed relationship, they decide to try simply having a little fun.

Defensive Jugglers are reacting to their experiences with men, rather than from an internal system of beliefs. If they could find it, they would prefer a serious, long-term, one-to-one relationship. Because they end up acting contrary to their own values, they often find after a period of juggling that they really aren't having much fun. There may be a lot of men around to flatter their egos, but they don't really enjoy sleeping with several men at once, and fragmenting themselves between a number of men.

The number of women who are Defensive Jugglers is quite large in today's world. More often than not after a period of experimenting with juggling, these women revert to behavior more in accord with their own values. They stop juggling,

see one man at a time, and take their chances. If the relationship doesn't work out, they go on to another one-to-one
relationship. Often it's a question of maturation. Women who
juggle while they're young, stop as they get older. Or it's a
matter of experimenting. They juggle to see if it works out
better for them, and stop if they find it's no better than
struggling with a single series of men not interested in
commitment.

Some women juggle in reaction to a specific man. If their
man is seeing other women, they start to see other men in
retaliation. They juggle with anger and hostility and are
delighted if the original man finds them with another escort.
They may even set it up so he does. These women juggle
with an I'll-show-you attitude. They may also see other men
in order to make the original man jealous, with the fantasy
that he will then realize how desirable they are to other men,
which will cause him to drop the other women in his life.

According to psychiatrists this rarely happens. In fact,
when the Juggler lets the man know she is seeing other men,
she is giving him permission to continue juggling himself.
They both continue to juggle, negating any chance that the
relationship will jell.

Many women these days, particularly young ones, accept
the notion that the man will juggle from the beginning. So
they juggle too, even though they may crave a one-to-one
relationship. They set it up from the outset that nothing will
ever happen to make the relationship more committed.

There are a large number of men today who are trying to
pressure women to juggle. These men turn juggling into a
philosophy. They claim that the desire for commitment means
the desire to possess, and therefore, a desire for commitment
is "sick." They explain to a woman that to want an exclusive
relationship is immature. Women want it because that is the
way they have been raised.

A few, but by no means all, feminist psychologists and
some practitioners in the human potential schools of psychology are pushing the same message. Women crave a one-to-one
relationship because of social conditioning. They may also
be more prone than men to want it because of intrinsic
biological differences—women bear children, men do not.

Women may want one-to-one relationships too simply because they are more connected to their emotions than men in our society. They often find spreading themselves out emotionally to be an unsatisfactory experience.

Whatever the reason, if a woman truly values a committed, one-to-one relationship, but juggles men because she can't find what her heart desires, she is behaving in a neurotic fashion. To act in reaction to others—in this case men—rather than from her own convictions is destructive to any woman's sense of well-being, and she shouldn't let anyone tell her otherwise.

The Grouper

There are women that are seen only with a cluster of men. They arrive at parties with two or three escorts. When they go on vacation they are accompanied by a group of males. They go to dinner with three men. They attend the theater as the only female in a party of-four. These are Groupers, women who need to be surrounded by an all male crowd. The group is generally made up of regulars, although other men may come and go.

Generally, Groupers are women who are very good-looking, have fabulous jobs, are well-connected, are wealthy or famous. A Grouper has a special glamour that attracts men who are willing to be part of a crowd rather than her one and only, or at least the men are willing to hang in there on the chance that they will finally be the one she chooses. To observers on the outside and the men on the inside, it is never clear which man in her crowd she is sleeping with, which among them is her favorite. Her attention shifts. She is always flirting with one or the other. They are all kept dangling.

The Grouper is a woman with insecurities about herself that make her feel safer when she is surrounded. She cannot send away even the least attractive man in her crowd because she's afraid of being rejected herself. The Grouper is not like the Juggler, who is desperate to make a choice and settle down. The Grouper knows she has a choice and her concern is about making the correct decision. She has an image of a perfect man, and like all women who harbor such idealized images, she finds it hard to find one man who can fit all the particulars of her fantasy. Therefore, she splits her fantasy up among the group. One man may have the looks she dreams about, another may have the wealth, a third may have the wit, a fourth may have the intelligence.

Groupers are women who find it difficult to give of themselves and share. Often they were pampered, only children. They feel entitled to take whatever they want out of life, and they give to themselves copiously. Everything is in excess. They have too many men; they often buy too many clothes. They like to eat well. Maintaining a group of men is a way of not sharing themselves—something they would have to do more of if they were in a one-to-one relationship.

Their inability to share is extended to other females. Rarely do they have female friends. They may have a surplus of men, but they don't want even the possibility of having to share one or hand one over to another woman.

Occasionally, a Grouper may know a woman she feels safe with—an ugly cousin, for example. Since she feels the ugly cousin isn't attractive enough to make off with one of her men, she may invite this out-of-the running female to join the group sometimes.

In one instance, a Grouper was taken by surprise. A very fat girl friend captured one of the men in her group. This taught the Grouper a lesson. Her group had been dwindling away with the course of time anyway. Men were leaving for more satisfying relationships with other women as they got older. At this point, the Grouper chose from among those left and married him.

Her fate is similar to that of many Groupers. The Grouper finds that as she and the group age, one by one the group will start to defect. The men get fed up and leave because they feel there is no point in hanging around, or they meet women more available to them personally. As the group grows smaller and smaller, the Grouper realizes that her way of life can't last forever. She then chooses one out of those remaining and learns to share with one man instead of spreading herself out among several. She is not a hopeless case.

The Sex Object

At a recent party, the door bell rang long after everyone else had arrived. The host answered it, and framed in the doorway was a woman with bright blond hair wearing a white cowboy hat, tight black satin pants, a bright red satin blouse under which she was obviously braless although her breasts were very large. The Sex Object had arrived.

As this woman entered, she immediately attracted the attention of every man in the room. As she downed drink after drink, men pawed her, made suggestive remarks. By the time the party was over, she had posed in a corner with men breathing heavily at her, sat in a chair with men sitting on either side, stroking her arms, shoulders and back. She was last seen sitting on the host's bed, very tipsy, saying, "Men are such shits!"

This blonde typifies the Sex Object. There is generally something fake and theatrical about Sex Objects—their clothing is too sexy, their manner too dramatic. They act seductive or even tartish.

Sex Objects operate like man traps and yet, if a man takes them at their unspoken word and makes a pass, they become indignant and resentful. They feel bitter and angry that men are after them only for sex—a fact that often is true because of the way they dress and conduct themselves. The hidden goal of Sex Objects is to attract men, and then reject them.

Sex Objects frequently come from deprived backgrounds. They feel their original family never gave them enough of anything. They are angry women, frequently aiming their hostility at men, whom they feel wield the power in this world. They want to cut men down. They do it by first luring them, then rejecting or humiliating them.

The Mess

Agnes is sitting in Maggie's house with another couple.
They have all been invited for dinner. They were asked to
arrive at 8 P.M. It is now 10:50 P.M. and Maggie is still in
the kitchen cooking. The other woman leans toward Agnes
and whispers, "Didn't you eat? Everybody who is invited to
Maggie's for dinner eats before they come." At midnight
dinner finally appears.

Besides never serving dinner until hours after dinnertime,
Maggie also gets lost on the telephone. She talks for hours
at a time. She drops by a friend's house, while another
friend may have arrived at Maggie's home, invited but
forgotten.

Maggie is a Mess. Messes are women with a defective
sense of time and place. They cannot create any kind of
structure or organization for themselves. They drift through
life in a chaotic fashion. Their homes are sometimes a mess
because they get distracted by other things when it's time to
clean, or because the Mess may get hung up on one task and
never get around to the others. The Mess frequently arrives
late for appointments; she is never dressed when a date
arrives. When she visits friends, she becomes oblivious of
time and often overstays her welcome.

Of course, there are degrees of Messes. The worst ones
drift from one living place to another. They drop out of sight
and friends lose track of them. They may switch jobs or
professions frequently. They can't stick with anything for
very long.

The better ones have a steady home base, but they create
chaos within them. They are capable of not getting dressed
from one end of the day to another. They disappear to visit or
run errands, and nobody knows where they are. A husband
comes home and finds friends visiting with his wife when she
is supposed to be preparing dinner.

Marilyn Monroe, as described by others, was a Mess.
When married to Arthur Miller she would often hang around

in a bathrobe all day. Susan Strassberg in her autobiography *Bittersweet* describes being invited to lunch at the home of Marilyn Monroe and Arthur Miller and arriving there at the designated time to find Marilyn still upstairs. When she finally drifted down, nothing had been prepared for lunch. She started to take something out of the freezer that would take hours to make. Marilyn Monroe was also known for remaining frozen in front of her dressing mirror while people waited an unconscionable amount of time for her.

Some Messes make a proud philosophy of their uncontrollable messiness. They consider themselves to be unconventional. These women are often dropouts from college. Their relationships are transitory, based on proximity. Messes often can't go through the difficulties of arranging to meet someone who doesn't live down the block. They aren't willing to deal with timetables for buses or trains. Their apartments, besides being totally messy, are often decorated in weird ways—each wall will be a different color, for example. Crowds of people drift in and out. They often forget to lock the door, so they are frequently burglarized. They move on whim or when the least little thing disturbs them about their present abode. It is difficult for them to become attached to any place or anyone for very long. They can be charming and seductive, and attract both men and women because they appear to be such colorful, free spirits.

Messes generally come from a background in which there was too much structure from one or both parents. They were overcontrolled as children with the result that they never learned to structure themselves—it was done for them. They were also angry at being overcontrolled so their lack of structure is a form of rebellion.

Frequently, there was inconsistent parenting in the early life of a Mess. Something happened to an important figure. A mother or father may have abandoned them or died. This resulted in a disorganized state in their early lives.

Messes keep trying for attachments, but their relationships often don't succeed for very long. There is an element of hostility in their personalities that can break out unexpectedly at any time. They generally are attracted to their opposites—people who are structured and organized. They admire discipline in others, but they are also antagonistic to people with these attributes. When they are asked to contribute a little structure to a relationship, show up on time, get organized, they become rebellious. They either turn on the person in anger, seemingly over an irrelevant thing, or they lose interest in the relationship when demands are placed on them, and they withdraw. They may also be abandoned by partners who find life impossible with them because they can never be found, they are always late, they are completely unpredictable. Their men get fed up, and don't want to put up with all that messiness anymore.

The Snow Queen

They are cool, aloof, elegant. There is never a hair out of place. They are very stylish, sophisticated, always know what the current trends are. They often have created their own unique style for which others admire them. They are imposing. They are the Snow Queens, women who are snobbish, unapproachable, judgmental and completely superficial. Life for the Snow Queen is all style and no content. Emotions are neither shown nor admired.

Snow Queens are concerned with how others look and conduct themselves. They want to know whether a person lives at the right address, has the right kind of furnishings, wears the right kind of clothing. The worst thing a person can do is have bad taste, be vulgar.

Their personal aim is to be better than the crowd—to be more sophisticated and more distinguished than others.

Snow Queens are often good-looking in a glacial way, or, if good looks are impossible, they turn their lack of looks into an asset. They become extremely stylish, extremely aristocratic. Snow Queens often have successful careers; they are generally good at what they do. They often become arbiters of what is currently in style. They can be doyennes of fashion, modern art or contemporary architecture, for example.

When the Snow Queen eats, she always has small portions, and her food must be served in a careful, controlled way. Snow Queens avoid foods they consider to be gross—no heaping platters of pasta or huge ice cream sundaes for them.

They never binge on food. Snow Queens spend very little time in their kitchens. They dislike cooking, eat out a lot, and prepare very simple fare for themselves at home.

Snow Queens are disconcerting to a good number of men, but other men, often sadistic ones, look at the Snow Queen as a challenge. They feel it would be an extra thrill to conquer her simply because she seems so aloof and inaccessible.

The men Snow Queens respond to have to be distinguished in some way. A renowned architect, a famous sculptor, a well-known financier would be acceptable to them. These are very snobbish women, and their men must appeal to this characteristic. Snow Queens despise ordinary people.

Some Snow Queens never marry, but most do. They often end up with men who are as style conscious and superficial as they are, or they may marry a man who is totally devoted to his career, likes the stylish way his domestic life will be conducted, and who simply doesn't want to be bothered with the emotional side of a relationship. The Snow Queen never shows emotion. She is a rigidly controlled person who dislikes weakness in herself and what she perceives as weakness in others: bad manners, lack of style, displays of emotion.

The Snow Queen rarely has female friends. Women generally don't like her snobbish, cold, superior manner. She often is alienated from her family. Either they dislike what she has become, or she despises and is ashamed of them.

Many Snow Queens don't have children. The whole process of birth and child-rearing appears disgusting to them.

The Snow Queen is a self-created creature. She generally grew up thinking she was worse-looking than most and as a result she suffers from a poor sense of self-esteem. In her youth the Snow Queen spent a great deal of time and energy improving her defects through dieting, plastic surgery, exercise—whatever she felt was needed to shape up. She also developed her own unique sense of style. She wanted to be superior to others as compensation for feeling inferior.

For all of the cold perfection of her current exterior, the Snow Queen is still the same girl who thinks she is unattractive. She appears much more self-contained and self-confident than she really is.

Star Gazers

Their pictures are in newspapers or magazines; their names appear occasionally in gossip columns. They are the unknown women on the arms of famous writers, directors, rock stars, television newsmen, actors, athletes. They are the Star Gazers, women who can't get interested in a man unless he is at the top of his profession and somehow in the public eye.

Star Gazers are almost always women of unusual beauty, but they have more to offer than beauty alone. They don't capture their men with a pretty face, and they don't use sex as a lure. These women generally have great intelligence, a social presence, and often a lot of talent besides. Although they are more competent than most people and realize it on one level, on a deeper level, they feel somehow deficient. And although they may have enough of what it takes to shine as a star themselves, they hold themselves back from going to the top of their own particular heap. They are often successful at what they do, but they are not star status. They suffer from the fear of too much success.

Although a Star Gazer will not sleep with anyone else except the star of the moment, she likes to have a star in reserve. If her boy friend has to go away on a business trip, for example, she may go out with another star, perhaps a lesser one whom she will regard as a friend. A Star Gazer needs the reassuring presence of stars in her life to feel all right.

Relationships with stars never last more than a few months. Her life is composed of a succession of monogamous affairs with prominent men. Generally, the Star Gazer herself is the cause of the breakup. She hides a lot of anger below the surface and it breaks out in outbursts of temper tantrums once she feels close to a star. A Star Gazer's anger is an attempt to push the star away. If he puts up with her outbursts, he loses luster in her eyes. She will exhibit her anger more and more, until she finally does succeed in driving him away. An even more frequent way that a Star Gazer ends her relationships is to suddenly see a defect in her star once she feels close to him. Suddenly, he is not smart enough, even though he is talented, or he isn't creative enough—just a hack—even though he is so successful, or he simply isn't worthy enough for her, and she rejects the star. If, as can happen, the star rejects her before she rejects him, then she feels very depressed and in her memory, he becomes overidealized. She mourns this wonderful man whom she has lost.

Star Gazers save sex for their serious relationships. Although they are responsive, they aren't sexual in orientation.

A Star Gazer never uses a star to further her own career in any way. It is a firm rule she is proud of. If a Star Gazer's friend tries to take advantage of her association with a star for some career gain, the Star Gazer will become livid. She doesn't think this is ethical.

A Star Gazer's female friends are generally chosen because in her eyes they are somehow inferior to her. In this way the Star Gazer can relax, put aside any possible feelings of competition or envy, and enjoy the friendship. She is a woman who strongly desires good, close relationships with other women.

The Star Gazer comes from a family in which there was a rejecting mother who never showed her any physical affection. Luckily, she had a father who could be maternal. He gave her the love and demonstrations of affection that were missing. Her father was invariably a powerful, very successful man. Within the Star Gazer's original family, there was generally a brother whom the mother obviously favored.

Her alliances with stars contain many echoes of the Star Gazer's original family. First of all, she responds to the star as a father figure. The star is not necessarily an older man, but he shares the attributes she associates with her father. He is as powerful and successful as her father, and in his public persona, he radiates warmth and intimacy.

A Star Gazer also sees the star as a representation of something impossible, larger than life and not really attainable. The Star, therefore represents her unobtainable mother as well as her father. She feels she is getting the love and attention from the star that she couldn't get from her mother. And since the star is also a favored person, he also represents her favored brother whom she is now able to attach herself to, and therefore be looked on with favor herself.

The Star Gazer's fear of success for herself is also overcome by the star. Although she cannot tolerate success in her own right, she can accept success if she is joined to it.

When the Star Gazer's anger erupts, it is really anger at her rejecting mother that she is expressing, although this motivation is unconscious. She is afraid she will not be accepted by someone close to her, just as she was not accepted by her mother.

If the star is an accepting person and tolerates her angry outbursts, he may become devalued in her mind because the only man she was ever really close to, her father, would not have put up with her rage. He would have withdrawn until she became good-tempered again. Therefore, if a star puts up with anger, he is defective because he is not like the Star Gazer's father.

However, if the star accepts her provocative behavior, he also stops being a star in her eyes. Stars are not understanding mortals; they are unattainable gods. Since the star does not match her original models for love, she tries harder and harder to push him away.

A Star Gazer generally tries to maintain some kind of relationship with her rejecting mother as an adult, but she also gets angry periodically at the source of her rage—mother. It is common for a Star Gazer not to speak to her mother for months on end. Generally the relationship gets patched up because her father intervenes.

Star Gazers start consorting with stars early in life, generally in their late teens. Their first stars may not be too prominent because world-renowned people are not yet in the Star Gazer's orbit, but they will attach themselves to the nearest star in their immediate environment.

Star Gazers are not to be confused with women, such as actresses, who use stars to further their own careers, or Groupies, those teenage girls and young women who sleep indiscriminately with rock stars, or sports stars.

Groupies

Groupies don't have ongoing relationships with prominent men the way Star Gazers do. They have quick sexual encounters. They allow themselves to be used by stars, but they are using their stars as well.

There is an exhibitionistic quality to the actions of groupies. "See, look what I got," is what they are, in essence, saying. They brag to friends and acquaintances about the rock stars they have slept with.

A Star Gazer never brags. Being seen in public with a star can sometimes be the thing she likes least about the relationship. It's the opposite for the Groupie. She does what she does for public consumption. Groupies sleep with stars to show the world how desirable they are and to receive admiration and approval.

Groupies generally have problems with how they feel about themselves. They think they are inadequate and they try to overcome such feelings by consorting with men who will show them to be more desirable than other women.

The Groupie generally learned her exhibitionistic behavior from her family. They may have been flashy in their dress or perhaps drove flashy cars. In some cases, the parents themselves are star struck.

Or the Groupie learned that exhibitionistic behavior won approval for her from her mother or father. She may have been ignored otherwise, but by dressing up and play-acting, she won praise, for example. The only way to get approval was to show off. Therefore, Groupies sleep with stars and talk about it to as many people as will listen and respond favorably.

Boss Gazers

Another kind of Star Gazer is found in more ordinary circles. She's the woman who sleeps with her boss, or the airline stewardess who sleeps with the pilot.

Boss Gazers respond to those who have power over them

or are in superior positions within their field as if their bosses were fathers. Boss Gazers generally had a father they yearned for as children sometimes because he didn't pay them enough attention. They need to latch onto the boss or other superior who becomes the father figure in their adult lives.

The Cosmetic Junkie

The late actress Billie Burke once mentioned that in all of the years of her marriage to Florenz Zeigfeld, she never let him see her once without makeup. Makeup Junkies are women like her who will never let anyone see them without lipstick, blusher, or whatever cosmetics they wear every day to improve their looks.

What makes a woman feel that her natural face should never be glimpsed by any mortal? Fear. Makeup is a metaphor for these women. Women who are Cosmetic Junkies fear that if their face, which they believe to be naturally unattractive, is revealed, then the real person beneath their skin will also be shown naked to the world. Since Cosmetic Junkies feel insignificant or defective in some way, they compensate by always wearing makeup. They are hiding their feelings of worthlessness behind cosmetics.

The strong impact of advertising from the cosmetics industry also leads women to feel unattractive without makeup. Generations of mothers have also raised their daughters never to set foot outside, even to go to the supermarket, without wearing makeup, just in case a man or a talent scout should cross their path. Nevertheless, the majority of women may feel better wearing cosmetics, but they don't become fanatics. They sometimes allow their natural faces to be seen by husband, lovers and friends, if not the world at large. The Cosmetic Junkie who won't ever allow herself to be seen without makeup is really hiding her inner self from public scrutiny.

So is a variation of the Cosmetic Junkie, the woman who always is seen, even in the black of night with dark sunglasses, or the woman who wears huge spectacles that hide most of her face usually together with clothing so baggy you can't tell what her body looks like underneath.

The Jealous Woman

Hank was married to Betty for six years. Throughout their marriage Betty was always accusing Hank of having affairs with other women. It was never true. He was a faithful husband, and he protested his innocence, but Betty would not believe him. She would fly into jealous rages. One day when Hank came home from work, Betty claimed once more that he had been with another woman. Without warning, she grabbed a knife and plunged it into his chest. Luckily Hank didn't die, but he never returned home after leaving the hospital.

Of all the human emotions, Dr. Ari Kiev, a New York psychiatrist, has called jealousy "the most painful."

There is jealousy which is caused by a real act on the part of a love partner. A man is actually seeing someone else or sleeping with another woman. The jealous reaction is legitimate and justifiable.

Then there is irrational jealousy. A Jealous Woman, like Betty, imagines that her lover is with another woman. She is always suspicious, forever on the alert for signs of infidelity, and finds herself in a constant jealous dither.

The Jealous Woman has an enormous fear of separation and loss. The Jealous Woman often projects onto the man her own unconscious wish to escape the relationship or to sleep with someone else, so she sees her man having sex with other women.

Often the Jealous Woman feels herself to be less attractive than her mate, and as a result, she feels that other women will take him from her.

A Jealous Woman was recently witnessed in action at a party. She was a rather bright, but overweight woman. Her husband was a tall, slender, good-looking man. They had been married fifteen years. After he had been dancing with his wife for some time, he asked another woman to dance. His new partner was a slim, nice-looking woman. They danced very well together. Suddenly, his wife shot up from the chair where she had been watching her husband. She ran to him, speaking loudly so everyone in the room could hear, "Stop patting her ass!" Her husband was stunned, and so was his dance partner. The husband had not touched the woman's posterior at all. It was all in this Jealous Woman's mind.

Another type of Jealous Woman isn't the victim of her own fantasies. Her jealousy is real. But, she sets herself up from the beginning to be jealous. She always picks men who are womanizers or already involved with another woman. These Jealous Women only feel attracted to a man when another woman is also in the picture.

Generally women like this are reliving a drama in their original family, when they, as little girls, felt themselves to be rivals with their mother for their father's love. By replaying the drama as adults, they are attempting to become the winner instead of the loser. However, by getting involved with womanizers, they assure the same outcome as in their past—they generally don't get their man. Nevertheless, they don't learn, and keep becoming part of a triangle, competing with another woman.

There is a difference in the jealousy of men and woman. As Dr. Leslie F. Farber, a New York psychiatrist and author of *Jealousy, Envy, Suicide, Drugs and the Good Life*, puts it: "A woman is more apt to conceive of the larger picture and fear displacement. A man is more likely to center his attention on the sexual fact."

In other words, a man most often feels jealousy in his groin. He feels his masculinity and sexuality threatened when he thinks his woman is carrying on with somebody else. A woman just feels terrified that the man is going to be taken away from her.

The Deadliner

Deadliners are women with a schedule for their lives. By age twenty they will lose their virginity. By twenty-one they will have graduated from college. By twenty-six they will be married. By thirty they will have two children. By age thirty-five they will return to work.

Deadliners are generally well-educated, intelligent women who need order and predictability in their lives—hence their rigid schedules.

Very often they have come from disorganized homes. They counteracted the messiness around them by creating neatness and orderliness in their own lives. In this way they learned to keep anxiety from overwhelming them.

A Deadliner will choose a man more to meet her self-imposed deadline than because the man is compatible. If a man has a suitable profession and is the right height and age, a Deadliner will marry him as her target date looms with no regard for the fact that he may come from a totally different background or believe in completely different things than she does.

The men attracted to Deadliners tend to be passive. They like her decisiveness. She is the dominant one in the relationship. But the spouses are often grossly incompatible because of the way in which they were chosen. This often forces the Deadliner to fit something into her schedule that she hadn't counted on—divorce.

CHAPTER 20

THE WELL-ADJUSTED WOMAN

Most of us have ideals of love based on movies, novels, television dramas and commercials, perhaps from the relationship of our parents. Our ideals, gathered willy-nilly from the world around us, are often fuzzy, unrealistic, overblown, and distorted. There is little in our society that presents a woman with a model of a healthy relationship.

How does a so-called normal woman, the "self-actualizing" woman as the late renowned psychiatrist Abraham Maslow called her, conduct her relationships with men?

Even if your own behavior doesn't match the healthy woman's in all respects, by knowing what ingredients go into a good relationship, you can set new goals for yourself and understand better what you may be doing wrong.

First, let's look at Ginnie and Jane at the beginning of a relationship.

Ginnie met Bill at the counter of a health food restaurant. He asked her if the vegetable casserole she was eating tasted good. Ginnie said it was delicious, and this was the beginning of a long conversation that lasted all through lunch. Ginnie found Bill to be intelligent and gentle, a combination she admired. She also found his blue eyes with dark hair very attractive. He reminded her of Paul Newman. Bill asked for her telephone number, as they were returning to their offices, and she gave it to him happily. When he called two days later and asked her out, she was delighted. At the end of her first date she was delirious with joy. She fell asleep dreaming about him. By the end of their third date, Ginnie was already involved in a fantasy. She fantasized that she and Bill were married and living in a smartly furnished apartment in a nice part of town with darling children and some tropical fish. In her fantasy Bill was always smart, witty, gentle, attentive and sexy. In her dream their love-making was always passionate and earth-shaking. In real life, ever since her first date with Bill, Ginnie had been sitting by the telephone waiting anxiously for him to call.

Now let's look at Jane. Jane met Don while they were both standing on a long line waiting to get tickets to a hit play. In that time Jane discovered that Don lived three blocks from her and that he, too, was a theater buff. She found out that Don had enjoyed the same plays as she that season. As they talked, Don made her laugh a lot—something she liked. When Don asked her to have coffee with him afterwards, Jane agreed. When he asked her for her telephone number, she gave it to him. On their first date a week later she learned that they came from similar backgrounds. By the end of the evening, Jane hoped to see Don again. She fell asleep peacefully, even though he had given no indication whether she would hear from him. She hoped he would call, but if he didn't, it was no tragedy. He called four days later.

By the end of her third date, Jane was not absorbed in any elaborate fantasy of being married to her new man. Unlike Ginnie, who was positive that Bill was Mr. Right very soon after meeting him, Jane was not yet sure.

Jane realized that the more she saw of Don, the more she liked him. His values and background were similar to her own, and she knew that was important. She enjoyed being with him, but she also realized that it was a new relationship, and there was a lot more she would have to know. Jane felt she had to get to know Don better before being serious about him. She was also, while seeing him, going on with the rest of her life. She was not afraid to leave the house or miss his phone calls.

Ginnie, like so many women, rushed into her relationship much too fast. After only three dates, she was ready to commit herself to Bill. Her interest in him was based more on her fantasy, rather than the reality.

On the other hand, Jane reserved judgment. She was not

swept away, nor did she envision love as being swept away. She recognized Don was someone she liked, but realized the relationship was still unfolding. Jane, a healthy, well-balanced woman, is able to wait patiently to see how things develop before contemplating a long-term commitment.

This does not mean that Jane is suspicious, and is waiting to find out what will turn out to be wrong with the current man. On the contrary, Jane is optimistic, but cautious at the beginning of her relationships.

Ginnie would have been devastated if Bill had not called her again. Jane would not have gone into a funk if Don disappeared. She realizes she has plenty of other resources, interests, and friends, and that her life will not become less meaningful if a man does not return her interest.

Like all Well-Adjusted Women, Jane has a strong sense of her own identity apart from her relationships. However, many women expect a man to create an identity for them. They feel like nothing unless they are someone's girl friend, wife, daughter, or mother. It's an attitude that society fosters in women, but it's one women should fight against if they want to operate in a healthy fashion. A sense of worth has to come from within oneself not from others. A woman needs to feel lovable about herself before she is able to truly love another person. Otherwise, she will expect a man to make up for or constantly reassure her in some manner about her own sense of worth.

Well-Adjusted Women don't expect a man to solve all their problems, make them feel more complete, rescue them from lives that are unfulfilling, or relieve them of the burden of having to take care of themselves. The Well-Adjusted Woman does not feel incomplete or like a victim in need of rescue.

Of course, feelings of helplessness are inculcated in women by society but they must begin to find their own individual strengths. "Love is confused with dependence," stated Rollo May, "but you can love only in proportion to your capacity for independence."

Because a Well-Adjusted Woman has a sense of worth apart from her relationships with men, there is no desperation in her search for a male partner, as there is in so many women. She does not spend all of her time man-hunting, but pursues her own interests. This does not mean that she sits home and hopes that by some miracle Mr. Right will beat a path to her door. If she sees someone who interests her, she tries to get to know him better; but at the same time, she has a lot of other things going in her life that count.

If she is rejected in a relationship, she still feels worthwhile and attractive, unlike so many women who think if a man ignores or rejects that they must be undesirable.

When a Well-Adjusted Woman has sex with a man, it grows out of her interest in him as a human being, not only because she thinks he is handsome or because she is afraid he will abandon her if she doesn't, or because she is lonely, or because she is trying to prove that she is desirable as a woman.

Once committed to a relationship, Well-Adjusted Women tend to be monogamous. This does not mean that they don't find other men attractive sometimes. They do. But they are able to keep from acting on the attraction, because they value and trust the relationship they have.

Well-Adjusted Women are able to be part of a solidly bonded couple, and still preserve a sense of their own autonomy and separateness in the relationship. They respect the individuality of their partner as well. They realize that relationships are not static. They are able to cope with change; they encourage and welcome growth in their mate rather than being in fear of it.

A Well-Adjusted Woman is not self-centered. She is not interested in having only her own needs fulfilled in a relationship. She is able to empathize and have genuine concern for the problems and joys in her mate's life, and she tries to take care of his needs and concerns as well as her own.

She is not jealous of the man's interests which do not include her, and she is able to pursue her own interests independently without fearing that the relationship will be threatened if she does. Well-Adjusted Women don't control their men or become clinging, stifling, or helpless in a relationship.

A Well-Adjusted Woman does not overidealize her mate,

nor does she ignore, belittle, berate, or criticize him for his failings. She always treats him with dignity.

She is able to recognize and openly admire a man's good qualities, but she is also able to see and graciously accept the fact that he may be less than perfect. She is able to understand and accept his faults, because she understands and accepts her own faults.

If there is something a Well-Adjusted Woman wants, she simply expresses her desire. She does not demand, or become manipulative, trying to get what she wants by devious means. Nor does she expect a man to be able to read her mind feeling disappointed if he can't.

There are moments of anger and dissatisfaction in the relationships of Well-Adjusted Women as there are in all relationships. They are able to face conflict directly. They don't suppress their anger, as so many women do when they are mad. They don't sulk, try to make a man feel guilty, give him the cold, silent treatment, withdraw into the bedroom to cry, or always give in in order to smooth things over. They talk the matter over and try to reach a mutually agreeable conclusion. Well-Adjusted Women let go of their anger after the argument is over, and they don't hold grudges.

A Well-Adjusted Woman is able to tolerate ambivalence in her relationships. She can accept bad moments and bad feelings along with good. This tolerance of ambivalence is vital to sustaining a long-term, stable relationship.

A Well-Adjusted Woman never uses a man to gain her own ends, and she doesn't put a price tag on her devotion, admiration, loyalty, love, or sex. She doesn't expect love in return for demands or sacrifices. For her, love is simply not to be traded or bargained. She gives freely of herself without expecting rewards.

A Well-Adjusted Woman looks for human qualities in a man rather than power, good looks, great wealth or a willingness on the man's part to always worship or cater to her. She does not consider herself to be inferior to men. She is always ready and able to openly express her love and appreciation of a man. When things go wrong in a relationship, rather than heaping blame on the man or herself, or lapsing into a depression, the Well-Adjusted Woman tries to analyze what went wrong and why and learn from it for the future.

The actions of Well-Adjusted Women in their relationships synthesized in the next chapter can serve as a guideline to anyone not only seeking love but also wishing to preserve it.

CHAPTER 21

FOURTEEN WAYS TO HAVE A GOOD RELATIONSHIP

1. Don't allow yourself to become submerged in a relationship or to take your identity from your man. It's important to retain a sense of autonomy—to know who you are apart from the relationship.

2. Realize that your partner has some interests of his own that will not necessarily include you, and don't feel left out or jealous if he does. This means that you see him as an individual as well as your partner.

3. Become aware of your mate's needs and feelings as well as your own. Good relationships are always two-sided.

4. When you want something, ask for it directly instead of demanding it, expecting that your partner will be able to read your mind or by trying to manipulate your partner indirectly.

5. Let your partner know you love and appreciate him.

6. Deal with conflict directly. Talk matters over, rather than running away, sulking, pouting, always giving in, or trying to force your opinion on your partner.

7. Realize that there are bad moments as well as good ones in all relationships and that disagreements don't mean that the relationship is failing. The ability to tolerate some ambivalent feelings toward a mate—occasional anger, fleeting moments of hatred—as well as love is crucial in being able to maintain a stable, long-term relationship. This tolerance is often the difference between those who can only fall in love and those who can stay in love.

8. Pick a man for his human qualities, his values, his compatibility with you, rather than for what he represents in

status, power, good looks, or even the fact that he is the only available man around at a time when you feel desperate to have a committed relationship. Make sure, too that you aren't choosing him because you feel he can make up for some emotional deprivation in your background, like the missing love or attention of a mother or father.

9. Don't overidealize your mate. Be aware that he is only human and has failings as well as good points. Disappointment will surely follow if you start out thinking of him as perfect.

10. Watch out that you don't become too dependent or clinging in a relationship. This happens most often if you fail to retain a sense of your own identity when you become attached to a man.

11. Don't expect a man to rescue you or marriage to solve all your problems in life.

12. Don't accept or reject a man too precipitously. Take your time to get to know a man before you make a decision about your future together.

13. Don't use a man for your own ends or expect rewards for sacrifice, service or love.

14. When things go wrong, try to figure out why. Don't blame it all on the other person, or on yourself. Put what you learn from your experience to work to create a better relationship in the future.

CHAPTER 22

WHAT MEN COMPLAIN ABOUT
IN WOMEN

Men love to complain about women almost as much as
women love to complain about men. Here are some common
male grievances that I would like to address.

1. *Women are only interested in a man with money*. Many
men feel that women are mercenary, interested in money for
money's sake. This may be true for some women, but for the
majority, the interest is in security.

Women have been forced to evaluate a man's potential as a
breadwinner because of their own position in society. In the
past, women had to depend on men economically to survive.
There were very few well-paying jobs available to women.
Today, there are certainly more jobs, and women are entering
the work force in unprecedented numbers, but the picture of
women's earnings remains grim.

For every dollar earned by a man, a woman earns sixty-
five cents. This is the same as it was 25 years ago. A male
high school dropout earns, on an average, $1600 more a year
than a female college graduate.

The overwhelming majority of women still hold low paying
clerical and service jobs. Women hold ninety-eight percent of
all secretarial jobs. Women comprise ninety-five percent of
private household workers. Women represent less than ten
percent of all skilled workers and less than five percent of all
top managers. In the professions that have been traditionally
open to females—social work or nursing, for example—the
wage scale is abysmally low, simply because these are pre-
dominantly female fields. Women do care about what a man

earns because society has made it imperative for them to think in these terms. Sociologist Willard Waller put it this way: "A man when he marries chooses a companion and perhaps a helpmate, but a woman chooses a companion and at the same time a standard of living. It is necessary for women to be mercenary."

2. *Her money is her money. My money is our money.* Although this is not true for all women, it is for many. This attitude grows out of several issues. First, it may be a way for a woman to hang onto her sense of femininity. If she is supported by a man, she still retains her female role, even though she may work, too. When a woman pools her earnings, she feels it is undermining her role as a woman, or her mate's as a man, if he takes her money. She feels uncomfortable with the whole concept.

Second, the issue may be one of power. A woman may feel more independent and assertive, if she has money of her own.

Even more important is the feeling among women that they will not be taken care of forever by a man. The picture of impoverished widowhood or divorce looms, and they put away their salaries in a separate account. Other women know they are earning a salary now, but in a typical female way of thinking, they have no faith in their long-run ability to be independent wage earners. This lack of faith in themselves is the result of generations of men treating women as if they could not take care of themselves. The message got through.

A woman's desire to have money of her own is not new. It existed in the past, even among housewives married to poor men. Many women somehow managed to put away a little from their household money. This nest egg was there just in case something happened, and it provided a woman with a tiny sense of independence. Often a husband found out about his wife's secret savings only during hard times. If he was in trouble, she would suddenly appear with her money and offer it to help out, or if a child needed money for something important, there was momma with her little bundle.

Issues about whose money is whose and how joint incomes should be spent are causing a lot of trouble in marriages today. Men have a long tradition of sharing their paychecks, and they don't understand women who won't. Men shared because they had to; their wives didn't work. They also did it because it was part of the male role. Giving money to his woman made a man feel more powerful and masculine. By contrast, giving money to a man, even a husband, often makes a woman feel insecure and less powerful.

3. *Women spend too much*. Reflecting this attitude are many jokes that picture women as spendthrifts. Women in this country became primarily consumers when they stopped being producers in the economy. Shopping became a pastime for women with little else to do. Men also often unconsciously encouraged women to spend. The same man who complains about his wife spending too much may also take secret pride in the amount of money she is able to spend. A wife's spending is a form of conspicuous consumption to show the world that the husband is a big earner. Just as having a beautiful woman provides status for a man, so does having a wife who spends a lot.

The advertising industry also encourages women to spend. Most ads are targeted just to females. Advertising campaigns often encourage a woman to spend, sometimes more than she can afford, in order to be in fashion so that she can feel secure about her appearance, and in order to be a successful housewife. Ads often cater to a woman's insecurities. They make a woman feel that without the product offered, she will not have laundry as clean as other wives (and her husband might leave her), she will smell bad (and men will shun or abandon her), or that her kitchen floor will be the shame of the neighborhood, and her kids won't want to bring their friends home. However, for every woman who spends too much there is her opposite—the woman who shops carefully and is frugal with the family budget.

4. *Women are manipulative*. Many women are manipulative but men rarely understand the cause of it. Women have been excluded from direct participation in power, and forbidden by their female role to ask for anything directly lest they be considered aggressive, castrating and bitchy. Thus, women learn to get what they want indirectly—through manipulation. It isn't as malevolent in origin as many men seem

to think it is. It is simply that some women see it as the only way available to get what they desire.

5. *Women are too emotional*. Women have not been trained to think logically and concretely as have men. Although some women manage to become concrete thinkers anyway, many are more emotional than logical. Another reason men think of women as emotional, perhaps more emotional than they really are, is because women use emotions on purpose to get their way with men. It's part of what is explained above— women are afraid to ask for things directly, and so they use indirect methods. Two sociologists, Paula Johnson and Jacqueline Goodchilds did a study in 1976 in which they asked over two hundred fifty men and women to write about "How I Get My Way." Fifty-four percent of the women, as opposed to only twenty-seven percent of the men, answered that they deliberately used some kind of emotional ploy. Forty percent of the women using emotions resorted to sulking, forty percent used tears, twenty percent used anger.

6. *Women use sex to control a man*. The man who complains that women have power "between their legs" is a very insecure male who feels that if he gives into his sexual drives, a woman will take advantage of him and will be able to control him. His complaint is a reflection of his own problems rather than a woman's.

There are other men who feel that when their woman turns them down sexually, it is a conscious ploy to obtain something. For example, the husband whose wife complains she is too tired for sex may think she is deliberately withholding sex in order to get him to give her the fur coat she said she wanted. There are a small number of women who do use sex in this way, but the majority of women who lose interest in a man do so for far more complex reasons. It may have to do with a problem within the relationship that is making her angry at her husband. Sometimes a woman's own personal psychological problems surface, and interfere with her desire. But men often fail to take into account any factors other than very concrete ones. They look at women as simple sexual creatures rather than complex human beings. They ignore the psychological dimensions of a relationship.

7. *Women are too demanding about sex these days*. Men

want a woman to be sexy, seductive and always available.
But when they find a woman who is openly interested in sex,
some men begin to feel threatened, fear they may not be able
to perform satisfactorily, and often think of her as insatiable
and overly aggressive. This reflects the ambivalence of many
men about women. They desire women, and at the same time
dread them. The origins of male dread go back to the powerful mother that every man had at the beginning of his life—
the woman who inevitably disciplined or frustrated him somewhere along the line. Of course, there are some women who
are overly demanding about sex these days. These are women
who are angry and hostile toward men, and they express it in
bed. But the number of men who fear the female is greater
than the number of angry women. Evil, insatiable women
have always been part of folklore, again reflecting a generalized fear of women and their sexuality.

   8. *Women are insincere or hypocritical.* Women have been
brought up to encourage men, to flatter them, to be always
accepting and compassionate, to be unassertive, to cater, and
to appear dumb when necessary. This results in a certain
amount of pretense on a woman's part which, of course,
makes her appear insincere and hypocritical. Women often
have two personalities—their natural one, and the one they
assume around men. Simone de Beauvoir in *The Second Sex,*
says, "Confronting man, woman is always play-acting."
Generally women are insincere in order to get love. Men are
insincere in order to get sex.

   9. *Women are often bossy, critical or nags.* A decent
number of women are overcritical, nagging and controlling.
Often this grows out of personal psychological problems. But
it also grows out of women's roles in society. Women have
always been charged with civilizing and domesticating men.
Some women feel they are just domesticating a man by
keeping after him to fix this or do that. Frequently a man sets
it up so that his wife nags. He agrees to do something and
then doesn't get around to it, causing her to ask him again
and again. This is generally part of an ongoing battle between
husband and wife.

   A controlling wife may also be a woman who is exercising

power in the only place she can—in her home. She can be a queen there, if nowhere else.

The sharp-tongued woman who appears so often in literature may also be expressing aggression. Women do not take out their aggression in physical ways against men because they are at a physical disadvantage. Their aggression, therefore, takes other forms, including verbal attack.

Studies have shown that women do become more aggressive and assertive about their own needs in their middle years, while men become more mellow and interested in affiliation. Women who become less docile with age are often accused of being malevolent and bitchy, when perhaps they are simply standing up for their own rights or are insisting on time for their own interests for the first time in their lives. If a wife is a true battle-ax she wouldn't have become one only in her latter years. She would have been one all along.

10. *Women are vain.* Women are overly concerned about their looks, but it isn't because they are vain. It is because they are often insecure about their appearances. They feel they need to look good to capture or retain the interest of men, and because the advertising industry, in order to sell makeup and other products plays on the insecurities of women.

11. *Women are becoming too choosy.* This is a new complaint among men. One man expressed his discomfort recently when he found at a resort that women didn't stand around the lobby of the hotel like they used to, waiting to be approached by men. Other men are amazed when women whom they ask out refuse more frequently than they did in the past. Women are becoming more choosy as they think more highly of themselves.

Certain women, very beautiful ones, very rich ones, were always choosy. There was always the girl that every boy lusted after, but she would only go out with the captain of the football team. The fact that more ordinary women won't go out with every man who asks them is a sign of our changing times. The fact that women play tennis, or swim, or take walks rather than stand around in resort hotel lobbies waiting to catch the eye of a man is progress in the lives of women.

Women aren't too choosy, they are simply more selective.

12. *Women today are too aggressive about chasing men.*

There are more women today than at any time in the past who call men and ask them out. Some men like it, some don't. If a man thinks that any kind of aggressive behavior is unfeminine, he will resent a woman calling him. The hardest part about being pursued by a woman is the fact that they have to turn her down if they are not interested. Men are learning how to say no to a woman, something they rarely had to do when they were the ones doing all the pursuing. And women are learning how to chance rejection, something that men have always had to face when they picked up the phone first.

SIXTEEN THINGS WOMEN DO WRONG IN RELATIONSHIPS

1. *They leap into relationships too fast.* After two or three dates many women start to try out a man's last name with their first name, or they mentally move the furniture around in his apartment to create a prettier nest for the two of them. Women start to fantasize about marriage much too early in the relationship—before they really know what kind of person this new man is.

2. *They want commitment too fast.* Many women who yearn for a solid relationship start to get anxious about it much too early—before the relationship has had a chance to develop. After two or three months, they begin to pressure a man about his intentions, or they decide on their own that it isn't going anywhere. This can happen before the woman knows how interested she herself is in the man. It's done almost routinely in any relationship. She acts prematurely out of her own anxiety about commitment.

3. *They deceive themselves.* Women often make more out of what is going on in the relationship than reality warrants. They often refuse to see clues that tell them the man is not really interested in commitment, that he isn't as serious as the woman is, or that he is engaged in behavior that would threaten the relationship if it were acknowledged. For example, it may be quite obvious that a man is seeing other women, but a woman ignores this fact, feeling that the relationship is as consuming to him as it is to her. She agonizes over him and wonders what she can do to nail him down. Or, a man tells her he doesn't want to get serious, but she treats

the relationship as if it were a life and death matter. Or, a man sees a woman occasionally, but she persists in thinking of him as a serious, steady boy friend. Or, a husband leaves plenty of clues around that he is having an affair, but the wife ignores them. The tendency to deceive oneself about the nature of the relationship or details within a relationship is a common one among women.

4. *They make excuses about the man's behavior*. Women make excuses which keep them from facing reality. They say to themselves, "He's only terrible to me because he is having such a hard time in business. He'll change when things get better." Or, "He's only afraid of commitment because he has such an awful mother. When he sees how different I am, how loving and wonderful, he will stop being afraid." Or, "He beats me up when he gets angry, but underneath it all, he's really a sweet man. If I keep treating him nicely, he will stop beating me." In other words, with a variety of excuses to fit the man's behavior, women often deliberately refuse to face facts. They pretend instead that the man is going to change and that everything is going to be all right.

5. *They stay in bad relationships much too long*. No matter if a husband or boy friend is abusive, if he is seeing other women, if he drinks too much, the woman tends to hang on to the bad relationship. Her fantasy is that this man will eventually change when he finally sees how wonderful she is and then things will get better. Instead of facing the reality that makes the relationship impossible, women continue to clutch at irrational hope. What generally keeps the woman in a bad relationship is fear of being alone. Yet, the better-any-man-than-no-man philosophy which makes a woman stay also prevents her from finding a more satisfying relationship.

6. *They suffer from the I'll-Never-Be-Able-To-Find-Another-Man Syndrome*. When a relationship breaks up, or a woman is even contemplating its end, she often begins to panic about her future. She is sure no man will ever find her attractive again. This fear is particularly strong among older women and women who don't consider themselves very attractive. Most women manage to establish relationships with men and find men to go out with, even if the relationships or the men aren't perfect. The terror of being alone forever is caused

more by a woman's own insecurities, her poor self-esteem rather than reality.

7. *They frequently have a fantasy of love which is impossible to fulfill.* Many women go around with an unconscious, overidealized fantasy of their father, and they search for a man who will fit this fantasy. Other women have a fusion fantasy of love—the man and the woman merge and become one. This is often based on a primitive love from infancy when mother and child, in the infant's mind, had no separation and were one entity. Women with a fantasy of love often set up impossible standards for the relationship. They may expect constant attention, or they may never want a man to have any separate activities. It is important for a woman to examine what she expects from a man in a love relationship. Does she want a replica of her father, or the father she never had? Does she want a powerful man, because she associates strength and power with her father? Does she have the feeling that love is an overwhelming experience in which she gets submerged and loses her identity—a scary prospect? She may harbor a dream that makes love impossible to find, or makes her fearful of it once she finds it.

8. *They center their lives too much on relationships and not enough on fulfilling themselves as individuals.* Too many women put their own lives in abeyance while they search for Mr. Right. Either consciously or unconsciously, they feel that when the right man comes along, he will fix whatever is wrong in their lives. As a result, they don't work on improving present conditions for themselves. Women frequently don't cultivate personal interests and hobbies that would make their lives fuller and more satisfying. They don't provide for their own futures economically, and often they don't pursue their own careers with enough interest or devotion because they feel a man will be taking care of them sometime in the future. Too many women spend their spare time man-hunting rather than doing things they enjoy as individuals. It is important for a woman to pay attention to her own life apart from men as well as her relationships with men. She should make it as satisfying and secure as possible. The fuller her own life is, the less desperate she will feel if there is no man around at the moment. She will be less tempted to hang onto bad

relationships, also. In our society women far outnumber men
and a certain number of women will never marry. Even if
woman does marry, divorce is rampant and men die at younger ages than women, so many women find themselves without a man in the end. Women have to learn to lead more
satisfying lives for themselves apart from men even though
men are certainly nice to have around.

9. *Women often try too hard to please men.* It is the way
women have been trained. Women cook elaborate meals for
men, try to build them up, comfort them, flatter them by
manner or words. Unfortunately, many women are so intent
on pleasing a man that they forget they have needs and
desires, too, which should be expressed and taken care of
within the context of a relationship. At its worst, wanting to
please results in a pattern of faked orgasms when a woman
pleases her man but not herself, swallowing anger or suffering
neglect or humiliation because she is afraid to speak up, for fear
of displeasing or losing the man in her life.

10. *They blame themselves and feel guilty when things go
wrong.* Women have been brought up to believe that it's their
duty to make relationships work, that they can make a man
totally happy—it is all in how they do it. Therefore, when
relationship doesn't work for one reason or another, women
tend to blame themselves. "If only I had been more giving or
caring, he would have loved me." "If only I had been patient
enough with him, he would have been nicer." "If only I
could have been wise enough to unravel the mystery of why
he was always so hostile, I would have found the good guy
underneath."

Another kind of self-blame women indulge in has to do
with their image. "If only I had been more beautiful or
glamorous or had bigger breasts or smaller thighs, he would
not have looked at anyone else and would have loved me."
This does not mean that women are without blame in the
failure of their relationships. Some kinds of female behavior
can indeed be destructive. Nevertheless, large numbers of
women automatically heap blame on themselves, whether it's
their fault or not, and feel guilty when a relationship fails.

11. *Women blame themselves if they don't have a husband.*
Women feel inadequate or like failures and often suffer from

anxiety and depression when they don't have a man of their own. This is because women were taught to make getting a man their primary goal in life; men were taught to go after success. The saying, "for every woman there's a man," implies if she doesn't get one, she is the problem. The truth is there are not enough men to go around in our society. Some women will not have a husband or a lifetime companion. This does not mean that they are defective or worthless or that life can't be fun or fulfilling in other ways.

12. *They expect romance to go on forever*. Women think of love as a technicolor experience—as being larger than life, as being swept away. Love is a "high" for women, and they are often not prepared for the fact that what goes up must also come down, at least somewhat. When life with a man becomes enmeshed with the daily routine of living, when sex becomes a matter of course, rather than the "grand event," when a man begins to take his mate for granted, too many women feel secretly or openly disappointed. New wives frequently have a letdown feeling before the first year of their marriage is over because they expected the high romance of courtship to continue forever. It is an unrealistic expectation that needlessly leads to disappointments in relationships. Intense romance can't go on forever with anyone. Relationships, by necessity, have to lapse into a routine.

13. *They often try to outmaneuver a man*. Many women worry about appearing too available. If they appear busy, they think it will make them seem more desirable. Other women try to make a man jealous. They date other men to push him into greater interest than he is exhibiting or to force a commitment. Playing games rarely works for any length of time. Men and women should try to be as authentic with each other as possible. When one tries to outfox the other, neither side wins.

14. *At certain times women grab at any man*. When a woman is alone, has gone through a dry spell in terms of relationships, she may grab at a man to whom she really doesn't respond, or who has a defect she is aware of from the beginning. What then happens is that the man, who has been grabbed more out of desperation than attraction, turns out to be imperfect, and the woman complains about him, often for

the same fault she saw from the beginning. Women need t
learn not to take any man just to avoid being alone. Learn t
live comfortably with oneself, instead. If a woman does gra
at just any man, she must be prepared to accept the conse
quences. She shouldn't dump unfair expectations or com
plaints on the man she chose because she was desperate. Tha
wasn't his fault. It was hers. Sometimes, the grab-at-any-ma
starts because a deadline age is approaching. It could b
thirty, it could be forty, it could be fifty. With a dread ag
looming the woman is tempted to hook up with any man wh
is available at the time.

15. *They obsess too much about love*. Women tend t
yearn too much for love. They feel more lonely than the
should without it, as if part of themselves is missing. It i
because women have been taught to think of themselves no
as individuals but as part of attachments. When in love
women tend to let the relationship take over every aspect o
their lives. It creeps into their work world, often interferin
with their ability to concentrate, or causing them to downpla
the importance of their work once a man enters the picture
The overevaluation of love, as the psychiatrist Karen Horne
called it, causes women to devalue the pleasures they coul
get from their work and other areas of their life becaus
everything seems second best when compared with love.

16. *They expect a man to read their mind*. Many wome
feel that if a man really loved them, he would know automat
ically what they want, without having to be told. This lead
to hurts and disappointments if a man fails to divine thei
thoughts. If a woman wants something she has to ask fo
it—nicely but directly. He's not going to know otherwise.

BIBLIOGRAPHY

Bardwick, Judith. *Psychology of Women.* New York: Harper & Row, 1971.

Barnett, Joseph, M.D. *Narcissism and Dependency in the Obsessional-Hysteric Marriage.* Family Process, Vol. 10, #1, Mar. 1971.

Bernard, Jessie. *The Female World.* New York: The Free Press, 1981.

Bernard, Jessie. *The Future of Marriage.* New York: Bantam, 1973.

Berne, Eric, M.D. *Games People Play.* New York: Ballantine, 1964.

Berne, Eric, M.D. *What Do You Say After You Say Hello?* New York: Bantam, 1981.

Deutsch, Helene. *Psychology of Women.* New York: Grune & Stratton, 1944.

de Beauvoir, Simone. *The Second Sex.* New York: Bantam, 1970.

Dinnerstein, Dorothy. *The Mermaid and the Minotaur.* New York: Harper Colophon Books, 1976.

Freeman, Lucy. *What Do Women Want?* New York: Human Sciences Press, 1977.

Friday, Nancy. *My Mother, My Self.* New York: Dell, 1977.

Fried, Edrita. *Active Passive.* New York: Harper Colophon Books, 1970.

Gornick, Vivian and Moran, Barbara K. editors, *Women in Sexist Society.* New York: A Mentor Book, New American Library, 1972.

Hammer, Signe. *Daughters & Mothers, Mothers & Daughters.* New York: Signet, 1976.

Harris, Thomas, M.D. *I'm OK, You're OK.* New York: Avon. 1969.

Hennig, Margaret and Jardin, Anne. *The Managerial Woman.* New York: Pocket Books, 1977.

Horney, Karen, M.D. *Feminine Psychology.* New York: Norton. 1967.

Horney, Karen. *Neurosis and Human Growth.* New York: Norton. 1950.

Horney, Karen. *The Neurotic Personality of Our Times.* New York: Norton. 1964.

Kernberg, Otto, M.D. "Barriers to Falling and Remaining in Love." *Journal of the American Psychoanalytic Association.* Vol 22, #3, 1974.

Kernberg, Otto, M.D. *Borderline Conditions and Pathological Narcissism.* New York: Jason Aronson. 1975.

Kernberg, Otto, M.D. "Mature Love: Prerequisites and Characteristics." *Journal of the American Psychoanalytic Association.* Vol 22, #4, 1974

Liebowitz, Michael, M.D. and Donald Klein, M.D. *Hysteroid Dysphoria.* Psychiatric Clinics of North America, Vol. 2, #3, December 1979

May, Robert. *Sex and Fantasy.* New York: Norton, 1980.

May, Rollo. *Love And Will.* New York: Delta, 1969.

Menninger, Karl, M.D. *Love Against Hate.* New York: Harcourt, Brace and World, 1970.

Miller, Jean Baker, M.D., editor *Psychoanalysis and Women.* New York: Penguin, 1977.

Miller, Jean Baker, M.D. *Toward a New Psychology of Women.* Boston: Beacon Press, 1976.

Maslow, Abraham H. *Toward a Psychology of Being.* New York: D. Van Nostrand, 1968.

Mintz, Elizabeth S. "Obsession With the Rejecting Beloved." *The Psychoanalytic Review.* Vol. 67, #4, pp. 479-492.

Mitchell, Juliet. *The Psychoanalysis and Feminism.* New York: Vintage, 1975.

Montagu, Ashley, editor. *The Practice of Love.* Prentice Hall, 1975.

Peele, Stanton with Archie Brodsky. *Love and Addiction.* New York: Taplinger, 1975.

Shapiro, David. *Neurotic Styles.* New York: Basic Books, 1965.

Steiner, Claude M. *Scripts People Live.* New York: Bantam, 1979.

Stein, Peter J., editor. *Single Life.* New York: St. Martin's Press, 1981.

Tavris, Carol and Offir, Carole. *The Longest War.* New York: Harcourt, Brace, Jovanovich, 1977.

Williams, Elizabeth Friar. *Notes of a Feminist Therapist.* New York: Dell, 1976.

Williams, Juanita. *Psychology of Women.* New York: Norton, 1977.

Wyckoff, Hogie. *Solving Women's Problems.* New York: Grove Press, 1977.

ABOUT THE AUTHOR

CAROL BOTWIN has written about human behavior, sex and other topics for such publications as *The New York Times Magazine*, *Family Circle*, and *Redbook*. In the late '60s, her by-line column, "Young World," appeared in *This Week* magazine, a Sunday supplement for 43 major newspapers. Her current column, "On Your Own," distributed by *The New York Times Syndicate*, appears in newspapers throughout the country. Carol lives in Manhattan and is the author of two previous books, *Sex and the Teenage Girl* and *The Love Crisis*.

We Deliver!
And So Do These Bestsellers.

Bantam
On Psychology

☐ 01419	**IF YOU CAN HEAR WHAT I CANNOT SAY** . . . Nathaniel Branden	$8.95
☐ 23043	**ACTIVE LOVING**—Ari Kiev, M.D.	$2.95
☐ 22576	**PATHFINDERS**, Gail Sheehy	$4.50
☐ 23234	**PASSAGES: PREDICTABLE CRISES OF ADULT LIFE**, Gail Sheehy	$4.50
☐ 23006	**THE FAMILY CRUCIBLE**, Dr. Napier	$4.50
☐ 20300	**A YEAR IN THE LIFE**, W. Bridges	$2.50
☐ 23399	**THE POWER OF YOUR SUBCONSCIOUS MIND**, Dr. J. Murphy	$3.95
☐ 23125	**FOCUSING**, E. Grendlin	$3.95
☐ 23079	**LOVE IS LETTING GO OF FEAR**, Gerald Jampolsky	$2.95
☐ 22503	**PEACE FROM NERVOUS SUFFERING**, Claire Weekes	$3.50
☐ 20540	**THE GESTALT APPROACH & EYE WITNESS TO THERAPY**, Fritz Perls	$3.50
☐ 20220	**THE BOOK OF HOPE**, DeRosis & Pellegrino	$3.95
☐ 23449	**THE PSYCHOLOGY OF SELF-ESTEEM: A New Concept of Man's Psychological Nature**, Nathaniel Branden	$3.95
☐ 23267	**WHAT DO YOU SAY AFTER YOU SAY HELLO?** Eric Berne, M.D.	$3.95
☐ 20774	**GESTALT THERAPY VERBATIM**, Fritz Perls	$3.50
☐ 22870	**PSYCHO-CYBERNETICS AND SELF-FULFILLMENT**, Maxwell Maltz, M.D.	$3.50
☐ 20873	**THE FIFTY-MINUTE HOUR**, Robert Linder	$2.95
☐ 22794	**THE DISOWNED SELF**, Nathaniel Branden	$3.50
☐ 23553	**CUTTING LOOSE: An Adult Guide for Coming to Terms With Your Parents**, Howard Halpern	$3.50
☐ 20977	**WHEN I SAY NO, I FEEL GUILTY**, Manuel Smith	$3.95

Buy them at your local bookstore or use this handy coupon for ordering: